WE CAN CHT . . .

. . . we must p̶ ̶. . . first.

The new age that we are in gives us tremendous opportunities. If you ignore them, then your life won't change much. You will stay on your average or below-average frequencies.

However, if you follow the laws of Karma, you will switch to a much more desirable frequency which will not only assure you of a better life in this incarnation, but it will result in more positive future lifetimes.

The choice, as always, is yours.

PAST LIVES, FUTURE LIVES

Dr. Bruce Goldberg

BALLANTINE BOOKS • NEW YORK

ISBN 0-345-35575-X

This edition published by arrangement with Newcastle Publishing Co., Inc.

Manufactured in the United States of America

First Ballantine Books Edition: November 1988

DEDICATION

This book is dedicated to all my patients
(past, present, and future), without
whom it would not have been possible.

Contents

ACKNOWLEDGMENTS

I would like to thank Harry Martin, Edie House, and all of the people who work at WBAL-TV, Sallee Rigler and WRC Radio, Charlie Donovan and WFBR Radio, my editors Victoria Pasternack and Douglas Menville, and others too numerous to mention, for their cooperation and thoughtfulness.

Introduction

THE PURPOSE OF *Past Lives—Future Lives* IS TO PRESENT the idea of reincarnation and karma to the reader in an attempt to explain why we are here and how we can all better ourselves. It is not my purpose to try to convert anyone to a belief in parapsychology or to interfere in any way with your particular religious or spiritual preferences.

If, however, you are not satisfied with traditional concepts of birth and death, then this book might very well change your life. Those of you who have ever wondered what it is like to die and what choices—if any—you will be given after death will begin to find answers to your questions.

In this book I use actual case histories of past life regression, along with progressions into future lives to help explain the laws of karma. Everyone has a karmic cycle, and the better we understand it, the easier our lives will be. This is my real purpose in writing this book—to help people understand why they do what they do and show them how to avoid making the same mistakes over and over again. If this book can help even one reader better his or her karmic cycle, then the time and energy spent in my research and writing will have been justified.

Whenever I use hypnosis to regress a patient into a past life or progress him or her into the future, I achieve a greater understanding of human behavior and the human mind than I could possibly obtain from any other source. In addition, the mechanisms of the karmic cycle begin to make so much more sense, and I am better able to offer my patients guidance.

It is not the purpose of this book to either prove or disprove the concept of reincarnation. Even with all the cases that have been recorded, there are still people who will doubt its validity. That is every person's right. It is my purpose, however, to enlighten the public to the effectiveness of hypnotic regression and progression. Even after the American Medical Association's formal acceptance of hypnosis in 1958, there have been relatively few practitioners of the technique. Misinformation about hypnosis must be replaced with accurate knowledge of this tremendously therapeutic discipline. The laws of supply and demand will then increase the number of hypnotherapists.

My own experience using hypnosis therapeutically has established and confirmed my belief in reincarnation. I've not been overly influenced by Eastern religion, gurus, or occultists. I have been influenced by the success I have had in helping people help themselves. Reincarnation and the laws of karma most logically explain the results I have witnessed using hypnotherapy.

If a patient's fear of heights, for example, can be traced back to falling off a cliff in a past life, and if reliving this scene permanently removes this fear, then who am I to question the validity of the scene? The most important point here is the elimination of the problem.

When trying to explain our purpose on this planet, traditional theories fall short, in my opinion. Karma is a logical explanation to me and I hope it will be informative to you.

Note: Some of the minor details in the case histories have been altered to protect the privacy of my patients. All the names used, except the chapters on the regressions and progressions of Harry Martin and Ken Manelis, have been altered. Everything else in these pages is true.

CHAPTER ONE

The Past Lives
of a TV Talk Show Host

ON A COLD AND OVERCAST WEDNESDAY AFTERNOON IN March of 1980, Harry Martin began his journey into the past.

From the moment he arrived at my office, Harry made it clear that he was very skeptical about hypnosis and even more skeptical about past life regressions. Yet I could tell that this twenty-eight-year-old TV talk show co-host was a highly intelligent man with great powers of concentration—which made him, potentially at least, an excellent candidate for hypnosis. (Being skeptical about regressions has very little to do with one's ability to be regressed. The suggestibility of the patient and the doctor-patient rapport determines success or failure in regression therapy.)

After explaining what hypnosis is—or rather, what it *isn't*—I induced a hypnotic trance, told Harry he would remember everything upon awakening, and used simple age regression to bring Harry back to the age of five. He described a scene in which he drew a circle on a cardboard box and pretended that it was a television set. He was trying to impress a six-year-old female playmate, an "older woman," of his communication abilities. Even at this young age Harry showed interest in television as a career. The details of this scene, as Harry remembered it, were very vivid. He described the clothes he was wearing, the color of the crayon that he used to draw the TV set, and the weather that day.

1

This was a very good session, and after it was over much of Harry's skepticism about hypnosis—though not about past life regression—had vanished. (Later Harry would tell me on my second "Hello Baltimore" appearance that if it hadn't been for my credentials as a dentist and my overall reputation he would never have participated in this project.)

The second session was held two weeks later. It was a lovely spring afternoon, and a second simple age regression was performed. This time Harry was taken back to age two. He saw and described some very detailed scenes at his grandmother's house. After the regression was over he expressed concern over some of the information he reported. For one thing, the color of the wallpaper in the bedroom he saw conflicted with what he consciously remembered. Second, the doorbell was different from what he could recall now.

I suggested he check out this information for its accuracy with his grandmother. I also gave him a "conditioning" tape for past life regression that consisted of a verbal induction into hypnosis and suggestions for the subconscious mind to explore its memory banks for any information that it would like to discover. The subconscious mind has a perfect memory bank. Since this vast storehouse is tappable only when the conscious mind proper (see Chapter 2) is relaxed and set aside, the use of a "conditioning" tape allows a patient to access this information more easily. I told Harry to play the tape in a completely waking state first, to make sure it wouldn't lead him into a life that was pure imagination. A completely waking state consists of the conscious mind proper functioning along with the subconscious mind. In the hypnotic state the subconscious mind works by itself (see Chapter 2). The tape contains no leading suggestions and by listening to it out of trance, the patient will feel more confident about the subsequent impressions he receives.

Before the next session, Harry called excitedly to inform me of several positive events. First, he had played my tape in a waking state and was satisfied with its purpose. Second, while playing the tape one night he experienced another age regression. Third, he had verified the details of the scene at his grandmother's house. The doorbell and the wallpaper were in fact as he saw them in the regression, not as he consciously remembered. (This demonstrates how uncannily accurate our subconscious mind's memory bank is.)

In the first week in April, Harry came to my office for what was to be his first past life regression. After some discussion about his progress with my "conditioning" tape, we went into my hypnotherapy room for the regression. Harry seemed quite calm, but indicated some surprise that he wasn't the least bit nervous. My hypnotherapy room is equipped with a recliner for the patient and a desk and chair for myself. I have a revolving disc that I have the patient look at to help induce a hypnotic trance. The temperature of the room is slightly warmer than normal, which also facilitates trance induction.

The trance was induced and I asked Harry what he saw. (Unfortunately these preliminary sessions weren't tape-recorded, but I recall details of the regressions.) He described a ship but couldn't make out any details at first. The scene he was describing was simply a ship approaching a dock on an island. Once the problem of orienting himself to this scene was overcome, much information concerning this scene and the surrounding circumstances was obtained.

This ship, called *The Dove*, was a cargo ship in the eighteenth century. Harry's name was Michael Bartholomew. In 1740, Michael was brought to this island to take over the shipping operation. The warehouse that stored the cargo was owned by Michael's uncle, but upon the uncle's death, Michael had inherited it.

Harry reported many scenes depicting Michael hard at work running the warehouse. Much of the physical work of loading and unloading cargo, as well as all of the supervisory functions, was carried out by Michael. (It is interesting to note that in his present life, Harry is an extremely hard worker and very much involved with the production end of television, along with being co-host of his talk show. His karmic pattern has remained consistent.)

After he came out of the trance, Harry made another observation. Just as I was about to ask him a question ("What is happening now?"), he told me the answer ("I'm going to the other side of the island to check on some workmen"). I considered it an illustration of telepathy. This is a common experience and does not require a very deep trance to be noted. All in all he was very pleased with this regression and so was I. It seemed to be evidence of a former life Harry had lived nearly 250 years before. Still, I don't know exactly how much of his skepticism concerning past life regression was removed. But I was convinced that progress was being made.

Harry was very enthusiastic that day as he left my office with an appointment to see me the following Monday for another past life regression.

When he came to my office for the next session, he looked a little tired but was still looking forward to the regression.

The second past life regression actually went better than the first. Harry was in a somewhat deeper trance and now he was used to the experience. But the first thing he saw—or didn't see—very much surprised him. Remember, these sessions were not taped, so only fragments of the actual dialogue will be given.

Dr. Goldberg: What do you see?
Harry: I, I don't see anything.
Dr. Goldberg: Take a moment and let any scene materialize slowly.
Harry: Oh, my God. The reason I can't see anything is because I am blind.

This illustrates an important principle of regression therapy. Even though Harry was blind in this particular life, he was made aware of that fact immediately and could still see the environment he was in. In other words, if you lack the use of your sight or hearing in a past life, you can still perceive your environment by the use of the hypnotic trance state.

It seems that Harry's name was Hap in this life, and he was born blind in 1847 on a farm in Utah. At the age of four he was brought to a small Western town where he learned to play the piano. Eventually he earned his living by playing piano in the bar of the hotel in which he lived. Even though he was blind, a situation that many people would find highly undesirable, he enjoyed his life. Harry described a scene in which Hap had gone for a walk in the woods just outside of the town and had gotten lost. It took him about three hours to use other highly developed senses to find his way back to town.

What is interesting to note about this past life is Hap's creativity. In his present life, Harry is very creative and, although he doesn't play the piano, he does play the drums. Harry is also writing a novel. Thus, his karmic pattern of creativity, as well as hard work, is consistently exhibited.

Near the end of Hap's life, he developed arthritis in both of his hands and was unable to play the piano. He described scenes in which he would go down to the bar and listen to the new piano player. Instead of feeling bitter or showing remorse, Hap's attitude was extremely positive and pleasant. This also coincides with Harry's present constructive attitude and pleasantness (obviously important qualities for a talk show host—the ability to make his guests feel welcome, relaxed, and to express interest and appreciation at all times).

Harry seemed very pleased with the results of this regression and said he could definitely relate to the emotions he felt as Hap.

It was two weeks later when I saw Harry again for another past life regression. This was to be his third and last regression, and you will shortly see that it was a most significant session.

The date was April 28, and it was a Monday. Earlier that day I had received a telephone call from one of my patients informing me that much of the information we obtained from her last age regression had checked out with members of her family. This is always most satisfying to hear, of course.

Harry arrived on time and after reviewing some of the karmic principles he illustrated in the previous two past life regressions, I induced him into a very deep trance.

Harry described a life as an English radio operator for the Royal Air Force during World War II. He was born in 1907. The plane he was flying was a bomber. He spent a great deal of time describing the plane. (Harry has no present interest in planes.) As the scenes progressed, it became obvious that this plane was to play an important part in this particular life.

Most of his World War II experience for the RAF centered on North Africa. The last year he mentioned to me was 1945, so I progressed him five years forward. This is what he reported:

Dr. Goldberg: Where do you find yourself now?
Harry: I am lying on this table of some sort and as I
                 look up all I can see is a large dome. It is hard
                 to make it out clearly because of the brightness
                 of the light.
Dr. Goldberg: What color is the light?
Harry: White.
Dr. Goldberg: Are you alone?
Harry: No. I can't see anyone, but I can hear people
                 talking about me.
Dr. Goldberg: What are they saying?
Harry: They are evaluating my life, my life as the ra-
                 dio operator. I must have died.

I then asked him to go back to the last day of his life as the radio operator.

Dr. Goldberg:	What do you see?
Harry:	I'm on a raft. The plane, it went down—crashed.
Dr. Goldberg:	Is anyone with you on the raft?
Harry:	No, I'm alone.
Dr. Goldberg:	What year is it?
Harry:	1949.

Harry reported having been on this raft for a number of days. His food and water supplies had run out and he was dying. He described his position on the raft as being "sprawled out," with his arms and legs hanging over the sides. He saw himself slowly die, but was not upset by it. (This is a common response because the patient realizes there is nothing he can do about the situation.) Harry then described a very dry feeling in his mouth and throat in the present time. I brought him to the point just after he had died and further questioned him.

Dr. Goldberg:	What do you feel now?
Harry:	I feel very strange. I feel as if I'm floating and it's as if I no longer have a body.
Dr. Goldberg:	How do your throat and mouth feel?
Harry:	I no longer feel thirsty. It's just very peaceful here.

This is again a common description. All physical discomforts are removed once the patient has died in the past life.

What is interesting to note about this regression is Harry's description of the in-between-life state. The dome that Harry described to me is similar to what has been told to me before by other patients. I have never seen it described in any other book or account of past life regression. Futhermore, Harry is admittedly very skeptical about reincarnation and has read no books about it. (He hadn't even heard of the Bridey Murphy story.) So this confirmed the authenticity of the regression for me.

Another interesting note about this regression is that Harry reported dying in 1949. In this life he was born on June 14, 1951. He had two years in between lives. This is a rather short time.

I asked him finally in trance what he felt he had achieved in his last life. He said he hadn't achieved enough; he felt bad about not leaving his mark on the world. As the RAF radio operator, he had never married and had no family to speak of. Today, Harry is married and is well on his way to leaving his mark on the world. His present life appears to be the culmination of a number of his past lives.

After the session was over, Harry and I discussed this particular regression in detail. He described the strange feeling he experienced in the dome as well as right after he had died. Still the plane stood out as the most significant aspect of that life.

This ended the past life regressions, but I wanted Harry to come back one more time to show how deep into his subconscious he could go without regressing into a former life. He was scheduled to return in ten days.

During that week I went to the library and found books with photographs of World War II airplanes from various countries. At his next visit, I showed these books to Harry. He immediately identified the plane he had seen during the hypnotic regression. It was indeed an English World War II bomber.

In this final session, Harry was induced into a very deep hypnotic trance. I gave him a series of relaxation suggestions but this time I did not say that he was to remember everything upon awakening, as I had said in all the previous sessions, though I didn't say that he was to forget anything either.

When he came out of the trance, he said he felt absolutely great. Also, he could not remember anything of what I said to him while he was in the trance. He felt as if he had been in trance for more than an hour. In actuality it was only about twenty minutes. This time distortion is quite common during trances, especially deeper trance levels.

We then discussed my appearing on his television show to educate the public about the clinical benefits of hypnosis. We agreed to meet and work out the details, and Harry left my office. On his way home an interesting thing happened. While stopped at a red light, Harry looked up and saw a World War II airplane very similar to the one he had seen in his last past life regression. He had never seen that plane before, either in Baltimore or anywhere else to the best of his knowledge. It seems this plane was out to haunt him, because a few days later he again saw this type of plane on a news assignment in Delaware. When Harry called me to report these events, my conclusion was simply that that particular past life was important to his

karmic growth, and the reappearance of the plane was a re-
minder of his lessons learned and those he has still to learn.

There is an ancient saying, "When the student is ready, the
teacher will be there." Until he met me, Harry had been very
skeptical about parapsychology and past life regressions. He
was not ready. After experiencing regressions personally, Harry
quickly learned how accurate and significant they can be. The
student was ready and the teacher was there.

My experience with Harry came about as a result of my desire
to clear up the public's misconceptions about hypnosis. Unfortunately, Hollywood films over the years had portrayed hypnosis
in a very negative and inaccurate fashion. Newspapers and mag-
azines have done a more credible job, but because of television's
massive appeal and influence over the American public, I wanted
to use the exposure of this medium to discuss hypnosis and its
use in past life regression.

The major obstacle I faced was how to interest a television
station in doing a show on hypnosis and regression in an ethical
and true-to-life depiction of the experience. I decided to call the
local NBC* affiliate in Baltimore to discuss the idea. I spoke
with the assignment editor in the news department and told her
I was a local dentist who had a separate practice in hypnotherapy. In addition, I mentioned my involvement with past life
regression therapy and my training from the American Society
of Clinical Hypnosis. She seemed intrigued by my story. She
asked me to come down to the studio to discuss it with her.

On a very cold Friday afternoon in early December of 1979,
I arrived at WBAL and spoke with the assignment editor,
Beverly Marable. She was very cordial, but concerned about
whether I could actually do what I said I could do with hypnosis.
I understood her attitude and suggested I regress an employee
of the studio to establish my credibility with them firsthand. She
agreed to this and volunteered herself as the patient. I was de-
lighted. If I regressed her, there could be no question of fraud
or collusion.

During our first appointment, Beverly was regressed to the
age of five and described, in very great detail, a trip to San
Francisco she had made by train. After the trance was over, she
was amazed at how she was able to recall all the details, details
that she would not have been able to recall consciously. A sec-

*On August 31, 1981, WBAL-TV changed its affiliation from NBC to CBS.

ond appointment was made. She left my office feeling refreshed and somewhat astonished at what she had just experienced.

Ms. Marable came to my office for her next session. All her skepticism had vanished. She was quite a good hypnotic patient, though the information that was obtained during her past life regression was somewhat sketchy. Nonetheless, she was impressed with the results.

The scene she described consisted of an early 1800s one-room schoolhouse. Since she was a devout city dweller, with no personal experience in rural settings, she knew that she could not have, or would not be likely to, imagine such a scene. She left my office feeling a bit mystified, but told me the producer of "Hello Baltimore" would call me and set up an appointment for one of their on-the-air personalities to experience a number of regressions so that he could describe his subjective experiences on the air. I couldn't ask for a more ideal situation. It would completely remove any thoughts of hoax, and provide me with an interviewer who could publicly verify the validity of his experience with me during hypnosis.

Harry Martin's case history, which began this chapter, established my credibility with the producers as a practitioner of past life regression hypnotherapy.

We were now prepared to do the show on Monday, May 19, 1980. I wasn't nervous (one of the many advantages of self-hypnosis), but I was very much excited about this appearance.

I arrived at the studio at 11:00 A.M., in time to get acquainted with the other co-host, Edie House, a very attractive young woman with a relaxed manner about her, immaculately dressed and very soft-spoken. We didn't have much time to talk before the show, but I knew that Harry had briefed her about my work and his experiences.

The show went rather well. The hosts and I discussed hypnosis and past life regression, and then I answered questions from viewers who called in.

The response to the show was unbelievable. Hundreds of telephone calls came into the studio and, to my surprise, all the calls were positive. The only complaints the studio received were that I was not on long enough. Viewers requested that the videotape of my interview be repeated.

Two days later, I received a telephone call from a talk show host of a Washington, D.C., radio show, wanting me to discuss hypnosis and past life regression a couple of weeks hence. I felt like a local celebrity.

My second appearance on "Hello Baltimore" was on July 28. When I arrived at the studio on this very hot and humid summer day, I could sense a difference in Harry and Edie. We all felt more relaxed and spontaneous.

During the show I established some of the basic concepts of reincarnation and illustrated how they could be used in hypnotherapy to remove the causes of certain habits, and especially phobias. Harry's skepticism about reincarnation again surfaced.

Harry: Even though I went through this, there is still
                a bit of skepticism about this. How do I know
                that what I really experienced isn't something
                that I experienced before, something that I read
                in a book or saw in a movie or on TV?

Dr. Goldberg: There are two differences between a regression
                and a fantasy, or just use of your own imagi-
                nation as in a daydream. One difference, and
                you can relate to the lives we took you through,
                is that in a regression you feel the scene. You
                don't just say you're in a Western scene or in
                an airplane; you actually feel the emotions in-
                volved. If you're happy, you feel happy and if
                you're sad, you feel sad. In a daydream if you
                see yourself on the beach, for example, you
                will imagine that scene but you won't sweat or
                feel thirsty. In a regression you feel the scene.
                The second thing is the ability to almost read
                minds. Harry, you illustrated this telepathy
                yourself. You were able to know even before I
                asked you a question what I was going to ask
                you. Do you remember that?

Harry: That's right. That did happen.

Dr. Goldberg: This form of telepathy cannot be imagined.

We don't know the exact mechanism of telepathy. It is sometimes exhibited in hypnotic trances, especially past life regression trances. However, we do know that the trance state
facilitates various forms of psychic phenomena. Telepathy is one
of these.

I do not profess to have made an absolute believer out of
Harry, nor was it my purpose. My purpose was simply to show
the difference between a fantasy and a regression. (The use of
regression has gained so much respect of late that it is some-

times used in court as evidence and by many police departments to enhance the memory of witnesses.)

Later that summer, Sallee Rigler, a psychic from Aberdeen, Maryland, appeared on "Hello Baltimore." I had occasion to watch the show and I was impressed with her. Sallee hosts a weekend radio show in Washington D.C. Just two days later I received a call from Sallee's producer at WRC radio. They wanted me to appear on Sallee's show to discuss past life regression. I could sense that all this exposure represented a new beginning for me and my work.

CHAPTER TWO

What Is Hypnosis?

HYPNOSIS IS A SUBJECT OF GREAT INTEREST TO NEARLY everyone. The fascination it holds is its promise to open a world of hidden treasure and self-improvement, as if by magic. And nearly everyone finds at some time a desire or need to improve oneself. Hypnosis sounds like an easy answer. After all, hypnotists have the power to make people do things (like learning a foreign language) or stop doing things (like smoking or overeating). Don't they?

Actually, hypnotists have no power and never did. They just have a special skill. Yet the misconception is understandable. Skilled hypnotists in the past were professional entertainers. They deliberately tried to give the false impression that they had a "remarkable power" over the subject and could force him or her to do bizarre things. The only real power behind hypnosis lies with the subject and his or her own mind.

MY OWN STORY

Many people ask me how a dentist got involved in such controversial fields as hypnosis and parapsychology (especially past life regression and progression into future lives). It didn't happen by coincidence, but by synchronicity.

As a child I always knew that dentistry was to be my career. By the age of six I had made this decision.

During my childhood and adolescence I showed no interest in parapsychology or hypnosis. By college age I chose a school that had an excellent biology department. As a biology major with a chemistry minor I was being well trained for dental school, but certainly not for work as a hypnotherapist.

During my four years at college I was exposed to many philosophies and belief systems; however, my attitude toward parapsychology was always objective. I didn't accept or reject it. Like a good scientist, I merely considered the data neutrally. Hypnosis and karma were simply not part of my interests.

My freshman year in dental school consisted of dentistry and little else. During my second year I investigated astrology by taking a course in it, and read my first accounts of past life regression using hypnosis. My interest stirred. During the remainder of my dental school career I spent more time researching parapsychology. I fed a lot of information into my subconscious memory banks.

What is of karmic significance is that I had natural talents in these disciplines. After graduation I entered a general practice dental residency at a Florida state hospital. (Residencies are not required in dentistry but they are nice to have as part of one's background.) It was here that an opportunity presented itself that was to change my life. A brochure from the American Society of Clinical Hypnosis offered a course in hypnosis to be given in Jackson, Mississippi. I had plenty of vacation time stored up, so I decided to attend. These courses are offered only to dentists, physicians, and psychologists. I was in good company. One of the psychiatrists who trained me told me I had a natural gift for hypnosis. He encouraged me to use it in my practice. My intention was to use in on my dental patients to reduce their apprehension and, in certain cases, to replace chemical anesthesia.

What he didn't know was that I had read up on past life regression, and one of the first things I intended to do after the course was completed was to use hypnosis to prove or disprove reincarnation—to my own satisfaction. It was no coincidence that I received the brochure from the American Society of Clinical Hypnosis at that time, and it was certainly no coincidence that the very first patient I hypnotized when I got back to Tallahassee regressed into a former lifetime.

The patient was a young lady I knew well. She expressed great interest in hypnosis and asked me to regress her. I agreed. She was a somnambule, a very deep hypnotic patient, and she described a number of past lives to me. She even spoke several foreign languages fluently while in the trance state. I knew enough of her background to know that she knew nothing about past lives, hypnosis, or foreign languages. These regressions occurred over a period of about three months. Each session lasted between forty-five minutes and an hour. She was able to overcome two habits and a phobia as a result of this therapy.

That did it. I was already excited by hypnosis, but more than that, I became a believer in reincarnation and karma from that day on.

From a mathematical point of view, the odds must be millions to one against my hypnosis training and my first hypnotic patient being so successful, all within a period of about three weeks. Immediately I began using hypnosis with my dental patients at the hospital for elimination of apprehension toward their dental treatment. In some cases I used hypnosis in place of chemical anesthesia (novocaine). The hospital approved of my hypnotic techniques and their application to dentistry.

I also used hypnosis for habit elimination, relief of minor medical problems, and then phobias on patients not connected with the hospital but referred to me by former patients. During this time I also successfully regressed various people into past lives. I was quickly obtaining a reputation concerning my clinical uses of hypnosis.

In June of 1976 I moved to Baltimore to set up my dental and hypnosis practices. In March of 1980, Harry Martin of WBAL-TV was in my office waiting to be taken back into a past life. It was part of my karmic cycle to succeed with him and to bring karma and past life regression via television and radio to the attention of the Baltimore-Washington metropolitan area.

HYPNOSIS AND THE INNER WORKINGS OF THE MIND

A simple definition of hypnosis is "a state of increased suggestibility accompanied by a focusing of one's concentration on one thought, idea, or person." When I say "increased suggestibility," I must explain that a person in a hypnotic trance will only accept suggestions that he or she might normally accept when not in a trance state. We all possess a moral and ethical code that cannot be violated regardless of the depth of the hypnotic trance.

To understand what hypnosis is, one must consider the inner workings of the human mind. Our mind is made up of four different levels of activity.

The first level or stage is called *beta*. This is the level of complete consciousness. We function in this level approximately sixteen hours each day. The main purpose of this level is to regulate our life-controlling bodily functions, such as heartbeat, breathing, kidney functions, digestion, etc. About 75 percent of the beta level, or conscious mind proper, is spent monitoring these vital bodily functions. Thus, only 25 percent of the conscious mind is left to deal with what we know as our conscious thoughts.

The second level is what we call *alpha*. Alpha corresponds to the subconscious mind, and this is what we deal with in hypnosis. This level is characterized by 95–100 percent concentration efficiency. This is far superior to the 25 percent efficiency of the conscious, or beta, level. Examples of activity on the alpha level are hypnosis, meditation, biofeedback, daydreaming, crossing over into natural sleep, and awakening. Hypnosis is a natural state of mind. It is not sleep. You are fully aware when you are hypnotized.

The next level of mental activity is called *theta*. This is the part of the unconscious mind that functions in light sleep. The term *conscious* means awake and aware; *unconscious* means unawake and unaware.

The last level is called *delta*. This corresponds to deep sleep. At this level, the unconscious mind is obtaining the greatest amount of rest. Suggestions will not be heard at this level. This level lasts approximately thirty to forty minutes each night.

In summary, the mind consists of four levels. When we get up in the morning we have just gone from natural hypnosis (alpha) to full consciousness (beta). When we go to sleep at night we go from beta (full consciousness) to alpha (natural hypnosis) to theta (light sleep) to delta (deep sleep) to theta (light sleep) to alpha, and the cycle repeats itself.

THE EXPERIENCE OF BEING HYPNOTIZED

If you are hypnotized, you will be in the alpha state. What will you experience? Exactly what is the hypnotic trance like?

Hypnosis is simply the setting aside of the conscious mind proper, and dealing with the subconscious mind directly. At no time will you be asleep.

When we are functioning at full consciousness (beta), both the subconscious and conscious mind proper are functioning. The physical experience in hypnosis will be identical to that of full consciousness, with three exceptions.

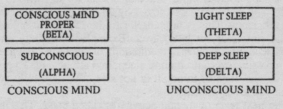

CONSCIOUS MIND   UNCONSCIOUS MIND

FIGURE 1

First, your concentration will be more focused, nearly 100 percent as compared to the 25 percent efficiency of the conscious mind proper. Second, every muscle in your body will feel relaxed. (Some people feel a floating sensation, others a warm or tingling feeling. Most people feel a heaviness, especially in the arms and legs.) Third, there is what I call "immobility." This is not technically accurate because one is always able to move any part of the body at any time. The patient in hypnosis doesn't *want* to move, so he or she doesn't. Many people have compared this effect to having laughing gas (nitrous oxide) in the dentist's office. This is quite accurate because nitrous oxide will place a patient in a hypnotic trance chemically.

Thus, a hypnotized patient will experience increased concentration, complete relaxation, and lack of movement. Also, our senses are more developed in trance, so that the sense of hearing, touch, smell, etc. will be more accurate in a hypnotic trance state. That's it. There will be no levitation, skyrockets, or any kind of sleep or zombie effect. Examples of natural, day-to-day hypnosis include daydreaming, crossing over into natural sleep at night, the beginning stages of waking up from natural sleep in the morning, watching most television, watching windshield wipers on a rainy night, watching light posts or white lines on a highway at night (highway hypnosis), reading a novel and getting so involved in the plot that you lose track of time.

Think about a daydream for a moment. When you daydream you are focusing your mind on a person, place, or event that is usually pleasant. You are not concerned about the weather, what time it is, or whether your clothes are too loose or too tight. If someone were in the same room with you while you were daydreaming, they would probably have to snap their fingers and call your name to get your attention. This is the alpha state and the best example of natural hypnosis. Everyone daydreams, and most people spend between three to four hours daydreaming every day. Thus, most people spend at least three hours every day in natural hypnosis. Hypnosis is thus a natural and normal state of mind. There is absolutely no danger involved. Without natural hypnosis the stress in our daily lives would kill us all.

In fact, since our senses are more developed or sharper, we are less prone to accidents or other forms of injury when we are in hypnosis. I am not aware of any instances in which hypnosis has ever resulted in either psychological or physical harm to a patient. A person who has a car accident late at night might be the victim of highway hypnosis, but only because he would normally have been asleep while he was behind the wheel.

In this book I will be showing you how hypnosis can be used to relive very traumatic incidents in a person's present, past, or future life with no negative side effects. In fact, many positive effects result, such as the elimination of fears, habits, and other negative tendencies.

THE LEVELS OF HYPNOSIS

Now, what about the different levels or stages of hypnosis? Today scientists classify over fifty different levels of hypnosis, but for simplicity I will divide hypnosis into three main levels.

The first is called *light trance*. In this level the patient is relaxed and probably won't feel that he or she is hypnotized. Although regressions and progressions can be accomplished at this level, the information obtained is very sketchy. In addition, when I work with phobias (fears), habits, depression, etc., this level has only limited efficiency in accepting very complex or difficult suggestions. Ninety-five percent to ninety-eight percent of the public can achieve this level.

The second level is called *medium trance*. This is the level in which I prefer to work. In this level the patient is more completely relaxed and more able to accept very difficult or complex suggestions. He or she can more easily relive and actually feel an event or scene in regression or progression. At this level the patient may be aware of outside noises but it will not distract him or her. About 70 percent of the public can achieve this level.

The last level is called *deep* or *somnambulistic trance*. This is the level of hypnosis a stage hypnotist likes to use because one characteristic of it is "hypnoamnesia." In other words, the patient will not remember what he or she did or said in trance unless specifically told to remember upon awakening. Only about 5 percent of the public can achieve this level. This level is also characterized by positive hallucinations (seeing an object that is not really there) as well as negative hallucinations (not being able to see an object that is there).

Even in this very deep level, however, the patient cannot be told to do or say anything that is against his or her moral or ethical code. So you see, a hypnotized person is never under anyone's control but his or her own. Unless I am interested in documenting a regression or involved in other types of research, I do not prefer to work with a patient at this level. It is not dangerous, merely unnecessary.

WHO CAN BE HYPNOTIZED?

As I have already mentioned, 95 percent of the public can be placed in at least a light hypnotic trance. People often ask me to describe the kind of people who make the best hypnotic patients and those who cannot be hypnotized. The best hypnotic patients are intelligent people (contrary to the popular misconception) who have an excellent memory, can focus their concentration, visualize scenes with great detail, can express emotions easily, are not overly critical, and who can go to a lecture or movie and become so deeply involved in the plot that time passes very quickly. Children make excellent patients because of their imagination, respect for authority, and lack of resistance or skepticism. The best hypnotic patients are children between the ages of eight and sixteen.

Those people who usually make the worst hypnotic patients are people who have very short attention spans, tend to focus on the past and future rather than the present, are overly critical, use logic instead of emotions, have lower IQs, and have great difficulty "letting themselves go." Mental retardation, senility, brain damage, inability to understand the language of the hypnotist, and overly cynical attitudes are also going to prevent the induction of a hypnotic trance.

SELF-HYPNOSIS

When I discuss hypnosis, I refer to *self-hypnosis*. All hypnosis is actually self-hypnosis. It is impossible to hypnotize someone against his or her will, unless certain drugs are used. I never recommend or use drugs. Thus, during a hypnotic session, a patient learns how to hypnotize him- or herself, utilizing the services of a hypnotherapist. The term for this is *heterohypnosis*, meaning hypnosis by another (*hetero* means "other"). Even the most skillful hypnotherapist is unable to hypnotize someone against his or her will. All hypnosis is thus self-hypnosis.

All of my patients are taught self-hypnosis so that they can condition themselves for deeper trance levels and shorten the time it takes to induce the hypnotic trance. I record cassette tapes for all of my patients so that they can be exposed daily to the suggestions I give them at their weekly sessions. There are many ways to learn self-hypnosis, but I find the use of cassette tapes are to be the most efficient.

OUR OWN NATURAL COMPUTER

Hypnosis takes place in the alpha state, or subconscious mind, which is best described as a computer. Just as a computer is programmed or fed information, the subconscious mind is constantly undergoing a programming process. Everything that our five senses can detect, as well as extrasensory perception (ESP), is permanently stored in the subconscious mind's memory bank. Since the subconscious mind, along with the conscious mind proper, functions for about sixteen hours each day, scientists estimate that the average human brain is exposed to, and stores, one million separate pieces of information every day.

Each piece of information is stored in what is termed a "memory trace" in the brain. If you multiply one million by 365, and then multiply this total by your age, then you have an idea of how many memory traces you are using. Scientists estimate that the average human mind contains seventy trillion memory traces. Since a trillion is a thousand billion, and a billion's is a thousand million, you can see that even a seventy-year-old person has barely used his potential of memory traces.

When I use hypnosis to regress patients into past lives, I attempt to tap into the memory traces of their subconscious minds and bring to their conscious awareness the stored sensory data that will reveal the origin of their present habits, phobias, or negative tendencies. By reliving these past experiences they can permanently eliminate fears or negative behavior.

STEPS IN HYPNOTHERAPY

People develop these tendencies because their self-image is lowered as a result of unpleasant past experiences. Thus, the first step in any form of hypnotherapy is to build up the patient's self-image. This is done by the use of what we call "ego strengthening suggestions." For example, I might say to a patient in a trance, "Every day, in every way, you are getting better, and better, and better. Negative thoughts and negative suggestions have absolutely no influence over you at any mind level."

In addition to adding to the patient's self-confidence, this results in an increase in his or her motivation, concentration, and energy levels. This is especially important when working with people who are anxious or depressed.

The second step I follow is to systematically reprogram the subconscious so that the problem, once removed, will not occur again. Eighty to ninety percent of cases of negative self-image can be cured by the use of regression and progression. Through systematic reprogramming suggestions, the problem can be eliminated permanently. This is important because many people think that removing a habit or phobia with the use of hypnosis will result in substitution of a new habit or phobia. Nothing could be further from the truth.

At least 80 percent of the patients who request regression or progression do so with the objective of eliminating a habit or phobia or negative tendency. There are hypnotherapists who claim "one-shot cures" for smoking, overeating, and other bad habits, using hypnotic suggestion. A habit that has been programmed for many years into the subconscious mind requires more than one exposure to effect its permanent elimination. Also, the old technique of using aversion suggestion ("If you smoke a cigarette, you will get nauseated") never really worked and doesn't work today. Instead, all suggestions should be positively worded ("I am steadily losing my desire for a cigarette each and every day").

There are many other common fallacies and needless fears about hypnosis. To summarize:

1. The fallacy of symptom substitution. As I have mentioned, by using regression to see the true causes of a negative tendency and by using systematic reprogramming suggestions to permanently eliminate the problem, symptoms are not substituted. They are permanently removed.

2. The fallacy of mind control. Earlier in this chapter I discussed the fact that absolutely nobody can be placed in a hypnotic trance against his or her will. Even a highly skilled hypnotherapist needs the cooperation of the patient in order to induce a trance. The only person capable of controlling a patient's subconscious mind is the patient. All hypnosis is self-hypnosis and is a natural phenomenon.

3. The fallacy of revealing secrets or other information in trance. Unless the patient wants to reveal the information, the information in a patient's subconscious mind will remain hidden. Psychologists use the phrase "the ego cannot be detached" to describe this. For example, in a past life regression, if you saw yourself in an embarrassing or even humiliating scene, you would relive this scene in your mind but would not discuss it, even if you were in a very deep trance, unless you wanted to.

4. The fear of not being dehypnotized. Because hypnosis is a natural process that the mind goes through each

and every day, and because we are constantly bringing ourselves into and out of trances, a patient can terminate a hypnotic trance anytime he or she wants to. Patients do not need a hypnotherapist to bring them out of a trance. I usually count from one to five to return the patient to the beta state, but this is not necessary. The patient will resume beta functioning by him- or herself. However, counting forward facilitates this process.

5. The fear of not remembering suggestions afterward. Unless you are a somnambule (capable of achieving a deep trance), you will always remember the suggestions or scenes afterward. I always give a posthypnotic suggestion (a suggestion that is meant to work long after the trance ends) for patients to remember everything they experienced or reexperienced upon awakening. The term "awakening" is a poor one, since the patient is not asleep, but most people can relate to this description.

   The only time I do not suggest a patient remember what he or she has experienced in a trance is when I am working with someone who is emotionally upset and the scene is especially traumatic. If I don't feel that the patient can handle the information, then I will suggest that he or she forget it (hypnoamnesia). In any event, the information or scene will be remembered by the patient eventually as the posthypnotic suggestion wears off (approximately four to ten days). Even somnambules will remember the scene if you give the appropriate posthypnotic suggestion.

6. The fear of regression. I know of no case where anyone has ever been harmed by the use of hypnosis in any form. I have done thousands of regressions and progressions and can personally testify to the many positive benefits. In all the time that I have used hypnosis, I have never seen or even heard of a negative effect or situation experienced by a patient. In my experience, the worst that can happen is nothing, i.e., no trance is induced.

Hypnosis is simply a way of relaxing and setting aside the conscious mind proper while at the same time activating the subconscious mind so that suggestions can be made directly to the subconscious, enabling the patient to act on these suggestions with greater ease and efficiency.

THE BENEFITS OF HYPNOSIS

From my double career as a dentist and a hypotherapist, I have found two major therapeutic applications of hypnosis: first, past life regression for the cure of unpleasant symptoms and negative behavior, and second, pain control. The second is an application that has been increasingly recognized by the Western medical community in recent years. Dentists and physicians are beginning to perform otherwise painful medical procedures using hypnosis instead of chemical anesthesia—with tremendous success.

I long ago postulated the idea of chemical mediators in hypnosis. Just as fear or excitement can cause the body, by way of the adrenal glands, to produce adrenaline (which acts to increase the heart rate and motivate a person toward quick and immediate action—so-called "fight or flight" mechanism), I felt that hypnosis might somehow stimulate the body to produce other types of chemical mediators. Recent research has proved this to be the case in the area of pain control.

Feeling pain consists of two processes. The first is the original pain signal that is transmitted to the brain from the point of stimulation, and the second is the interpretation of that signal by the brain. Hypnosis seems to alter the brain's interpretation of the pain signal by stimulating the brain's production of a chemical called *endorphin*.* Recent biochemical research has identified the chemical structure of endorphin as resembling that of morphine, except that it is ten times more potent than morphine, with none of morphine's addictive side effects. The brain also produces a chemical that destroys the effects of endorphin, so that the protective function of our pain-interpreting mechanisms can resume their normal functions.

Thus, current biochemistry has established the first link between hypnosis and an explanation of how it works. In the coming years, I expect many more chemical mediators in the brain

*Recent research has shown that endorphin cannot be the mechanism for hypnotic pain control since naloxene (a narcotic antagonist) doesn't reverse hypnoanalgesia.

to be discovered and analyzed to explain the many other positive actions and effects of hypnosis.

Below I've compiled a partial list of the many other benefits that hypnotherapy can be useful in achieving. Among these are:

1. increased relaxation and the elimination of tension

2. increased and focused concentration

3. improved memory ("hypernesia")

4. improved reflexes

5. increased self-confidence

6. pain control

7. improved sex life

8. increased organization and efficiency

9. increased motivation

10. improved interpersonal relationships

11. slowing down the aging process

12. harmony of the mind, body, and spirit

13. elimination of habits, phobias, and other negative tendencies

14. improved psychic awareness—ESP, meditation, astral projection (out-of-body experience), telepathy

15. elimination of the fear of death by viewing one's past and future lives.

I hope this chapter has helped make you aware of at least the basics behind hypnotherapy and its uses in regression and progression. Throughout the rest of this book I will be referring to the principles that have just been discussed.

Before one can truly benefit from actual case histories, a background on karma is necessary. In the next chapter I will explain what karma is and how the mechanisms of past and future lives work.

CHAPTER THREE

What Is Karma?
Historical Foundations
and Popular Concepts

T HE PURPOSE OF MY DISCUSSION OF KARMA, REINCARNA-
tion, progression, or any other aspects of parapsychology is to inform you of a very exciting field. It is not my intention to try to convert anyone to my beliefs nor do I want to state
dogmatically that there is only one answer to the question of
rebirth. In my work as a hypnotherapist, I have learned to keep
an open mind. My concepts and opinions have changed through
the years and will change again as new ideas and theories develop. This book and the knowledge it contains is an expression
of my background, personality, interests, and experiences.

Karma is simply cause and effect. If you throw a rock through
a window, putting a hole in the window, you have a cause
(throwing the rock) and an effect (a hole in the window). Every
effect that exists has some cause. If you are unhappy about your
life, your financial situation, your relationships, your health,
etc., then you must realize that causes exist. These causes can
be traced back to past lives. Your subconscious mind retains all
of these causes because it has a perfect memory bank. The
subconscious mind also survives death, so that a new life means
merely exchanging one body for another. You have the same
subconscious, only now it has learned some lessons and grown
spiritually.

All of the things you have or have not done in this and all of
your past lives will generate certain effects in this life as well as
in future lifetimes. The laws of karma are perfectly just. The

soul always has free will. Karma can bring you happiness or sadness depending upon the causes you have earned, and the paths you have chosen to take. It is not the purpose of karma to reward or punish. Its purpose is to educate the subconscious, to purify it. Once the subconscious is purified, it no longer needs karma, or the "karmic cycle," as we refer to it. The karmic cycle is the chain of lives we live to work out all of the negativity we have earned in previous lifetimes.

The balance sheet or final result of the karmic cycle is zero. When all of the positive causes we've earned cancel out all of the negative causes, and we have learned all of the lessons that we are supposed to learn, then we have completed our karmic cycle. The balance sheet is zero and the subconscious is purified. We then no longer need to come back again to learn.

If, however, we react to certain tests in our lives negatively (with hatred, revenge, jealousy, pettiness, or some other negative emotion), then we have not learned our lesson but have failed the test and will have to retake this test in either this or a future lifetime.

KARMA—AN EASTERN TRADITION WITH A WESTERN APPLICATION

The belief in the preexistence of an individual soul (or subconscious) has been called by many names. The terms *metempsychosis, transmigration, reincarnation, rebirth*, and *reembodiment* have been used to describe this mechanism. *Karma* is a Sanskrit word that literally means "action." (Sanskrit is an ancient Indo-European written language, dating from about 1500 B.C.) Karma is the force that leads to reincarnation. *Destiny* is another synonym for karma. In any one life we plant the seeds of the personality that will grow during that and subsequent incarnations (lifetimes). Thus, reincarnation is the mechanism by which karma works. The two must be considered together.

The basic law of karma has come to mean action and reaction, or cause and effect. This is equivalent to the Christian philosophy: "As ye do unto others, so shall it be done unto you." Any action that is considered harmful or evil to the well-being of another is recompensed exactly in proportion to the harm done.

One of the basic principles of karma is that every soul (entity) has free will. There is always freedom of choice. Each soul is drawn to parents who can provide the biological heredity and physical environment needed to learn karmic lessons. Psychic genetics is more important than biological genetics in determining the character of our lives. In addition, all lessons and deeds are recorded in the entity's Akashic records, which are used to determine each new lifetime. These records are the sum total of our past, present, and future lives and are stored in our subconscious.

A law of retribution extends over the entire karmic cycle. This law allows an entity to enjoy, in one lifetime, what it has earned in previous incarnations.

Often people will say that they are incapable of doing something because of their karma. In this case karma is being used as a crutch. Karma neither rewards nor punishes. This universal law of cause and effect gives meaning to all actions. Nothing happens by chance. It is only through ignorance and misuse that karma results in destruction, pain, sorrow, and suffering.

The concept of *transmigration* is included in Eastern karmic thought. Transmigration is the passage of the human soul from the mineral kingdom to lower animals and finally to man. Many Eastern philosophers reject this concept, as do the majority of Western karmic followers. Even those who do accept transmigration feel that it is impossible to revert back to the lower animal form once human form is achieved. I personally do not accept transmigration, and none of the 25,000 regressions and progressions that I have personally conducted have revealed a nonhuman existence.

Every culture since ancient times has accepted the idea of karma in some form or other. I will now trace the origin of karma from the East to the West. Then I will present some current popular explanations of the phenomenon.

EASTERN KARMA

Hinduism

The Hindus called the soul atman, which survives many lifetimes until it accomplishes its destiny of perfection, enlightenment, and joy and finally attains direct insight into its identity with Brahman, the World Spirit, and thus eliminates the necessity of rebirth.

Krishna states in the *Bhagavad-Gita*, the ancient Hindu script,

"Man doth not perish here or hereafter. The man dwells for an immensity of years and is then born again on Earth. Being thus born again he comes in contact with the knowledge which belonged to him in his former body and from that time he struggles more diligently to perfection."

The Laws of Manu, Book V, states: "On the departure of the individual soul from his body and its new birth in another womb, and on its wanderings through ten thousand millions of existences . . .

On the infliction of pain on embodied spirits, which is caused by demerit, and the gain of eternal bliss, which is caused by the attainment of their highest aim through spiritual merit . . ."

Tibetan Buddhism

The *skandhas* (heaps of attributes or elements of limited existence) play a most important part in the transmission of "unfinished business" in Buddhist philosophy. These karmic connections between lives (skandhas) are similar in function to the DNA that makes up the chromosomes responsible for inherited characteristics in the physical body. These skandhas remain at death as karmic remnants and attach themselves to the subconscious and subsequently are reincarnated along with the subconscious.

The *Tibetan Book of the Dead*, written thousands of years ago by advanced yogis, describes the different types of experiences a soul (subconscious) will have after death. According to this text, a soul passes through many nonphysical worlds before coming back to earth to be reincarnated. The amount of time spent in each of these worlds depends entirely on one's state of spiritual development.

A soul may linger in its former environment on Earth and visit familiar places of its past, or just observe its previous body before entering one of the nonphysical worlds. Eventually the soul enters a world of souls where it reevaluates its last lifetime and, after a certain period of time, is reborn into a new body.

One striking difference between the Hindus and the Buddhists in their concept of karma is that the former believe in a permanent soul, whereas the latter maintains that everything in the universe is in a state of change. Buddhists consider the soul to be a conglomeration of habit patterns, attachments, and instincts which are all subject to change. Thus, Buddhists feel that there is no permanent soul, just a pulsating subconscious that goes from lifetime to lifetime learning lessons until it achieves its liberation by attaining enlightenment. Buddhists say that the existence of the three "fires" of craving, ill-will, and ignorance bring about rebirth. The extinction of these "fires" is symbolized by the word *nirvana*, meaning "perfection."

Zoroastrianism

The teachings of Zoroaster of ancient Persia are preserved today by the *Parsis of India*. Mezoam separated man from the other animals by the presence of a soul. This soul is free and without a body or anything material. It is through the soul that man reaches God. Jam-i-Kaikhoshra stated, "After leaving this body a virtuous man acquires a still better place and body and his wisdom constantly increaseth."

The Koran

Under Islamic influence, Spain was a great center of philosophy. Avicebron, a Spanish Jew, brought the long forgotten teachings of Plato—who believed in a soul—back to European thought. During the Dark Ages in Europe, when the knowledge of Greece and Rome was all but lost, the doctrine of rebirth was being taught in the East by Al-Ghazālī and Al-Batagni in the schools of Baghdad. However, the Sufis, a Muslim mystical sect, did the most to preserve reincarnational thought in the East. The Sufis claimed to possess the esoteric philosophy of Islam. Saadi, Rumi, and Hafiz were Persian Sufi poets. A quote from the Koran, the sacred text of Islam, illustrates karma: "God generates beings, and sends them back over and over again, till they return to Him."

WESTERN KARMA

Stone-Age Karma

Primitive civilizations have often included human sacrifice as part of their rituals. They believed that only the body and not the soul was being sacrificed. Some North American and Central American Indians felt that human sacrifice helped the individual's karmic cycle.

In Great Britain, the ancient Celtic religion of witchcraft, or

Wicca, was eventually replaced by the incorporation of reincarnation into their religious beliefs. This also applied to France and Scandinavia.

Egypt

According to Egyptian beliefs, transmigration was the accepted mechanism of reincarnation. After a person died, he or she would reincarnate as an animal for as long as 3,000 years until the soul became purified. Only then could this soul return to the human form. The *Books of Hermes* state, "From one soul of the Universe are all Souls derived. . . . Of these Souls there are many changes, some into a more fortunate estate, and some quite contrary. The Soul passeth from form to form; and the mansions of her pilgrimage are manifold."

Greece

Orpheus was the founder of Greek theology. He taught the Greeks various sacred rites. Plato and Pythagoras used Orpheus as a source for their own philosophies.

In the *Life of Pythagoras* by Diogenes Laertius we find Pythagoras reviewing his previous lifetimes. He states that he was Aethalides and then Euphorbus, who was wounded by Menelaus at the siege of Troy and died there. As Aethalides, Pythagoras (582–507 B.C.) received the memory of his soul's incarnations as a gift from Mercury (God of Wisdom).

Plato (427–347 B.C.) states in *Phaedrus*, "Every soul is immortal. All that is soul presides over all that is without soul and patrols all Heaven, now appearing in one form and now in another. Every man's soul has by the law of his birth been a spectator of eternal truth, or it would never have passed into this our mortal frame, yet still it is no easy matter for all to be reminded of their past by their present existence."

In *Laws*, Book X, Plato states, "Know that if you become worse you will go to the worse souls, or if better to the better, and in every succession of life and death you will do and suffer what like may fitly suffer at the hands of like."

Ancient Judaism

Josephus, the Hebrew historian, states that there were three sects of philosophy among the Jews. These were termed the Essenes, the Pharisees, and the Sadducees. The Sadducees believed that the soul died when the body died but both the Essenes and the Pharisees believed in rebirth.

Philo Judaeus (20 B.C.-A.D. 54) says in *DeSomniis*, "The air is full of souls; those who are nearest to Earth descending to be tied to mortal bodies return to other bodies, desiring to live in them."

The Kabala is a sacred text supposedly representing the hidden wisdom behind the Hebrew scriptures. It was derived by the rabbis of the Middle Ages from older doctrines. Reincarnation often appears in the Kabala and was further developed in Hasidism. According to these teachings, all human souls have a common origin from primordial man (Adam Kadmon). Parts of Adam's soul (*nitzotzoth*) form every individual soul. Adam's original sin brought higher and lower souls into confusion. As a result, every soul had to pass through a series of incarnations before returning to God.

The ancient Jews believed that Moses was the reincarnation of Abel, the son of Adam. Their Messiah was to be the reincarnation of Adam himself, who had already come a second time as David.

Rome

The poet Ennius introduced karma to the Romans. In his *Annals*, Ennius tells how Homer appeared to him in a dream and told him that their two bodies had the same soul. Virgil (70–19 B.C.) in the *Aeneid* says, "All these souls, after they have passed away a thousand years, are summoned by the divine ones in a great array, to the Lethean river. In this way they become forgetful of the former earthlife, and re-visit the vaulted realms of the world, willing to return again into living bodies."

Christianity

An early Christian philosopher by the name of Origen (A.D. 185–254), considered by some historians to be one of the most prominent of all of the Church fathers, in his *Contra Celsum*, states, "Is it not more in conformity with reason that every soul for certain mysterious reasons is introduced into a body, and introduced according to is deserts and former actions? The soul, which is immaterial and invisible in its nature, exists in no material place without having a body suited to the nature of that place; accordingly, it at one time puts off one body, which was necessary before, but which is no longer adequate in its changed state, and it exchanges it for a second.''

Saint Augustine (A.D. 354–430), in *Contra Academicos*, discussed Plato's reincarnation by saying, ''The message of Plato, the purest and most luminous in all philosophy, has at last scattered the darkness of error, and now shines forth mainly in Plotinus, a follower of Plato so like his master that one would think they lived together, or rather—since so long a period of time separates them—that Plato is born again in Plotinus.''

There were many disputes over issues of Christian doctrine—especially over the preexistence of the soul—in the 500 years after the death of Christ. During the Dark Ages, the doctrine of reincarnation became hidden but fortunately did not disappear. Heretical Christian groups kept reincarnation and karma alive in the West.

In A.D. 529, Emperor Justinian closed the Neoplatonic School in Athens and banished the last of the Neoplatonists. For nearly a thousand years, with the exception of the Christian heretics, the concept of reincarnation disappeared from Christian Europe. Not until the fifteenth century in Florence, Italy, under the protection of the House of Medici, were the teachings of Plato and the concept of reincarnation revived.

George Gemistus (1355–1450) is credited with being the first person to reintroduce Plato to the Western world. Gemistus wrote, ''As to ourselves, our soul remains immortal and eternal. . . . Attached to a mortal envelope, it is sent by the gods now into one body, now into another, in order that the union of the mortal and immortal elements in human nature may contribute to the unity of the whole.''

Theosophy in the United States

In the last quarter of the nineteenth century, the Theosophical Society was founded in New York City by Mme. H. P. Blavatsky, Col. H. S. Olcott, William Q. Judge, and others. It marked the first widespread movement in the modern Western world to investigate and study reincarnation and related concepts. This represented a synthesis of religion, philosophy, science, and psychology.

Reincarnation in the East was thought of as a means to escape as quickly as possible from the wheel of rebirth and to attain nirvana. Westerners considered the return to earth life as a penance or as a means of purging oneself of impurities. Theosophists regarded reincarnation as the universal law of evolutionary progress, holding that in an infinite universe there must be infinite possibilities for growth and development. Thus, one would never outgrow the need for new cycles of rebirth.

H. P. Blavatsky (1831–1891) expressed her views by stating, "The doctrine of Metempsychosis (reincarnation) has been abundantly ridiculed by men of science and rejected by theologians, yet if it had been properly understood in its application to the indestructibility of matter and the immortality of spirit, it would have been perceived that it is a sublime conception."

SUMMARIZING REINCARNATION AND KARMA

Karma means "action" or "reaction." Another way to define it is to state it simply as cause and effect. Christians say, "Do unto others as it should be done unto you." The Christian philosophy views this cause and effect as occurring during a single lifetime. Followers of karma and reincarnation carry it over from lifetime to lifetime.

The law of karma states that any single entity is born into a particular lifetime under the exact set of circumstances and with the exact set of capabilities to best utilize his or her karmic cycle. These qualities were the result of previous incarnations.

The law of retribution encompasses the entire karmic cycle. Thus the soul may benefit or suffer in one lifetime from the events of its previous lifetimes.

The law of karma has many advantages for its students. It offers an understanding of the frustrations and obstacles that are experienced by people who don't seem to deserve this environment. Second, it offers a more scientific explanation for the teachings of Christ and all other religious leaders. Third, it acts as a deterrent to selfish, thoughtless, and harmful actions. Fourth, it facilitates the belief in an orderly universe, one in which law and order and a sense of moral purpose dominate.

One of the very attractive qualities about reincarnation and karma is the opportunity to meet challenges in new lives and to have a great deal of control over one's destiny. You might consider it a concept of evolution based on the laws of cause and effect. "As you sow, so shall you reap."

SOME POPULAR EXPLANATIONS OF KARMA AND THEIR BASIC PRINCIPLES

Below are some of the more popular concepts that attempt to explain karma and their major principles. I will not list every concept, because there seem to be more concepts than regressive hypnotherapists, but I will describe the most logical (in my opinion) and popular ones.

Before I do this, let me caution you about cults. During the past twenty years, many cults, or pseudoreligions, as I call them, have surfaced and tried to sell their philosophies to unsuspecting Americans. If you allow anyone to control your thinking there will undoubtedly be negative karma generated as a result of this experience. The rule of thumb that I use whenever an organization presents itself with the "answers" to all human problems, and especially if a single leader is offered who will show you "the way," then that group is a cult.

The answers to one's karmic cycle lie within one's subconscious. Any human being who immodestly takes credit for your accomplishments either has an ego problem or a great misconception of karma or both. Shakespeare said it best when he wrote, "To thine own self be true."

Here are the concepts as promised.

The Plane Concept

According to the plane concept, our karmic cycle is worked out on five lower planes. On each of these lower planes an entity (soul) has a level of awareness or vibrational rate. In order to go to a higher plane, your vibrational rate must have reached a certain level. Each successive plane requires a higher vibrational rate. If it is not at this level, then the entity will go to the plane that best fits its level.

The Lower Five Planes:

1. *The earth plane* or *physical plane*. This is the plane that we function in now. The body is most material or physical at this level. The greatest amount of karma can be erased or added on at this level. This is by far the most difficult level.

	GOD, OR NAMELESS, PLANE (PLANE 13)	
SEVEN	PLANE 12	
HIGHER	PLANE 11	
PLANES	PLANE 10	
	PLANE 9	
	PLANE 8	
	PLANE 7	

SOUL PLANE (PLANE 6)

KARMIC	ETHERIC PLANE (PLANE 5)	
CYCLE	MENTAL PLANE (PLANE 4)	
(LOWER 5	CAUSAL PLANE (PLANE 3)	AKASHIC RECORDS
PLANES)	ASTRAL PLANE (PLANE 2)	
	EARTH PLANE (PLANE 1)	*YOU ARE HERE*

FIGURE 2

2. *The astral plane.* The body is less material here. This is where the subconscious, or soul, goes immediately following death or crossing over. Ghosts are examples of astral bodies.

3. *The causal plane.* The body is even less material at this level. The Akashic records are kept here. This is where a medium projects him- or herself when he or she reads your past or future.

4. *The mental plane.* This is the plane of pure intellect.

5. *The etheric plane.* The body is least material at this level. On this place truth and beauty are most important.

The amount of time spent on these lower planes will depend entirely on the soul's achievements and remaining karmic debts. If you must develop intellectually then you would select the mental plane. If truth is most important to your karmic cycle then the etheric plane would be your choice. The earth plane represents the plane of greatest elimination of or addition to our karmic debts.

The Moment of Death

From the moment of death, the entity is placed in a very pre-carious position. This is a transition or adjustment period. We must first be made aware that we have died. This is accomplished by the very helpful guidance from highly evolved entities called Masters and Guides. These Masters and Guides have completed their karmic cycles many centuries ago. Their main purpose is to help us adjust to our death and to lead us to the white light that will take us to the intermediate realm of the sixth, or soul plane, where we will evaluate the last life and choose the next one. At this time, we may also see and com-municate by telepathy with friends or relatives who have previ-ously died. These entities will also try to persuade us to enter the white light.

If you don't enter the white light, you will remain on the astral plane as a troubled spirit. Most recently departed entities will find comfort in the last surrounding they inhabited on the earth plane. Thus, they will stay around their house or apartment. Some of their family may be made aware of their presence and would interpret this as a ghost haunting their house. Indeed, many cases of haunted houses are explained in this fashion.

The Soul or Sixth Plane

Eventually you will enter the white light and your destination will be the soul plane. Upon arriving at the soul plane you will be greeted by special guides who are assigned specifically to you for the purpose of orientation. Your guides will spend as much time as necessary to explain the nature of reality to you and your present purpose on this plane. You will be shown in detail the events from your last life and how they fit into your karmic patterns. Also, you will be shown scenes from past and future lives and your purpose will be to study these events in detail. It is as if you were a football player studying films of the team that you were scheduled to play that Sunday. Instead of preparing for a football game, you are preparing to choose your next life.

You are given a tremendous amount of help and advice by your Masters and Guides in these all-important decisions. First, you will have to select an era of time for your next life.

The historical time period that you choose is of great impor-tance. Those of us here in the twentieth century are supposed to have been around during the days of Atlantis. I have regressed many patients back to the days of Atlantis (a highly advanced civilization probably located in the Bermuda Triangle) and Lemuria (a highly advanced civilization theorized to have been in the Pacific Ocean, and predating Atlantis—50,000 B.C.)—both of which are now lost to us in the present. There are certain lessons that can best be learned during more primitive historical eras, such as the Dark Ages. The beginning of the Industrial Revolution would offer a stage for quite different challenges. Finally, the twentieth century, with nuclear power, space shuttles, laser beams, and other technological achievements, offers quite a different arena for our karmic lessons.

The length of time between lives varies greatly. When I regress patients back to the Middle Ages, it can be centuries in between lives. Regressions of the eighteenth and nineteenth centuries usually result in about seventy-five years from the end of one life to the beginning of the next. Twentieth-century regressions are the fastest in that there seems to be a range of from one year to twenty-five years between lives. Apparently, our vibrational rates and karmic lessons to learn are such that coming back rapidly is necessary in this century.

Astrology plays a major role in deciding a time period for your next life. The exact time, place, and date of birth will be very important. If you have artistic lessons to learn and sensitivity is to be experienced, then coming back as a Pisces would be indicated. Learning lessons as an executive or leader might dictate coming back as a Scorpio, Capricorn, or Leo. Of course, your other planetary influences such as the moon, ascendant, Mars, Mercury, Venus, etc., must also be carefully selected.

In addition to astrology, "subcycles" must also be taken into consideration before any decision concerning the overall karmic cycle can be made. Within our karmic cycles, these smaller subcycles, such as certain emotional, intellectual, creative, and physical tasks, when completed, finish a certain phase within the total karmic cycle. Some parapsychologists say that every twelve lives makes up a subcycle. These twelve lives correspond to the zodiac signs in astrology. Theoretically, we choose a different astrological sign in each of these twelve lives to complete the cycle.

There is something called a "karmic chart," which can be constructed from your birth date, time, and place. This is quite different from a regular astrological or natal chart in that it specifies what your subcycle is and can give you great insight into your overall karmic cycle.

On the soul plane, you will also be choosing your parents, brothers, sisters, and other family members, as well as planning all the major events in your life. These events must take into consideration the karmic cycle of these other people. Using the football analogy again, it would be like trying to formulate the schedule for the National Football League. Imagine how difficult it would be to formulate the schedule of so many teams, with conference, interconference, and other factors to consider to fulfill league requirements and at the same time try to make each team happy with its schedule.

Not only must you be fully aware of your own karmic cycle but you must be at least familiar with the karmic cycles of the many significant people whom you will come into contact with in your new life. Whether you will be rich or poor, an only child or a member of a large family, black or white, weak or strong, will all depend on a very complicated selection process that your past life history will decide. Your Akashic records have all of this information and they will be your constant reference on the soul plane.

Akashic Records

These Akashic records are reportedly kept on the causal plane, but we do have access to them on the soul plane. They represent a file on the soul's growth and development throughout its many lives. They contain what the soul has learned and not learned. Thus, the soul's progression through its karmic cycle is what the Akashic records will show. By using these records we have intimate knowledge of what we have done and what we have to do. This is a most valuable aid.

For example, because of past karmic debts, in your next life you might need to stress the intellect. The emotional side of living would be underplayed so that the intellect could be developed to its maximum potential. Or the opposite situation might present itself. Your physical status is also important. A handicap, although it seems an obvious disadvantage in your new life, gives you the opportunity to learn certain lessons that would be difficult to learn if no such defect existed.

The Principle of Forgiveness

What is interesting to note about working out our karma is the principle of forgiveness. When I have the patient speak from the superconscious (the highest level of the subconscious) mind level I am informed of how this principle works. Assume that you lived during the time of the Vikings, about 1,200 years ago. Raiding villages, burning buildings, raping the women, and murdering the villagers would have been commonplace. This would incur much negative karma. If during one of these raids a certain group of villagers would have their lives spared because of your kindness, then you would earn positive karma. It wouldn't be just one positive episode against many negative ones. The fact that you showed this kindness would erase many negative episodes during that particular incarnation. If you spent the rest of that life helping other people, all of the past murders, thefts, and other crimes could be removed from your karmic cycle.

Free Will

Since the soul always has free will, it is our decision to be born at a certain time and place. It is our decision to choose our parents, friends, lovers, and enemies. We cannot blame other people or a bad childhood or marriage for our present problems. We are directly responsible for our lives because we have chosen the environment. The basic framework of your new life will be preplanned by you, but you can't plan every situation. Not only does *your* soul have free will, but so do *all* the souls that you will come into contact with in this new life. The main point there is that you choose the tests.

Group Karma

We do not just reincarnate individually. Rather, as I have been suggesting, our own separate karmic cycles are intertwined with many others. For example, your parents may have been your children in a former life. Your wife may have been your brother or son, etc. This is not to say that karma involves any form of incest or other such moral judgment. It simply implies that our lessons are intermingled with the lessons of other entities. These lessons have an effect between entities and among others around them.

Group karma applies to everything we do. People who are killed in airplane crashes, wars, or other catastrophes actually chose that time and place to die. Case histories later in the book will develop this concept further.

Masters and Guides

We are aided in making these decisions by our Masters and Guides. These highly evolved entities have completed their karmic cycles and their purpose is simply to help and advise us as to our next lives. They do not moralize or pass judgment. They simply counsel us and try to help us as best they can. The individual soul always has free will to ignore their advice. Many of our decisions are poorly made for this very reason. These Masters and Guides also receive advice from even higher entities with higher vibrational rates in the seven higher planes. These much more advanced entities receive their advice from even more evolved sources, the ultimate authority being God or ALL THAT IS (as many parapsychologists refer to God). The final result is, of course, excellent guidance. When we listen to these guides, we make better decisions and work out our karmic cycles faster and with much less trauma.

Choosing a New Body

This is a very complicated process and group karmic considerations must be met. That is, you have to consider the karmic cycle of dozens of other entities before you can finalize your plans. These other entities must agree with your plans because they also have free will. This veto power can cause untold delays in the final framework of your and their next lives.

There can even be competition for certain bodies. Let's assume that you have completed your design of the basic framework for your next life. Now you must choose a newborn to enter. But let's say that another entity desires this same newborn for his or her karmic cycle and gets the right to inhabit it. You still have a karmic cycle to work out with the parents and other members of that newborn's family. You will now have to find another suitable newborn and devise a way to relate karmically to the parents and other family members of the newborn you were prevented from entering. We don't know exactly how the order on the waiting list for bodies is decided. It is probably based on a priority system giving those souls with the most important karmic lessons to learn first priority.

Once you have carefully chosen your next body and designed the basic framework of your next life, you are ready for the soul's entrance into the newborn. During the course of the pregnancy, each soul may visit its future body. Indeed, many souls actually enter the developing fetus, and this is why many people have prenatal memories that can be tapped through the use of hypnosis.

One reason that the soul can come and go as it pleases at this time is because the fetus's nervous system has not fully developed yet. There are openings in the skull (cranium) called "fontanels" that allow the soul, or subconscious, to enter or leave the body. These openings will not close until the child is about two-and-a-half years old. (Some people refer to these openings as a "chakra.") This helps explain the psychic nature of children.

The soul or subconscious, actually enters the body of the newborn within twenty-four hours before or after the birth of the child. Many times during our childhood the soul will leave the body. This will occur during the waking hours as well as at night as the entity sleeps. All throughout our life the soul will leave the body during our sleep state, because it is during this sleep state that our Masters and Guides can continue teaching and advising us on our earthly progress. Thus, we are never really without the benefit of our guides, and the process of learning that began in between our lives never really ends.

Other Decisions on the Soul Plane

Much counsel is given to an entity on the soul plane. However, even with all this advice and plenty of time to make these decisions, some people choose to reincarnate before they are advised to. This is unfortunate because the necessary planning has not occurred. Instead of saving time, much time will be wasted and many errors will be made.

Relationships represent important decisions on the soul plane. Telepathic communication between you and the other entities involved will establish the details of who you will relate with and how in your next life. Your son in this life may be your father in your next life. Your wife or husband may be your brother or employer or parent.

Soul mates, or people with whom you have had very significant love relationships over many lifetimes, will be handled carefully. These soul mates represent the culmination of many lifetimes of being together and of sharing the most valuable emotion of all. You will not, however, be with your soul mates in every life.

In choosing your next life, the earth plane may not be to your liking. In that case you might choose any of the other lower planes (astral, causal, mental, or etheric) to work out your karmic cycle. Life on these other planes isn't very different from that on the earth plane. People get married, have children, divorce, love, hate, etc. on all of the lower planes.

There are some entities that will not reincarnate immediately. They may act as teachers or a kind of guide themselves. Of course, only entities who are more highly evolved with higher vibrational rates will be able to take this karmic vacation. Eventually they too must come back and resume their karmic cycle.

The Seven Higher Planes

You may choose any of the lower five planes to work out your karma, but as long as you have a karmic cycle you cannot enter the seven higher planes—your vibrational rate would be too low to allow this to happen.

The lower five planes exist simultaneously but function at different frequencies. The frequencies are similar to a radio signal. Let's assume that the earth plane is at frequency 5000 and the astral plane is at frequency 5200. As long as your vibrational rate is 5000, you will not ascend to the astral plane.

Beyond the soul plane there are seven higher planes, with the highest plane being the nameless, or God, plane. On the God plane the essence of all of us resides. What this concept is saying is that God is within all of us, we are all creators, and we create our own realities. God is also called ALL THAT IS by the followers of this concept. Thus, this God plane is the equivalent of heaven.

What I find particularly appealing about this concept is that there is no hell. Hell is merely the temporary negative aspects of one's lives on the lower five planes. However, there is a heaven in this concept. Many people assume parapsychology to be an atheistic (no belief in God) or agnostic (not believing in God unless proof of its existence can be obtained) discipline, but nothing could be further from the truth. When we reach the God plane we are perfect. The subconscious—or soul—is pure.

As with the lower five planes, it is your vibrational rate that determines which of the seven higher planes you enter. If your vibrational rate is for the eighth plane, then that is where you would reside. Your level of consciousness—your thoughts and actions—determines your vibrational rate.

Please refer back to Figure 2 for an illustration of the plane concept.

SOME OTHER POPULAR CONCEPTS OF KARMA

The Oversoul Concept

This particular karmic concept claims that you are part of a larger soul. You are merely an extension of this complete soul. In order for this oversoul to learn many different lessons, it creates smaller souls so that it is living many lives simultaneously. Past, present, and future occur simultaneously, according to this concept.

One interpretation of this concept places the oversoul on the God plane. Thus, although we are functioning on the lower planes, we are all directly part of God. We would then all be Gods.

Some regressions have uncovered parallel lives or one entity reporting two former lives at the same dates but in different locations, lending credence to this view.

Simultaneous Multiple Incarnation Concept

As the earth's frequency begins to accelerate with technological advancements, more and more of the older souls will now be attracted to coming back to this era of time. These very mature souls have the ability to inhabit many bodies at one time. Thus, they can speed up our evolutionary process.

Also, many parapsychologists feel that only highly evolved souls with certain vibrational rates would be able to survive in the twentieth century.

The Space-Time Continuum

FIGURE 3

This concept states that there is no such thing as the past, present, or future, as we know it. All of our various lives are being lived at the same moment but at different frequencies. Thus, your past lives are occurring right now on a different frequency along with your present and future lives. They are all affecting one another. You are thus able to change the past and future by changing the present.

To illustrate this concept, imagine yourself in a spaceship leaving the Earth. As you look back down on the Earth you see the present occurring in Europe, the past in South America, and the future in North America. As you return to the Earth you choose which era, or continent, by this example, you want to function in. Einstein's Theory of Relativity, which tells us that there is only the probability—not the certainty—of the existence of matter at any point in time, is in line with this concept.

The Linear Concept of Reincarnation

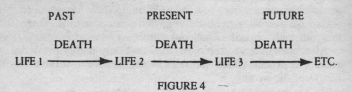

FIGURE 4

This concept simply states that the past is history, the present is occurring now, and the future hasn't occurred yet. This is the notion of time we are most familiar with. Thus, your past and future lives have no direct effect on your present life, and vice versa. This is, of course, in conflict with the classical concept of karma, on which this book is based.

The Extraterrestrial Concept

This concept assumes that sometime between 100,000 B.C. and 50,000 B.C. the Earth was visited by beings from another planet. Their purpose was to observe the Earth. These beings were pure energy and had no bodies, as we know them. They were curious about what it would be like to have a body, so they took over the bodies of humans at that time. These extraterrestrials were able to leave the body at any time. However, because they misused the body and committed all kinds of negative acts, they were punished by being trapped inside the body. Their own karma was preestablished, and all they had to do was work out this minimal karmic debt and they would be free to leave the body upon its death. However, their karma was increased by further negative actions and thus we have our current karmic cycle.

This concept offers some interesting explanations. Our immediate predecessors (Cro-Magnon man) lived from about 40,000 B.C. to about 25,000 B.C. Neanderthal man preceded Cro-Magnon man and lived from about 75,000 B.C. to about 40,000 B.C.—during the time the extraterrestrials are said to have come to Earth. One interesting note about the evolution of modern man (*Homo sapiens*) is that we evolved far faster than we should have. Evolution is a very slow process, yet the difference between Cro-Magnon man and modern man is enormous. Since I don't believe in coincidence or mere chance, it is obvious that some other factors were at work in our evolution. A possible explanation for this rapid evolution is that these extraterrestrials, by means of some form of genetic engineering, altered the makeup of Neanderthal and Cro-Magnon's brain cells to allow more intelligent thought patterns to be exhibited.

The ancient civilizations of Atlantis (in the Atlantic Ocean) and Lemuria (in the Pacific Ocean) were said to have begun between 75,000 B.C. and 50,000 B.C. There have been many books published suggesting the physical evidence of visitors from other planets. If the idea interests you, by all means pursue it.

I have only attempted to sketch in some background data concerning karma. As far as your belief in a particular concept goes, you may choose from these or form your own opinion. Whatever you do, keep an open mind. When the student is ready the teacher will be there. If you don't believe in karma or reincarnation, don't worry. You probably will in your next life.

CHAPTER FOUR

Documented Proof
of Reincarnation

I S IT POSSIBLE TO PROVE THE CONCEPT OF REINCARNATION beyond any shadow of doubt? The answer must be no, with the present limitations of our available data. Even with all of the documented cases, no matter how many facets of a case check out, there will always be skeptics who will try to explain the results by coincidence or some other outdated answer.

It is physically impossible to determine just how much of what a patient has read or been exposed to is mistakenly reported as the impression of past life during hypnotherapy. Still, when a child reports information in a regression using the vocabulary of an adult or speaks in foreign languages that he or she has never been exposed to, I find no other explanation more plausible than reincarnation.

In this chapter I will present just a few of the best documented cases of reincarnation. These should make some of the skeptics think twice.

BRIDEY MURPHY—FACT OR FICTION

The Bridey Murphy story is not the first documented case of a previous lifetime, but it is by far the best known. Morey Bernstein, a businessman in Pueblo, Colorado, regressed Mrs. Virginia Burns Tighe (called Ruth Simmons in the book) between

November 29, 1952 and August 29, 1953. Mrs. Tighe's past life was in Belfast, Ireland, in the 1800s and her name was Bridey Murphy. The results of these six tape-recorded hypnotic regressions were published in 1956 by Doubleday and Company as *The Search for Bridey Murphy*.

Morey Bernstein had learned to use hypnosis and for ten years prior to his regressing Mrs. Tighe, he had offered his services as a hypnotist without charge to local physicians. At first Mr. Bernstein was very skeptical about the idea of past life regression. As the sessions continued, he became convinced that Mrs. Tighe had, in fact, lived before.

In 1952 Virginia Tighe was married. She and her husband were only casually acquainted with the Bernsteins. Mrs. Tighe was born in 1923 and lived in Madison, Wisconsin, until she was three years old. At that time she moved to Chicago, where she grew up. After attending Northwestern University for a year and a half, she married an army air corpsman who was killed in World War II in 1944. After moving to Denver, she married businessman Hugh Brian Tighe and raised three children in Pueblo, Colorado.

Morey Bernstein chose Mrs. Tighe as his subject because he had hypnotized her twice before and realized that she was capable of achieving a very deep hypnotic trance. She also knew nothing of Morey's interest in reincarnation. Neither Bernstein nor Virginia Tighe had ever traveled to Ireland.

In trance, Mrs. Tighe described her life in Ireland. She was born in Cork in 1798, the daughter of a barrister named Duncan Murphy and his wife, Kathleen. Virginia's name in this life was Bridey Murphy and she had a brother named Duncan Blaine Murphy. Bridey attended a school run by a Mrs. Strayne. Duncan eventually married Mrs. Strayne's daughter Aimee. Bridey had a second brother who died as a baby. She was Protestant, and at age twenty married Sean Brian Joseph McCarthy, the Catholic son of a Cork barrister. The young couple later moved to Belfast, where Brian attended law school and taught law at Queen's University. There had been no children during their life together. In 1864 Bridey died at the age of sixty-six.

There were many attempts to prove and disprove the accounts of Mrs. Tighe's six regressions. I will discuss only those facts that were verified and which leave little doubt as to the authenticity of this case.

Bridey mentioned Farr's and John Carrigan as two Belfast grocers from whom she bought food. John Bebbington, the chief librarian in Belfast, verified this fact. In addition, these two men were the only individuals of those names who were in the food-stuff business in Belfast at that time. Bridey also mentioned a rope company and a tobacco house that were operating in Belfast. These also have been verified.

Some of the statements that Bridey made were refuted by experts based on known facts but were later shown to be correct after all. An example of this is the statement by Bridey that as a child she received a spanking for scratching all of the paint off her metal bed. Experts reported that iron beds were not introduced into Ireland until at least 1850. The Encyclopaedia Britannica stated that iron beds appeared in Ireland in the eighteenth century.

Second, Bridey called the place in which she lived "the Meadows." A map of Cork in 1801 showed an area named Mardlike Meadows, where about half a dozen houses were indicated. Third, she stated that her husband taught law at the Queen's University in Belfast in 1847. Experts said that Queen's College was not founded until 1849 and Queen's University wasn't established until 1908. Subsequent research found that on December 19, 1845, Queen Victoria declared that "there shall and may be erected . . . one college for students in arts, law, physics . . . which shall be called Queen's College, Belfast." On August 15, 1850, Queen Victoria founded Queen's University in Ireland and stated "that the said Queen's Colleges shall be, and . . . are hereby constituted colleges of our said university."

Fourth, Bridey mentioned little sacks of rice that were tied to the leg as a sign of purity. *Life* magazine's expert on folklore, Richard Hayward, refuted this by saying that rice had never been part of Irish folk traditions. But rice was, in fact, imported into Ireland at about 1750. Since rice is white it would naturally suggest purity and this custom is quite possibly accurate.

Fifth, Bridey talked about reading a book called *The Sorrows of Deirdre*. Experts stated that according to the English catalog of books published between 1800 and the present, the first appearance of this book was in 1905. Later it was discovered that an inexpensive paperback was published in 1808 by Bolton entitled *The Song of Deirdre and the Death of the Sons of Usnach*.

Sixth, she mentioned the tuppence as one of the coins used in her day. This proved to be correct but only very few people knew that this particular coin was in use in Ireland only from 1797 to 1850. There were many other rather obscure facts that were initially disputed by experts but were subsequently corroborated upon further investigation.

It is interesting to note that throughout these six recorded sessions, Bridey gossiped and exaggerated her actual position in life. It soon became obvious that she was a member of the lower class (probably a coachman's wife or the wife of a messenger for a barrister). Her attempts to raise herself to the middle class and the awe and jealousy that she exhibited toward the middle class are natural responses. However, these qualities would hardly have been presented as such if this were all a hoax.

One final note on this case is the session centering on the last years of Bridey's life in Belfast. Mrs. Tighe spoke with a weary, half whine and a throaty Irish accent that defies all explanation other than reincarnation. She could hardly have been exposed to it in this life, since the accent of the Belfast slums has never been used by American actors. Also, to have mastered such an accent, Mrs. Tighe would have had to be a very accomplished actress. As a "typical American housewife," she possessed none of these qualities. In my opinion, these last tapes illustrating this accent are more convincing of her life as Bridey Murphy than many of the controversial facts she stated that have subsequently been verified.

THE RESEARCH OF DR. IAN STEVENSON

Dr. Ian Stevenson was born in Montreal, Canada, on October 31, 1918. He received his medical training at McGill University and was later associated with the Alton Ochsner Medical Foundation of New Orleans and Cornell Medical College. From 1949 to 1957 Dr. Stevenson was assistant and associate professor of Psychiatry at the Louisiana State University School of Medicine. From 1957 to 1967 he was chairman of neurology and psychiatry at the University of Virginia Medical School. Since then he has been alumni professor in psychiatry.

Much of Dr. Stevenson's research has been in reincarnation. His book entitled *Twenty Cases Suggestive of Reincarnation* deals with interviews of children whose memories very strongly suggested reincarnation. Dr. Stevenson is recognized as one of the world's foremost authorities on reincarnation.

The case of a five-year-old Lebanese boy named Imad Elawar, who in 1964 lived in the village of Kornayal, provides an interesting example of documented reincarnation. Imad claimed to have been in his last life Ibrahim Bouhanzy, who died of tuberculosis on September 8, 1944, at the age of twenty-five. After eliminating the possibility of the child receiving information of this family from travelers or other family members, Dr. Stevenson questioned Imad about his past life. Imad claimed to recall his former family and the place where he had lived. He mentioned the names Mahmoud and Jamile (whom he described as beautiful, well-dressed, and wearing a red dress that he had given her). A sister named Huda was mentioned, along with Amin, Mehibe, Adil, Talil, Toufic, Salim, Kamel, and Said, whom he referred to as brothers.

A total of fifty-seven claims had been made; fifty-one proved to be correct. Imad did not visit the village of Khriby of his former life until Dr. Stevenson came onto the scene. Jamile, it seems, had been Ibrahim's mistress. When Imad was four, he rushed up to a stranger and hugged him. Imad stated that they were neighbors. The stranger had, in fact, lived in Khriby and had been a neighbor of Ibrahim Bouhanzy.

Dr. J. G. Pratt, an associate of Dr. Stevenson's at the University of Virginia Medical School, aided Dr. Stevenson in his analysis of this most remarkable case. They both concluded that it was not practically possible for Imad to have traveled to Khriby, because of the topography. Fraud was also dismissed after a careful analysis was made of the evidence collected. Neither family stood to gain and both stood to lose by lying.

Another interesting case is William George. George was a Tlingits Indian fisherman in Alaska who at the age of sixty (in 1949) told his son and daughter-in-law that he would return as their son. He stated that they would recognize him by his present birthmarks, and he gave them a gold watch to hold for him. William George disappeared while fishing shortly afterward. Less than a year later his daughter-in-law had a son who had the exact same birthmarks as William George.

As the boy grew up, he mimicked his grandfather in many ways, including a limp that William George had incurred in a basketball game. The boy also correctly identified the gold watch by picking it out of his mother's jewelry box unprompted. He also constantly referred to his uncles as "sons" and his great-aunt as "sister."

Dr. Stevenson wrote: "He shows a precocious knowledge of fishing and boats. He also shows greater than average fear of water for boys of his age. He is more grave and sensible than other children of his group.''

A PSYCHIATRIST EXPLORES HIS OWN PAST LIFE

Dr. Arthur Guirdham, an eminent British psychiatrist, stated in 1977 that he and one of his patients shared a past life together and that he was convinced that reincarnation was a fact.

In 1962 a patient called Mrs. Smith came to see Dr. Guirdham about nightmares that she had been having. These scenes always involved her lying on a floor in a room awaiting some terrible event. Soon after seeing Dr. Guirdham the nightmares stopped but memories of a past life emerged.

She reported a life as a member of the Cathar sect, a persecuted religious cult in thirteenth-century France. Mrs. Smith stated that Dr. Guirdham was her lover, that his name was Rogiet, and he was a blue-robed priest of the Cathars.

Dr. Guirdham contacted a noted French historian, Professor René Nelli, and asked him to investigate this matter. Professor Nelli is on the faculty at Toulouse University in France and he is an authority on thirteenth-century French history. Each fact that Dr. Guirdham provided Professor Nelli from Mrs. Smith's visions checked out.

The clinching item seemed to be the blue robes of the Cathar priests. Scholars had for centuries maintained that these robes were black. Professor Nelli's research proved Mrs. Smith correct and the scholars incorrect. No history book contained this information. Only ancient records written in a language that Mrs. Smith had no knowledge of contained this all-important information. Mrs. Smith could not possibly have known about the blue robes beforehand.

THE CASE OF JONATHAN POWELL

When George Field was fifteen years old and living in Hinsdale, New Hampshire, he was hypnotized by the late Loring G. Williams into a past life as Jonathan Powell. George stated that his father's name was William Powell and his paternal grandmother was Mary Powell. They were Quakers who lived in the village of Jefferson in Ashe County, North Carolina. Their house was near the "Big Hill."

During the Civil War Jonathan had to work for the Northern army soldiers. He hated those "damn Yankee soldiers." One day, when he refused to sell five sacks of potatoes to these soldiers because they offered him such a low price, they shot him in the stomach and killed him.

Williams, George Field, and a number of others drove down to Ashe County to verify this account. Powell was an uncommon name during that time in Ashe County. A local historian, Eleanor Baker Reeves, confirmed that a Jonathan Powell had actually lived.

After being regressed again George Field was asked questions by Ms. Reeves. She confirmed that George had an accurate knowledge of fifteen of the twenty people she asked him about. Well over sixty percent of the answers George gave to her questions were found to be correct. Field also exhibited great knowledge of the changes in the topography of Ashe County from 1860 to 1965.

George Field had never been to Ashe County before. He also described a river called South Fork, which did not show up on the maps of his home state (New Hampshire), but did show up on local North Carolina maps. Also, most of the residents of the village were Baptists but there were a few Quakers present.

A woman whose maiden name was Powell was located, and she claimed to be Jonathan Powell's great-grandniece. She stated that her great-granduncle had been killed by Union soldiers during the Civil War, but she didn't know the details about his death.

Last, George Field spoke of Yankee soldiers wearing gray uniforms. Eleanor Reeves stated that even though Union soldiers normally wore blue uniforms, at that time there were bands of renegade soldiers who came from the North, wore gray uniforms, and raided and plundered some Southern villages. Jonathan Powell could have easily been killed by one of these renegade soldiers.

THE CASE OF HENRIETTE WEISZ-ROOS

Henriette Roos was a portrait artist and concert pianist who lived in New York. She recalls that she was Rossaritta Weisz, a miniature portrait painter, in Bordeaux, France, during the 1820s. She also claims to have given asylum to the famous Spanish painter Goya when he was exiled from Spain.

Henriette showed great skill as an artist as a child in Holland, although she never had any formal training in art. She married a Hungarian pianist and composer named Franz Weisz at the age of seventeen.

After showing some of her work to the Royal Dutch Academy in Amsterdam, Henriette was enrolled there as a student and graduated with honors. She divorced Weisz soon after, but kept his name, contrary to the local custom, and was now called Henriette Weisz-Roos. She had a strange attraction to the name Weisz.

In the summer of 1936 in Paris, Henriette, unable to sleep, was compelled to paint in the dark. She did this for several hours and then went back to bed. When she awoke the next morning she discovered that she had painted a beautiful portrait of a young woman. It was the best work she had ever done. She contacted a medium and found out that Goya was repaying the kindness, which she had shown him by offering him asylum in 1820 in France, by guiding her art career.

Several days later, Henriette found a book about the life of Goya. She learned that a woman named Leocardia Weisz gave Goya asylum during his exile from Spain. Leocardia had a daughter named Rossaritta Weisz who was a miniature portrait painter and who looked after Goya. After reading this account, she dropped the name Weisz from her surname.

What is interesting to note is the following:

1. Both Henriette and Rossaritta were miniature portrait painters.

2. Both Henriette and Rossaritta were fond of cats.

3. Both Henriette and Rossaritta were sympathetic toward the poor.

4. Rossaritta was crushed to death in a crowd at the age of twenty-seven. Henriette was always afraid of crowds.

5. Henriette came from a family without any interest or background in painting, yet she showed natural talents in this field.

6. Henriette never made it public that she was directly inspired by Goya. Her silence showed that she never tried to profit from her past life, thus discounting the accusation of fraud.

7. Henriette's portrait style is very similar to that of Goya.

8. Henriette was unusually attracted to her married name of Weisz, and she violated a local custom in keeping that name for some time after her divorce.

EDGAR CAYCE

Edgar Cayce was an uneducated man who spent most of his life in Virginia Beach, Virginia. He is one of the world's best-known psychics. His specialty was in diagnosing medical conditions of people he had never met. When placed in a hypnotic trance, Cayce would not only correctly diagnose the patient's medical problem but would recommend the correct treatment in approximately 99 percent of the cases he handled. He would receive a letter from someone he did not know, and just from the patient's name, would recite the diagnosis and prescription. Mr. Cayce had no conscious knowledge of medicine nor did he even believe in reincarnation until very late in his life.

At the time of his death in 1945 Edgar Cayce had given more than 14,000 telepathic-clairvoyant readings; 2,500 of these are called "life readings." These "life readings" traced the past lives of individuals and aided them greatly in understanding their present problems. These discourses have fortunately been preserved and are kept in the library of the Association for Research and Enlightenment at Virginia Beach. Each reading is carefully indexed and notes the name of the stenographer, the conductor of the session, and all witnesses present. In addition, each reading is accompanied by background information, if there is any, along with follow-up correspondence with the individual, his or her doctor, or family. I highly recommend reading the story of his life and other books that have been written about him.

XENOGLOSSY

Xenoglossy is the speaking and/or writing of a foreign language in trance by a person who possesses no conscious knowledge of this language. When children are regressed and speak or write foreign languages fluently, which they have not been exposed to in this life, I consider this proof of reincarnation. One could rationalize a word or phrase being mastered in a foreign language by a child, but not an entire language. There is no way that a person's subconscious mind could have been exposed to an entire foreign language without conscious awareness of this. When adults or children start writing in hieroglyphics or other dead languages, I start thinking about past lives.

The case histories that fill the bulk of this book are my own documented experiences with past and future lives. All the evidence has been collected during private sessions with my patients, and much of the dialogue is transcribed directly from tape recordings made with my patients' full knowledge and permission.

The potential benefits from regression therapy are limitless, as you shall shortly see. With the background you have acquired from these first four chapters you are now ready for a more detailed explanation about what regression is and how it works.

CHAPTER FIVE

On a Clear Day
You Can See Yesterday:
Age Regression with Hypnosis

WHY DO PATIENTS SEEK PAST LIFE REGRESSION HYPNOTHERAPY?

There are a multitude of experiences from past lives that can negatively affect us in our present daily lives. A fear of water can be the result of drowning in a past life. A woman who died in a desert sandstorm when she was a nomad in her last life now has an unusual fear of wind.

Insomnia was treated in a middle-aged woman by revealing a previous lifetime as a male Civil War sentry for the South who fell asleep at his post. Union soldiers killed the sentry and his fellow soldiers, so the karmic association of going to sleep and death was well established. Fortunately, reliving that lifetime removed the insomnia.

An overweight man starved to death in a past life. Another man wondered why he was such an overprotective father until he found out that he had deserted his family in two previous incarnations.

A teenage girl came to see me because she was afraid of meeting new people. In the 1700s she was a little girl confined to a hospital in France for three weeks. Every time she had a visitor, the nurse would wash her face very roughly, getting soap in her eyes and nose. It was not surprising to learn that in this life every time she met someone new her nose began to hurt.

A workaholic in this life witnessed his family starving to death in Greece hundreds of years ago because he was not able to adequately provide for them. By overworking himself in this life, he was preventing that from ever happening again. Fortunately for him, his past life regressions removed his workaholic compulsions permanently.

A woman suffering from frigidity in this life found out that she was rejected by her husband in a past life because she was raped. Her husband in this life was the same entity as her husband in that past life. By being frigid, she was repaying him for his actions. Today, she is no longer frigid thanks to past life regression.

I personally feel that there isn't a problem or negative tendency that past life regression therapy cannot help. I also feel that this is the very best and most efficient form of therapy that has ever been devised. The case histories presented in this book are just a sample of the kinds of real-life problems that can be helped with past life regression.

The most important benefit of regression and progression therapy is not the retelling of scenes from past or future lives. It is a change in perspectives on life, an enlightenment as to who you are and what you are supposed to be doing here. The realization of constant evolution to something bigger, better, and more fulfilling is very beautiful to witness. I witness this every week of my life.

AGE REGRESSION

Regression is simply going back in time. If you think about what you had for lunch yesterday, you are regressing with your conscious mind proper. Hypnotic regression is going back in time utilizing the subconscious mind with its perfect memory bank. I will use the term *simple age regression* to refer to going back in time in this lifetime. The term *past life regression* will refer to the going back in time in a prior lifetime.

Simple age regression is by no means a simple procedure. The patient is guided back in time by systematic disorientation as to the present year, months, and day. Appropriate suggestions are then given to reach the earlier age. Personality traits characteristic of this age will often be exhibited by the regressed patient. For example, speech patterns, handwriting, and other characteristics of that earlier age become evident.

There are two types of age regression. The first type is called *revivification*. In this type the hypnotized patient actually relives or reexperiences the events of his or her life at an earlier age. For the duration of the trance, all memories following the regressed age are removed. Only somnambules (patients capable of very deep trance) are capable of achieving this deep-level trance. Although it is easier to obtain desired information at this level, it is not necessary to attain this level to use simple age regression.

The second type of age regression is called *pseudo-revivification*. This type is characterized by the patient being able to relive scenes from an earlier age, but the memories following this age are not forgotten. In other words, patients are aware that they are still in the present but the scenes are from the past. Their speech, handwriting, and other characteristics will not have changed from those they possess currently. This is by far the most common form of age regression, and much detailed information can be obtained. In this type of regression, as with any type of regression, the patient will reexperience the emotions of the scenes he or she is reliving.

At no time is the patient in danger of being trapped in this earlier age. Even in true revivification the patient can come back to the present at any time he or she wants to.

One characteristic of both types of regression is *hypermnesia*, or heightened recall. The memory banks of the subconscious mind are now being tapped and the patient can recall literally anything that he or she has seen, heard, touched, smelled, or tasted. As long as you physically experienced something, age regression can bring the information back. In fact, the use of hypnosis in criminal investigation has received much attention during the past twenty years—for just the reason we have been discussing: the strength of recall under hypnosis. From remembering license plate numbers to recalling the details of a rape or murder case, hypnosis has been accepted as an important evidence-gathering technique by many police departments. The fact that courts have utilized the services of hypnotherapists shows the change in the public opinion as to the validity of this technique.

Not long ago, I had occasion to use hypermnesia in a legal case. The patient, whom I shall refer to as Ralph, was involved in a car accident on New Year's Day in the early morning hours.

He was referred to me by a former hypnosis patient. Ralph, a very likable man in his late thirties, simply could not recall the details of what happened on that fateful morning. Since this was a legal case and since the details of the accident were crucial to determine insurance liabilities, my services were requested.

Ralph went to a New Year's Eve dance with his wife, Susan, and three other couples. At about 3:00 A.M. Ralph and Susan decided to go to a bar called Dunhills to wish Happy New Year to a friend of theirs who owned the bar. After parking their car on Calvert Street they walked across the street to Dunhills. As they crossed the street a large van hit Ralph, and Ralph completely repressed (pushed the scene back into the subconscious) all knowledge of the actual accident itself. The next thing that he remembered was being in a hospital at about 5:00 A.M. that morning.

Nearly a year later, Ralph, Susan, and their attorney came to my office for the initial session. At this time I explained what hypnosis was and wasn't and an initial trance was induced. The attorney was impressed with Ralph's relaxed state during the trance.

The second session was held on November 20th, but I was unable to obtain any information. Ralph came alone to this and the successive sessions. I was not surprised at this initial failure since I was attempting to reexplore a very traumatic event. Regression conditioning suggestions were given and he was dismissed. During the next two sessions, Ralph recalled scenes from December 26th through December 31st, but I was still unable to reexplore the moment of impact.

On December 15th the entire accident was relived and this session was recorded. I repeated the regression on December 22nd and also recorded the session. Here are some excerpts from this last session:

Dr. G.:   Carefully, step by step, tell me what you experienced next.
Ralph: I felt something hit me.
Dr. G.:   On what side did you feel something hit you?
Ralph: On my right side.
Dr. G.:   Did you hear any noise before the impact?
Ralph: No.
Dr. G.:   Did you see what hit you?
Ralph: No. No, I was facing the other way, looking to my left.

Dr. G.:   What do you see at the moment of impact?

Ralph: I can see myself trying to catch my balance, but I'm falling and knocking Susan down.

Dr. G.:   When you are on the ground where is the vehicle that hit you?

Ralph: It, it is to my right.

Dr. G.:   Where are the wheels of this vehicle in relation to the central white line on Calvert Street?

Ralph: The right wheels of the van are on the Dunhills side of the white line, but the left wheels are on the other side of the line.

Dr. G.:   How do you feel now?

Ralph: I hurt all over. I can barely move and all I can feel is constant pain.

Dr. G.:   Sleep now and rest and detach yourself from all discomforts. Focus now on my voice. When I reach the count of five you will awaken refreshed, relaxed, and will recall everything you reexperienced. One, two, three, four, five, awaken.

As you can see, Ralph was able to provide much information as to the moment of impact and the events that followed.

The use of age regression in treating habits and phobias makes use of this reexperience effect to help the patient understand why he or she acquired a particular negative tendency and what emotions were felt at the time. This last point is particularly important because the repressed emotions seem to account for about 80 percent of the causes of a patient's problem. The repressed scene alone accounts for the remaining 20 percent. By using age regression, a patient can relive the visual memories along with the emotions, and by bringing up these repressed emotions, he or she is effecting the cure to the problem. Simple age regression can also be used to help recover lost items, especially if related to a traumatic event.

The reason we develop symptoms of headaches, backaches, arthritis, colitis, allergies, asthma, and many others is because of a breakdown in our conscious mind proper's repression mechanism. If we experience a particularly negative scene along with unpleasant emotions, the conscious mind has a natural tendency to repress or bury these memories and emotions in the subconscious mind. However, with time this repression mechanism breaks down and the memories begin to surface. The surfacing of these memories without the emotions is too much for the conscious mind to take. It decides against dealing with this scene. In order to divert its attention, a negative physical symptom is created. By reliving the scene and reexperiencing the repressed emotions, many physical symptoms can be permanently removed.

PAST LIFE REGRESSION

The use of past life regression can eliminate the causes of other habits, phobias, and negative tendencies. There are many techniques to regress a patient into a past life. Some therapists use simple age regression to go back to the birth experience and then suggest the next logical step—going back into a past life.

I don't feel this is necessary. For one thing, birth is a traumatic experience for everyone. Second, the subconscious mind knows all about your past lives and doesn't need a map to find them. I simply ask the patient's subconscious in trance to go back to the origin of a particular problem or to relive a prior life that would give insight and understanding to the patient's present life.

Many people are curious about what they will experience in a past life regression. There are many possible experiences. First, you may see a scene and at the same time be aware of information related to this scene. I refer to this as both an audio and visual experience and it results in excellent data. Fortunately, it is the most common experience with my patients. It's as if you are watching a movie or television show.

The second type of experience consists of seeing cloudy or quick impressions that tend to disappear just as you are about to understand them. Another reaction is appearing to "know" or be aware of the environment without actually seeing or hearing anything. Feeling as if someone were whispering in your ear is another possibility. Reading words that appear before your inner eyes is a very rare type of experience, although this may be how some people know what the date is or what country they are living in.

Although there are people who regress large groups of people into past lives, I am a believer in individual regressions. I have done both individual and group past life regressions and I have experienced much better detailed information with individuals. When I work with a patient individually I can be much more effective in helping him or her to overcome a problem or just find out more about him or herself and his or her karmic cycle. A number of so-called coincidences can be traced back to prior lives, and these scenes can be most helpful to patients in helping to explain why certain things have happened to them.

Shielding or protective techniques are always applied to a patient undergoing a past life regression. In all of the thousands of regressions that I have done, I have never had a traumatic episode or any type of negative experience. I shield with what I call "spiritual protection." This technique consists of having the patient imagine a pure white light entering the top of the head and filling the entire body, surrounding each and every muscle, bone, and organ. That is all there is to it. This white light is to protect the patient from any harm or negativity that he or she might experience.

The case of Andy will illustrate the benefits of this technique. Andy is a blue-collar worker who joined a coven in Baltimore because of his wife's interest in witchcraft. He quickly lost interest in this coven because of the many negative things that they were doing. He and his wife stopped going to the meetings but he started having hallucinations. At his job he would hear voices of people who weren't there and see shadows of people that would disappear when he turned around. One day he received a call from the coven leader telling him that these hallucinations would not stop until he rejoined the coven.

Andy came to me for help. He proved to be an excellent hypnotic patient, and after three sessions of spiritual protection his problems ceased. All I did was to protect Andy from the psychic attack he was receiving from the coven leader and his followers. The white light is to ward off any negative influence, regardless of the source. After a time the coven leader realized Andy was protected and no longer attempted to harass him with this form of negativity. Andy was free. (Let me say at this time that I advise everyone to stay away from any form of witchcraft, black or white magic, and especially covens. They are all negative and your karma, as well as your present life, may be made unpleasant by these groups.)

PROGRESSION

Now that you understand the basics behind regression, let us discuss progression. Progression is going forward in time. It is used in any kind of regression to return the patient to the present. For example, let us assume you were regressed to the age of five. If I then wanted to move you forward to the age of eight, I would progress you three years on the count of five. Finally, I would progress you back to the present, just prior to concluding the session. This is called progression. You are never in danger of being trapped in the future.

Progression also has other uses. It can be used to see how a particular decision that a patient is considering will come out. For example, let us assume you are considering changing your job. You progress yourself two years in the future and you can find out if you did change jobs and whether or not it worked out to your advantage. Let me make clear that I am not referring to psychic experiences. I do not consider myself a medium or reader of the future. It is merely the use of hypnotic progression that enables me to help patients help themselves. I quite realize that there is no way to prove a progression other than waiting to see if a particular event occurs as seen in the progression.

Many people consider progression a form of wishful thinking. I will be the first to admit that the viewing of a scene in the future could possibly be the workings of hopes and desires of a subconscious mind, except for one fact. The viewing of scenes in the future of which the patient could have no control over establishing. An example of this would be reading a newspaper headline that exists five years in the future describing a natural disaster or the election of a president or a war, and having that event occur in five years just as it was read in trance five years before. No other explanation, in my opinion, could even come close.

SIMULTANEOUS TIME

In the last chapter, I briefly mentioned the lack-of-time concept. This concept offers us an interesting explanation as to the mechanism of a progression.

The lack-of-time concept states that the past, present, or future do not exist as isolated blocks of time. The past, present, and future occur simultaneously and each can affect the other. Just because we are taught all through our academic years to think of the past as having occurred, the present as occurring, and the future as about to occur, that is less than proof-positive of the way things are. Einstein's Theory of Relativity and quantum physics offer us far different possibilities of time.

If we assume for a moment that all time is occurring right now, then it is easy to see how one can read the future or past almost as easily as one reads the present. The placing of one's self in a hypnotic trance merely removes the usual barriers of time and allows for more complex observations.

The main problem in understanding the lack-of-time concept is that we function in a three-dimensional reality. There are many other dimensions that are illustrated by various forms of psychic phenomena. Time as we know it is merely an illusion created by our own physical senses. Our five senses perceive reality as occurring a little bit at a time. It thus appears that one event exists and is gone forever and is replaced by the next event which also disappears. Since our perception is limited, we nicely place time into three separate components called past, present, and future.

An example of this concept is the dream state. Imagine having several dreams in a particular night. Each dream may encompass one hundred earth years but to you, the dreamer, only minutes have passed. During the dream state your subconscious mind is freed of the dimension in which time, as we know it, exists.

Since what we term past, present, and future events appear to us in sequence, we find the idea of simultaneous time difficult to accept. Since, in that scheme, all events would occur at the same moment, a past event really doesn't cause a present one, nor does a present event cause a future one. Thus, our past and future lives really don't have to happen as we think they do. By changing our present circumstances we can effectively change our karma.

Think of how much karma could be removed by dealing with the past, present, and future lives all at the same time. By the same token, think of how much karma can be added on instead of removed. This should actually give us more incentive to become a better person now.

Let me use the dream state again to illustrate the concept of no time. Some parapsychologists feel that when we dream we are being advised by our Masters and Guides on another dimensional plane. Since we are on a different plane, time has no meaning for us. We are shown how to work out our karma. We are taken to what we on the earth plane would call the future.

Many people tell of having dreams of flying or of falling great distances. It has been postulated that this is a conscious remnant of the projection into the future that we experience in our dream state. The term *astral projection*, or *out-of-body experience* (OBE), has also been used to describe this state. We all leave our body when we dream. The dream state for all of us is a communication between our dimension, or reality, and others'.

To understand the concept of creating your own reality, review the lack-of-time concept. If the present can directly change the past and future, you create your own reality every moment you exist. You alone are totally responsible for your life and the environment in which you live. Look within yourself for the causes of your good or bad fortune. Remember, karma is cause and effect.

DÉJÀ VU VERSUS SYNCHRONICITY

When I give lectures on karma, I am often asked about the many coincidences that seem to occur in people's lives. As a parapsychologist I long ago dropped the term *coincidence* from my vocabulary. The term *synchronicity* is far more accurate.

Carl Jung, the Swiss psychiatrist, coined the word *synchronicity*. He used it to describe particularly meaningful occurrences without any apparent cause. This synchronicity seems to happen to people just at the right time and place. When you most require a certain chain of events to occur and they do, despite seemingly impossible odds, then you are experiencing synchronicity. ESP, telekinesis, psychokinesis, astrology, omens, déjà vu, and precognitive dreams are examples of this principle.

The following is a possible physiological explanation of synchronicity: There are two hemispheres of the brain, the left and the right. Synchronicity actually entails the communication of the intuitive right brain (the subconscious and superconscious) with the analytical left brain (the conscious mind) through the use of symbolic events. Thus, these so-called coincidences represent the purposeful communication of the subconscious and superconscious minds with our conscious minds. Since the right hemisphere of our brain contains all knowledge of past, present, and future lives through the Akashic records, and since the left hemisphere of our brain barely keeps up with our present life, it is no wonder that consciously we call these events a "coincidence" and dismiss them from further thought or consideration. I personally feel that absolutely nothing happens by mere chance or coincidence.

Everyone has had experiences with déjà vu. When you walk into a building that you know you have never seen or been in before but somehow feel that you have been there, you are experiencing what pyschologists call déjà vu. The classical explanation states that in this building you may see some furniture, paintings, curtains, or other structures with which you are familiar. The mind then simply extrapolates (extends beyond this association) the entire environment as being familiar.

In my opinion, this explanation just doesn't work. Many times patients have reported to me that absolutely nothing in the building seemed familiar—yet they knew they had been there before. It is my theory that one of two things has occurred. The most likely possibility is a progression. Perhaps a week before you visited this building, your subconscious mind read this event. Then, when the event became a reality, you felt strangely familiar with it. This sometimes happens to me in reference to conversations. I could be talking to someone and all of a sudden I know exactly what they are about to say next.

The second explanation, occurring less often, is the possibility that you had a past life in this building or a significant past life event occurred in or around the building. This has explained many of the spontaneous regressions that have been reported to me.

A good example is a young woman who came to me for a past life regression in 1978. She told me nothing about her background or experiences before I hypnotized her. Then, in the trance state, she described in detail a life in medieval Germany. She had traveled to Germany the previous summer on a vacation and was supposed to leave for Belgium, but was delayed unexpectedly for twenty-four hours. To kill time she went to a castle that had been converted into a museum. While in this castle she viewed a portrait of one of its residents, dating back to the thirteenth century. She spontaneously went into a regression and relived the life of this woman. She couldn't move a muscle during the experience, which lasted about forty-five minutes.

Her purpose in coming to me was to confirm certain details about the regression, which she fortunately was able to do. Since this young woman was from Baltimore and had absolutely no interest or background in German history, I cannot accept the classical explanation of déjà vu for this spontaneous regression.

DOCUMENTATION

Many people have asked me to use progression to predict the outcome of elections, stock market prices, etc. I will not do this for many obvious reasons, most important being the possible influence on the public as well as the creation of panic if a natural disaster is foreseen. Until this field is thoroughly investigated, I, myself, have more questions than answers.

When dealing with past life regression, the question of verification always comes up. Of course, many regressions have been thoroughly documented. A simple progression can be documented if you are patient enough to wait until the expected event is to happen. But how do you document a future life progression? The answer is simple—you don't. Waiting a few lifetimes or hundreds of years goes beyond even my patience. One day science may come up with an answer, but until that time this must remain an unsolved mystery.

In June of 1981 I conducted a rather unusual experiment. Charlie Donovan is the host of an evening talk show on WFBR radio in Baltimore. Since February of 1981 I have been the show's contributing editor on hypnotherapy and have many times discussed regression and progression on the air. Charlie called me on Friday, June 5, to request my help in breaking the Baltimore Oriole's five-game losing streak. The Orioles were to play the California Angels that weekend in Anaheim. Prior to that day the Orioles had lost three straight games to the New York Yankees. I progressed myself to the following day to see if I could visualize the box score of the game. The score I came up with was 6 to 3 in favor of the Orioles. During dinner that evening I thought of the score of 6 to 4 but dismissed it because the first impression is usually more accurate.

At 9:15 P.M. Eastern Standard Time I went on the air and had the listeners concentrate on the score "Baltimore 6 and California 3." I do not in any way consider myself to be a psychic, merely a hypnotherapist. For approximately one minute there was silence on WFBR as about 125,000 people concentrated on this score. At 9:25 P.M. I said good-bye to Charlie and my fans. The game began at 10:30 EST.

The score was 6 to 3 in favor of the Orioles by the middle of the seventh inning. A passed ball by the Baltimore catcher in the bottom of the seventh inning resulted in the final score being Baltimore 6 and California 4. The box score read as follows:

BALTIMORE	3	0	0	1	0	2	0	0	0	6
CALIFORNIA	0	0	1	0	0	2	1	0	0	4

Mass utilization of 125,000 subconscious minds seemed to have broken their losing streak.

There were 125,000 witnesses to this live demonstration of progression. I don't know exactly why or how this experiment worked, but there may someday be an answer.

CHAPTER SIX

Didn't We Meet
in a Past Life?

L OVE RELATIONSHIPS ARE BY FAR THE MOST REWARDING of all karmic entanglements. Couples quickly find out that they have been together before in many past lives. They will also be together again in future lives. When there is a problem in a relationship, past life regressions can often pinpoint the exact cause of the problem. One partner may have deserted his wife in a past life and thus incurred a karmic debt. In the life prior to that one the wife that was deserted may have deserted her husband or perhaps she accidentally caused his death. Thus, a cycle of karmic debt and retribution was established.

This cycle will continue until all of the lessons are learned and all of negativity is balanced by positivity. The principle of forgiveness will help speed up this process, but the cooperation of both members is necessary. Carl's case nicely illustrates these principles.

Carl came to see me several years ago. He was bothered by what is referred to as secondary impotency. This means that Carl was able to function sexually at some times, but not at other times. Physiologically there was nothing wrong with Carl, but psychologically he had problems. He was very much distressed when he came to my office. His voice was always soft and somewhat high-pitched.

After working with Carl for six weeks I felt that the cause of his impotency was rather straightforward. A simple age regression revealed a scene in which Carl was in his present wife's

(Martha) apartment. Martha was divorced at that time and she and Carl had been dating for about six months. On a fateful Sunday morning in June, Carl was in bed with Martha when his sleep was disturbed by a loud knock on Martha's front door. Carl was very groggy at the time so that he didn't consciously remember this incident, although he readily reexplored it in trance. Martha's ex-husband was at the door. He saw Carl's truck out front and he was threatening Martha. He said that he knew that Carl was in her bedroom and if he ever caught them making love he would kill Carl. Carl's subconscious mind heard this and it was the beginning of their sexual problems.

Carl was rather impressed with this regression because his impotency episodes almost completely disappeared within two weeks. However, I was not satisfied that this was the true cause of Carl's impotency and I suggested past life regression. Carl was not sure about reincarnation, but he was willing to try anything that might solve his sexual problems.

Several weeks later Carl had his first past life regression. He described a life in the eighteenth century in France. Carl was the son of a fisherman in a small seaport on the east coast of France. His name was Ladin. Gene was his best friend and Gene's father owned most of the boats in this town. At the age of fourteen Carl's (Ladin) father died and Carl became a fisherman working with Gene. The following conversation represents Ladin at age twenty-four:

Dr. G.:   Are you still working for Gene's father?
Carl: No.
Dr. G.:   What happened?
Carl: Gene, he's got all of the boats. His father died. Gene is my buddy. I got my own boat now.
Dr. G.:   Do you enjoy your work?
Carl: Yeah. Especially when she goes with me.
Dr. G.:   Who is she?
Carl: Jeanne, my girl, Jeanne.
Dr. G.:   How long have you known Jeanne?
Carl: About two years.

Carl's voice had dropped to a very low level at this time. He now spoke with great confidence.

Dr. G.:   I want you to move forward to a very important event that occurs between you and Jeanne on the count of

	five. One . . . two . . . three . . . four . . . five. What do you see now?
Carl:	We're sitting right there at the table. She is going to the doctor.
Dr. G.:	What is wrong with Jeanne?
Carl:	She doesn't have long.
Dr. G.:	She doesn't have long to live?
Carl:	No. That's not it. She's pregnant, but they're not sure whether the baby will make it.
Dr. G.:	Are you married to Jeanne now?
Carl:	Yeah.
Dr. G.:	I want you to move forward to after the time Jeanne sees the doctor. One . . . two . . . three . . . four . . . five. What do you see now?
Carl:	The doctor—he must be a quack.
Dr. G.:	Why?
Carl:	He don't know nothin'. He don't know what to do. I have to stay with her all the time.

I progressed Carl to the day of the birth of his child.

Dr. G.:	What is happening now?
Carl:	Jeanne, she is screaming.
Dr. G.:	Where is the doctor?
Carl:	He's not there. There's some woman there instead.
Dr. G.:	What happens now?
Carl:	It's all over. My baby is lost (crying).
Dr. G.:	All right, Ladin, detach yourself from any negative emotions and tell me exactly what happened.
Carl:	They couldn't save him. I, I feel it's my fault. Oh, my God, Jeanne's dead! She died giving birth to a dead baby. It was a boy. I'll never go through that again.

Carl made up his mind not to have children again. His subconscious mind could very well have interpreted that literally by causing him to be impotent. After progressing Ladin ahead five years in time, the following information was obtained:

Dr. G.:	Where are you living now?
Carl:	I'm living in town.
Dr. G.:	What are you doing?
Carl:	I got a shop. I make fishing nets. I'm respectable.
Dr. G.:	How is business?

Carl: Pretty good. My pa, he should have done this.
Dr. G.:   What happened to Gene?
Carl: I, I don't see him.
Dr. G.:   Where does Gene get his nets from?
Carl: He sure doesn't get them from me.

Carl was progressed to his death. I then contacted his super-conscious mind and questioned him about his life as Ladin.

Dr. G.:   How does Gene relate to your life as Carl?
Carl: Gene is Randy.
Dr. G.:   Who is Randy?
Carl: My little brother.
Dr. G.:   Who is the entity known as Jeanne?
Carl: She's my wife, Martha.
Dr. G.:   Who was your father, the fisherman?
Carl: He is my Uncle Charlie.

From the superconscious mind level the patient can identify people from a past or future life and inform me who they are in their present life. Carl as Ladin blamed himself for Jeanne's (Martha's) death as well as that of their baby boy. By becoming impotent he eliminated the possibility of putting Martha through another traumatic pregnancy.

The less experienced therapist might be satisfied with this regression as the cause of Carl's present impotency. However, there are usually a series of lives and incidents relating to any problem. One must go beyond this regression and continue to search for other causes. On December 29 Carl was regressed into another past life. He described a life in the fourteenth century in Germany.

Dr. G.:   What is your name?
Carl: Hans.
Dr. G.:   What is it that you do?
Carl: I take care of the castle.
Dr. G.:   Where do you live?
Carl: In a small room in the back of the castle.
Dr. G.:   Who owns the castle?
Carl: The lord. He lives there with his wife.
Dr. G.:   How old are you now?
Carl: Fifteen.

Carl was progressed to the age of twenty.

Dr. G.:	What do you do for a living?
Carl:	I'm a soldier.
Dr. G.:	Where do you fight?
Carl:	I protect the castle.
Dr. G.:	From whom?
Carl:	Beggars and invaders.
Dr. G.:	Move forward five years on the count of five. One . . . two . . . three . . . four . . . five. Are you still a soldier?
Carl:	Yes. I command 300 men.
Dr. G.:	Do you have a woman?
Carl:	Helena. Helena is the most beautiful woman in the world.
Dr. G.:	Are you married to Helena?
Carl:	No. She is the daughter of the lord (the owner of the castle).
Dr. G.:	On the count of five, I want you to move forward to a significant event, if any, that occurs between you and Helena. One . . . two . . . three . . . four . . . five. What do you see now?
Carl:	I'm all dressed up. I've got my shields on.
Dr. G.:	What is the occasion?
Carl:	I'm marrying Helena.
Dr. G.:	How do you feel?
Carl:	I feel great (very excited).

Carl was then progressed to the birth of his first child.

Dr. G.:	What do you see now?
Carl:	My baby.
Dr. G.:	Is it a boy or a girl?
Carl:	It's a boy, a baby boy.
Dr. G.:	Where are you living now?
Carl:	I have a small house near the castle.
Dr. G.:	Who lives in the castle now?
Carl:	The lord's wife. The lord died and now his wife lives there.
Dr. G.:	Are you still a soldier?
Carl:	Yes, and I'm damn good at it, too.
Dr. G.:	How do you get along with the lord's wife?

Carl: I don't like her. I told her to get out of the castle. It's mine and I want it.

I progressed Carl forward to a scene which would show a resolution of this problem, if any existed. He was now forty-five years old.

Dr. G.:   Where are you living now?
Carl: In the castle.
Dr. G.:   Where is the lord's wife?
Carl: I threw her out. She's crazy.
Dr. G.:   Why do you say that?
Carl: My soldiers forced her and her people out, but she makes trouble.
Dr. G.:   What kind of trouble?
Carl: She says things about me and she is trying to organize another army to attack my castle.

Carl was progressed forward to a scene that would signify a resolution to the problem with the lord's wife. He reported an attack on the castle.

Dr. G.:   What is happening now?
Carl: The soldiers are inside my castle and they're killing my men.
Dr. G.:   Do you recognize these soldiers?
Carl: Yes. They came once before with her (the lord's wife) about two years ago to try and get me to leave the castle. I wouldn't leave. It's my castle and I'm not leaving.
Dr. G.:   Where are your wife and child now?
Carl: Oh, dear God, they're dead! She (the lord's wife) did this. I'll get back at her if it's the last thing I do.

Carl died that day. He was killed by one of the soldiers, and the lord's wife eventually moved back into the castle. When I spoke to Carl's superconscious mind, I found out that the lord's wife in that lifetime is his present wife (Martha). His statement concerning getting back at her was represented by his impotency. Carl was married before and never had any sexual problems until he met Martha. He was thirty-five years old when he met his present wife.

On January 19, 1979, I regressed Carl back into another lifetime.

Dr. G.:	What do you see?
Carl:	Smoke. I see smoke.
Dr. G.:	Anything else?
Carl:	Tall trees. Many, many tall trees.
Dr. G.:	Are you in the woods?
Carl:	Yes. I'm outside my cabin. It's cold out and I'm gathering wood for the fireplace.
Dr. G.:	Can you see yourself?
Carl:	Yes.
Dr. G.:	What do you look like?
Carl:	I'm, I've got very long hair.
Dr. G.:	What color?
Carl:	Brown.
Dr. G.:	What is your name?
Carl:	Jake.
Dr. G.:	How old are you?
Carl:	Eleven.

Jake was born in 1802 in a cabin in Maine. His father's name was John and his mother was named Hilda. Jake did not go to school. He had a sister named Becky.

Dr. G.:	Can you read and write?
Carl:	Yes.
Dr. G.:	Who taught you?
Carl:	An old lady comes up from the village to learn me.
Dr. G.:	Do you like her?
Carl:	Yes, but sometimes she hits me on my fingers with a stick when I say something wrong.
Dr. G.:	What do you do with your time?
Carl:	I hunt. I like to hunt.
Dr. G.:	Who do you hunt with?
Carl:	I most hunt with Pa, but I like hunting with my buddy, Sam.
Dr. G.:	What do you hunt?
Carl:	Deer, mostly.

Jake was progressed ten years in time.

Dr. G.:	How old are you now?
Carl:	Twenty-two.
Dr. G.:	Do you have a girlfriend?

Carl:	Yeah.
Dr. G.:	What is her name?
Carl:	Amy.
Dr. G.:	How did you meet her?
Carl:	She works in the general store in the village. I met her there.
Dr. G.:	How do you get along?
Carl:	She likes me a lot but she doesn't want me to hunt.

I progressed Jake ahead five years to the age of twenty-seven. His father had died and he had left home to start his own life. He and Sam bought a small farm and hunted together often.

Dr. G.:	Where are you now, Jake?
Carl:	I'm in my room, thinking. [Jake's voice was very deep.]
Dr. G.:	What are you thinking about?
Carl:	I killed a fox yesterday. I hate them foxes.
Dr. G.:	Where is Amy?
Carl:	I don't got time to fool with no woman. She wouldn't come with me when I moved here.
Dr. G.:	Where is Sam?
Carl:	He's out hunting deer.
Dr. G.:	Why aren't you hunting with him?
Carl:	I didn't feel like it today. I just want to think awhile.
Dr. G.:	What are you thinking about?
Carl:	Things.
Dr. G.:	What kind of things.
Carl:	Last week I almost shot Sam. He got real mad at me.
Dr. G.:	Is that why you didn't go hunting with Sam today?
Carl:	Yeah. Hey, why all these damn questions? Just who the hell are you anyway?

This sometimes occurs in trance. If a patient is reliving an uncomfortable scene, he or she may become somewhat indignant to my voice. They will demand to know who I am. Fortunately, this effect is temporary and questioning can resume in a few minutes.

| Dr. G.: | How are you and Sam going to solve this problem the next time you go hunting? |
| Carl: | We worked out some signals. When me or him whistle a certain way that means it's us and not some damn animal. |

Jake was then progressed ahead to an important event that occurred between him and Sam.

Dr. G.:	Where are you now?
Carl:	I'm in the woods.
Dr. G.:	What are you doing?
Carl:	I'm hunting. What else would I be doing here?
Dr. G.:	Are you alone?
Carl:	Nah, Sam is hunting with me. He's out somewhere ahead of me.
Dr. G.:	How does Sam feel about hunting with you again?
Carl:	Oh, he's okay. We worked out a plan to get some deer. We haven't killed a deer in over two weeks.
Dr. G.:	Where exactly are you now?
Carl:	Quiet.
Dr. G.:	What's happening.
Carl:	Be quiet. Can't you hear that?
Dr. G.:	No. What is it? What do you hear?
Carl:	There's something moving in the bushes. I'm gonna get me one of them deer.
Dr. G.:	Did you kill it?
Carl:	I don't know. I shot it and the bushes stopped moving. I better see if I got it.
Dr. G.:	Did you kill the deer?
Carl:	Oh, my God. I shot Sam. He's hurt real bad. Why the hell didn't he whistle?
Dr. G.:	What is happening now?
Carl:	I'm trying to get him back to the house.
Dr. G.:	What is he saying to you?
Carl:	Nothing. He's unconscious.
Dr. G.:	How far are you from the house?
Carl:	Just a couple of miles.
Dr. G.:	Move forward to the time when you and Sam are back in the house at the count of three. One . . . two . . . three. What is happening now?
Carl:	I'm going into the village to get the doc. I sure wish I didn't have to leave Sam here alone.
Dr. G.:	Is he still unconscious?
Carl:	Yeah. He don't look good.

I progressed Jake to the completion of this event. It seems that he had a difficult time finding the doctor. A local bar was

where the elderly physician spent much of his time. Jake found
him there shooting pool and finally convinced him to come out
to the cabin. The doctor attended to Sam, but it was hopeless.
It was just a matter of time before Sam died.

Dr. G.:   What is going on at this time, Jake?
Carl: The doc, he can't do much for Sam. Sam's gonna die.
           It's all my fault.
Dr. G.:   Is Sam conscious now?
Carl: He's lost a lot of blood. He can barely talk.
Dr. G.:   What is he saying?
Carl: He says that it all happened so fast. He didn't know
           where I was.
Dr. G.:   What does he say to you?
Carl: He says 'Don't touch me.' He tells me I'm stupid and
           that he wished he never knew me. He looks so pale.
Dr. G.:   How do you feel, Jake?
Carl: I'm so ashamed. It's all my fault. I should have whis-
           tled before I shot into the bushes.

    I removed Jake from this scene and progressed him forward.
It seemed that Jake's life went downhill after Sam died. He left
the farm and moved into the mountains. He built a small cabin
there and hunted and fished most of the time. It was a very
lonely life and Jake was most relieved when death finally came.
I took him to the superconscious mind level and asked him some
final questions:

Dr. G.:   How do you feel about your life Jake?
Carl: I didn't do anything right. I was so lonely. If only I
           didn't shoot Sam.
Dr. G.:   Who was Hilda? Who is Hilda in your present life?
Carl: The secretary, Pam, down at work. That's who Hilda
           is.
Dr. G.:   What about John? Who is John?
Carl: Daniel. He's one of my buddies at the plant.
Dr. G.:   Who is Becky?
Carl: She's my sister-in-law.
Dr. G.:   What about Amy? Who is she?
Carl: Emily.
Dr. G.:   Who is Emily?
Carl: She was a girl that I dated when I was in high school.

Dr. G.:   Who was Sam?
Carl: Martha. Sam is Martha.

What is most important about this life is the death scene with Sam. Sam said to Jake, "Don't touch me." He made Jake feel guilty and useless. Carl's subconscious mind remembered this, and his present impotency was a direct result of this incident.

This case illustrates the principle of changing sexes. Martha was a male in her last life as Sam. Although most of your lives will be lived as one sex, the karmic cycle requires at least one change of sex.

When Carl was Ladin in the eighteenth century in France, he blamed himself for Martha's (Jeanne's) death. She died in labor and Carl promised himself that he wouldn't go through that experience again. He didn't want to have any more children. In his next life as Jake he would never marry. One might say that he indirectly caused the death of Martha as Ladin, but as Jake he directly caused Martha's (Sam's) death by accidentally shooting him. The amount of guilt that Carl brought with him from these past lives was enormous.

In the lifetime as Hans, Carl forced Martha (the lord's wife) out of the castle. Martha won in the end and caused the death of Carl. Carl swore that he would get back at her if it was the last thing he ever did. He was good to his word as he sought karmic retribution indirectly during his next two lives as Ladin and Jake. His present life as Carl might have ended up the same way. Fortunately, Carl was able to see the causes of his sexual difficulties. If I had regressed him further, I'm sure I would have found other lives in which Martha let him down and vice versa.

It doesn't matter who started the problem. All that really matters is that the problems get resolved. Today, Martha and Carl have no sexual problems. They love each other very much and have finally learned to live together in peace. It takes many lifetimes for most couples to finally resolve their difficulties.

CHAPTER SEVEN

Bob and the "Light People"

THERE ARE MANY THEORIES ABOUT THE ORIGIN OF OUR
species. Anthropologists and paleontologists have strong
opinions about Africa as the birthplace of humankind. Religious
leaders have equally strong and conflicting theories. Parapsychologists have yet a very different explanation. Earlier in the
book I spoke of the extraterrestrial concept of evolution and
reincarnation. Although this is one of the most controversial
aspects of parapsychology, Bob's case history might lend some
credence to this theory.

Every so often I regress patients only to find that they are not
in a physical form. They do not possess a body. They are pure
energy. The most common form of energy is light. The term
"light people" has been used to describe entities that do not
take physical form. Bob's case is actually quite typical of a "light
people" regression.

In November of 1979 Bob called my office for an appointment. For the first time in his time in his life he was suffering
from insomnia. For the past two months, recurring nightmares
had kept waking him in the middle of the night and he had found
it difficult to fall asleep again. When he awoke the following
morning he felt drained. It was obvious to him that he had experienced some traumatic dream during the night, but he did
not remember the content. Also, his lack of energy was affecting
his work.

Bob came to my office for his first appointment on a cold

November afternoon. A medical technologist by profession, Bob was a highly intelligent and well-educated man in his late thirties. Parapsychology was not one of Bob's interests and he seemed somewhat anxious about being hypnotized. After hearing my explanations about hypnosis and asking some background questions, Bob settled down and was induced into a trance. At no time during this initial session did I discuss past life regression. Most cases of insomnia can be treated easily enough without the use of regression. In routine cases I simply record a cassette tape that would relax the patient and program him to think of only pleasant thoughts before going to bed.

Bob was seen once a week for the next month and his insomnia disappeared. He was able to sleep soundly for the first time in three months. However, he did report an unusual dream to me, the only one he could remember. The environment of the dream was impossible to put into words. When he stated that all he could see around him were beams of light, I knew I had another "light people" regression in the making.

I explained the process of regression to Bob, being careful not to discuss past life regression of the "light people." The reason I handled this case in this way was twofold. First, I didn't want to impose my belief system onto Bob. Second, I wanted him to enter a regression without any preconceived notions about extraterrestrials.

Bob was quite willing to explore regression therapy. By this time he trusted me and held hypnosis in much higher esteem than he had the preceding month. After two sessions of simple age regression. Bob felt very comfortable with the technique. He was a good medium-trance patient and a pleasure to work with. Highly intelligent people with excellent powers of concentration make the best hypnotic patients. Bob had both of these qualities in abundance.

On December 20, Bob was to be the recipient of a most unusual Christmas present. I always allocate additional time when I know in advance that this type of regression is going to be performed. The reason for this, as you will see shortly, is that there are many obstacles to a free flow of information. In most regressions, once a patient begins to answer questions, the information begins to flow rather freely. This is definitely not the case with a "light people" regression. After Bob was induced into good medium trance, I asked him to go back to the origin of the nightmares that he had been experiencing. He reported a most unusual story.

Dr. G.:   What do you see at this time?
Bob: What is your vibrational rate?
Dr.G.:   Where are you now?
Bob: I, I can't see your essence. What is your vibrational rate?
Dr. G.:   It is your function to report your progress to me at this time. Your vibrational rate will be altered downward if you don't cooperate.
Bob: I have just been in the evaluation chamber. They won't tell me my exact progress.
Dr. G.:   Who are they?
Bob: [Silence.]
Dr. G.:   Who are they?
Bob: The Planners. Aren't you one of the Planners? No, I'm being directed not to tell you anything.

Before I continue with this regression I should explain that the "light people" are very restricted in what they can say. It is almost as if there is some sort of magnetic field around them that severely limits their ability to communicate. My vocabulary may seem different during this regression. The reason I am able to elicit any information whatsoever is because I have performed a number of these "light people" regressions and I can relate to them on their level of awareness.

Dr. G.:   What is your name?
Bob: I, I have no name. I am merely a source with a vibrational rate.
Dr. G.:   What is your vibrational rate?
Bob: [Silence.]
Dr. G.:   What is your vibrational rate?
Bob: I am not permitted to release that information. They won't let me. I know that you're not a Planner. Why can't I see your essence?
Dr. G.:   I am not a Planner but I do monitor your progress. My vibrational rate is well beyond yours so that you cannot detect my essence. Now tell me about your experiences on the planet.
Bob: I don't want to go back. The physical form is not pleasant. I don't like it.
Dr. G.:   What do you see around you at this moment?
Bob: I am in a chamber of some sort. I have never been in this place before. My source is yellow. There are other

	sources of different colors present. We are in forma-tion. The Planners are giving us orders.
Dr. G.:	Can you describe the room that you are in?
Bob:	The chamber is white. There are no distinct borders. Everything is hazy. There is much movement of different sources. We are being judged.
Dr. G.:	Who is judging you?
Bob:	The Planners. They are evaluating our trials with the physical form on the planet. I know I've done poorly.
Dr. G.:	Why do you say that?
Bob:	It's awkward being in those things. Why do they want us to be physical? Can you help me?
Dr. G.:	You know I can't. I'm not permitted to interfere with the Planners. My purpose is strictly to gather information. What is happening now?
Bob:	The Planners have not allowed us to leave our places. I can't move. One of the sources is being reduced for his actions on the planet.
Dr. G.:	What do you mean by reduced?
Bob:	The vibrational rate is being lowered. It will mean more time in the physical form.
Dr. G.:	Where are you from?
Bob:	We are not from this galaxy. I am not permitted to give you any more details about our planet.
Dr. G.:	Why did you come to this planet?
Bob:	To explore. The Master Planners want us to experience the physical form. It is our mission. We are supposed to help those forms on the planet. I just want to go home but they won't let me.
Dr. G.:	Has any other source returned home?
Bob:	No. We will stay here until the mission is complete.

My interpretation of further discussion with Bob is as follows: It seems that these "light people" were sent to Earth to experience the human body. They were supposed to help our evolutionary progress. Many of these sources, or lights, failed in their initial attempts at taking over the body. Apparently, it was easy for them to come and go as they pleased. At regular intervals they were removed from the bodies and brought to some sort of examination room (although this was not a physical room as we know it). Their progress was evaluated by a group of monitors or Planners. If they did well, their vibrational rate was raised, but if they failed, it was reduced. These Planners were directed by Master Planners who communicated with them from the home planet many galaxies away.

Dr. G.:   Why have you disturbed the entity known as Bob with these scenes during his rest period?

Bob: It was time he knew.

Dr. G.:   Why now?

Bob: Before his vibrational rate was too low. It is now high enough for him to receive this data.

Dr. G.:   Why not let him experience this data during his waking state?

Bob: I can't answer that. Only the Planners know that. I am not a Planner.

Dr. G.:   How did you do on your last evaluation?

Bob: I failed some of the tests. I am going to have to spend more time in the physical form.

Dr. G.:   Are you being disciplined?

Bob: Spending more time in the physical form is always a punishment. I must not fail again.

Dr. G.:   What happens if you continue to fail?

Bob: I will not be able to leave the physical form. Can't you communicate with them and explain . . . ?

Dr. G.:   I cannot communicate with a Planner. What is it like in a physical form?

Bob: [Silence.]

Dr. G.:   What is it like in a physical form?

Bob: They won't allow me to communicate. Only the Planners can know that. You must accept that.

Dr. G.:   I understand.

Bob was progressed forward in time to the final outcome of his experiences as one of the "light people." He reported having failed many additional tests and was not permitted to leave the human body. During the latter stages of this regression, it became increasingly difficult to obtain any information. Bob was being censored. The words came out slowly and only with great difficulty. I brought him back to the present and gave him many suggestions for relaxation.

Dr. G.:   Well, Bob, how did it feel?

Bob: I, I don't know what to make of it. I felt as if I was in a bubble of some sort. My every thought was being

controlled. It is by far the most unusual experience I
can ever recall.

Dr. G.:   Did you know who I was?

Bob: Absolutely not. Your voice bothered me at first be-
            cause I couldn't see your light. I don't know why that
            was particularly important, but it was.

Dr. G.:   Did you feel more comfortable after I identified my-
            self?

Bob: Yes. I felt more relaxed for a while, but sometime
            later that feeling of being controlled came back and I
            couldn't answer your questions. What does it all
            mean?

I explained the "light people" to Bob and told him why I had
kept him in the dark about this concept. Although he was quite
skeptical at first, he seemed to understand and was grateful for
the progress he had made.

During the next six months Bob kept in contact with me. His
insomnia did not recur and the nightmares stopped. Apparently,
he was free of this situation.

The nightmares had been scenes of his former incarnation as
one of the "light people." By reviewing these scenes in a hypnotic trance the information from his prior life as one of the
"light people" was given to him. This eliminated the need for
further nightmares. Bob, to this day, is still quite skeptical about
"light people." He is merely happy that he no longer has a
sleeping problem.

"Light people" regressions are infrequent, but they always
seem to occur at a significant time in a person's life. The state
described may or may not be the cause of a problem, but the
information that is received is always helpful to the patient. It
seems that when the student is ready, the "light people" will
be there. Usually, these "light people" explore their first incarnation on Earth. Most patients who have these types of experiences show very little interest in extraterrestrial life. They usually
seek my services for habit elimination or some other problem.

There are many interesting concepts that "light people"
regressions illustrate. All communication was done by telepathy. Some of the silences were attempts of the hypnotized patient
to communicate with me by telepathy. These sources of light
function on a different dimensional plane. The term *room*
has a different meaning to them. These beings were pure light
energy. The only things that could confine them were magnetic

fields and thought patterns controlled by the Planners. A Planner could immobilize one of the "light people" merely by directing certain thoughts at them.

I have my own theories as to the origin of the "light people." Obviously, they are entities from another planet. Since the information that I have received is fairly consistent, I have ruled out hallucinations or overactive imaginations. One can only guess as to why our planet was chosen by these "light people." Perhaps we are fortunate that our evolution was tampered with by these aliens. Our present technology might have been impossible without their aid. In addition, these aliens may have added to, if not caused, our present karmic cycle by interfering with our development.

I wonder about our future. Scientists today feel that evolution will eventually eliminate the need for a physical body. Are we then all going to end up as "light people"? If we do, I hope we learn from the mistakes of our predecessors.

CHAPTER EIGHT

Hubert Meets Aliens
in Ancient Egypt

H UBERT IS A RATHER KINDLY, SIXTY-YEAR-OLD SOUTH-
ern gentleman from Virginia. He called me in August
of 1978 to request a past life regression. It seemed that he had
been in Baltimore visiting his sister and had looked up hypnotists in the Yellow Pages. When he saw my name he wrote it
down but did not call me before he left town. Out of the twenty
names listed under hypnotists he picked mine. Synchronicity
was working again.

It was a very humid afternoon when he called me from Virginia and asked if I did past life regressions. Interestingly
enough, I am the only hypnotherapist in Baltimore who does
engage in past life regressions. Hubert told me that he would be
back in Baltimore in October, and he set up an appointment.
He wanted to see my every day for a week before he left for
Virginia. This is a most unusual request, but I honored it, and
I'm glad that I did.

Hubert has recently heard of the concept of hypnotic regressions and was most eager to begin. One important note about
Hubert's background was that he was alone in this life. His wife
had died about ten years earlier and his sister in Baltimore was
one of his last living relatives. As a retired salesman Hubert felt
very lonely.

We discussed hypnosis and past life regression at length during this initial session. During his second session, a simple age
regression was performed. I was not overly impressed with the

results. During the third and fourth sessions, however, Hubert entered into deeper trance levels and revealed a past life in Egypt.

Dr. G.:   What do you see now?

Hubert: I'm standing in front of the pyramid.

Dr. G.:   Is there anything else that you can see at this time?

Hubert: I see the Sphinx in the distance.

Dr. G.:   Which object do you feel closer to?

Hubert: The pyramid, definitely.

Dr. G.:   How many pyramids do you see?

Hubert: Just the one.

Dr. G.:   Can you describe the pyramid?

Hubert: It is only partly built.

Dr. G.:   Can you see yourself in this scene?

Hubert: Yes. I seem to be lifting a large stone.

Dr. G.:   Are you alone?

Hubert: No. I am one of many workers involved in moving this rather large block of stone.

Dr. G.:   Is there anyone directing you?

Hubert: No, not at this moment. We seem to know what we're doing.

Dr. G.:   How are you moving these stones?

Hubert: We're moving them the wrong way. We're lifting them by brute strength. It is not being done scientifically. We are trying to get them into position to place ropes around them.

Hubert appeared to be very much bothered by the fact that there was little efficiency in the movement of these stone blocks. He felt he knew a better way but realized that nobody would listen to a mere worker.

Dr. G.:   How much of the pyramid is complete?

Hubert: About one-third, roughly.

Dr. G.:   Are you living with anyone at this time?

Hubert: Yes, I'm married to a beautiful but shy woman.

Dr. G.:   Can you describe her to me?

Hubert: She's dark-skinned and almost my age (eighteen years old). Her hair is long and black. We love each other very much.

Dr. G.:   How tall is she?

Hubert: About five feet four inches. She is about two inches shorter than me.

Dr. G.:   Do you have any children?

Hubert: No, it's just us two.

Dr. G.:   At the count of five I want you to move forward to a
          very important event in your life. One . . . two . . .
          three . . . four . . . five. What do you see now?

Hubert: I'm in our tent and I'm playing with our child. He is
          a great source of pleasure to us.

Dr. G.:   Where are you living now?

Hubert: We are not far from the river. Our tent is small.

Dr. G.:   What kind of work do you do now?

Hubert: I'm a stoneworker for the Great Pyramid.

Dr. G.:   How old are you?

Hubert: Thirty-one.

Dr. G.:   What exactly does your position involve?

Hubert: I cut slots into the stones so that they will fit into the
          pyramid.

Dr. G.:   Do you like your job?

Hubert: I'm very skillful at my work, but they won't listen to
          my ideas about moving the stones.

Dr. G.:   Who are they?

Hubert: The directors.

Dr. G.:   Can you describe these directors?

Hubert: They are very tall, around seven or eight feet tall.
          They have large heads and long fingers.

These seem to be aliens directing the construction of the pyramids. When I asked Hubert how they moved about from place
to place, he described no vehicle. It seems that they just appeared at various sites about the pyramid and directed crucial
steps in its construction. They then disappeared.

Dr. G.:   How do the directors communicate with you?

Hubert: They don't talk at all. They seem to send out some
          sort of thought signal which compels me to obey them.
          I, I don't feel that I can resist them at all.

Dr. G.:   How much of the pyramid is built at this time?

Hubert: About two-thirds.

Dr. G.:   I want you to move forward by at least ten years on
          the count of five. One . . . two . . . three . . . four
          . . . five. Can you tell me what you see now?

Hubert: I'm much older. My shoulders are rounded and most
          of my hair is gone.

Dr. G.:   Are you still working on the pyramids?

Hubert: Yes, but not as much now. They (the directors) realize
           that I couldn't work as hard as I did when I was
           younger, but they need my experience.

Dr. G.:   Where are your children now?

Hubert: My daughter is home and my older son works with a
           different crew on the pyramid.

Dr. G.:   Where is your younger son?

Hubert: He is not with me. He left home and I feel lonely
           without him.

Dr. G.:   Let's go back to the directors. How do they help you
           build the pyramid?

Hubert: They provide us with instructions and special equip-
           ment.

Dr. G.:   What kind of equipment?

Hubert: They have special ropes. I've never seen rope like it
           before. It is very strong and doesn't seem to break.
           They also have a cranelike apparatus that runs on a
           battery of some sort.

Dr. G.:   How many directors are present at one time?

Hubert: Three.

Dr. G.:   How much of the pyramid is built now?

Hubert: It's almost complete. Thank God. I feel as if my very
           soul went into that pile of stone.

The Great Pyramid of Giza was built by the pharaoh called
Khufu. There were three pyramids constructed between 2600
and 2500 B.C. The largest and oldest is called Giza. The ancient
Greeks referred to Khufu by the name of Cheops. This pyramid
is located in the desert along the Nile River, about ten miles
south of Cairo in Egypt. The pyramid is about 481 feet high and
its square base measures 755 feet on each side.

Inside the bottom of the pyramid are large rooms that were
used as tombs for the royal family. These rooms contained gold,
precious gems, beautifully carved furniture, and other valuable
objects. The Egyptians believed that the dead could take earthly
possessions to heaven with them.

It is rather hard to imagine that the ancient Egyptians (almost
five thousand years ago) were able to build this monumental
structure without the aid of modern cranes and engines that we
use in building today. Historians believe that the Great Pyramid
of Giza took about twenty years to build and that at least 100,000
men labored to complete it. Most of these men were slaves who

worked endlessly, hauling the large stones and somehow putting them in place.

Engineers have stated that in order for such a structure to remain standing after almost five thousand years, great accuracy must have been used in the placing of the stone blocks. An error in placement of about a quarter of an inch could have caused the complete collapse of this great pyramid in just a few hundred years. The average error on each side, however, is less than a ten-thousandth of an inch in squareness and in level.

Hubert was progressed another five years.

Dr. G.:   What important event, if any, has occurred?
Hubert: My daughter got married. She moved out of our tent and I feel so alone now. The pyramid is completed and I have nothing to do.
Dr. G.:   What happened to your two sons?
Hubert: The younger one never came back and my older son died in an accident while working on the pyramid. He was crushed—oh, dear Lord, it was pitiful—by a large stone.
Dr. G.:   What do you look like now?
Hubert: I'm a broken-down old man. I have no hair. My wife is dead. Two of my children have gone. My daughter moved away. I don't like being alone.
Dr. G.:   What kind of food do you eat?
Hubert: It's some sort of grain with water. Garlic is also part of my diet. Sometimes I eat fish.
Dr. G.:   What do you drink?
Hubert: Water. Just water.

The remainder of Hubert's life was uneventful. He described his existence as that of a welfare recipient. He received no money but food and clothes were given to him. He was moved into a small hut where he lived out the rest of his life by the Great Pyramid. The directors used him now and then to teach the young stoneworkers. Hubert enjoyed the company of these young workers. This part-time occupation kept him from feeling totally useless and alone.

The last step in this regression was to take Hubert to the superconscious mind level to find out how these people fit into his karmic cycle. We discovered that his wife in Egypt was his wife in this life. His daughter and younger son had no connection with him in this life. The older son, however, was a sales manager of his about twenty years ago.

It is interesting to note Hubert's loneliness both in Egypt and in his present life. In his Egyptian life his wife died just a few years before he did, yet he felt alone and lonely much of his life. Hubert had a great deal of love for his children, but they never returned his affection.

There are many parallels between Hubert's Egyptian life and his present life. Today he is a very soft-spoken and shy man who wants so much to contribute, but nobody seems to listen. As a salesman his suggestions were often rejected by his younger sales manager (his older Egyptian son reincarnated). In the regression, he was afraid to mention his ideas about moving the stones for fear of punishment. Throughout his life, Hubert exhibited fear of authority figures. Initially, he was even afraid to call me for an appointment.

If there is one karmic lesson that Hubert learned from this life it was patience. He is by far one of the most patient people I have ever known. Loneliness was another experience that Hubert was to explore in both lives. He seemed to accept his present situation without bitterness or regret.

A few months after his last session, I received a latter from Hubert, telling me that he had become involved in a local charity. His life seemed to take on more meaning. Younger people he worked with as a volunteer showed him a lot of respect, and Hubert now felt wanted. He gave much of the credit to me and my work, but it was Hubert who helped himself. All I did was to provide some guidance.

CHAPTER NINE

The Baby That Was
200 Years Overdue

E VELYN IS A REGISTERED NURSE WHO WORKS IN A BALTI-more County hospital. She had seen me on a local television talk show (''Hello Baltimore'') and she wanted to be regressed into past lives. She had some personal questions she wanted answered, and she felt that past life regression was indicated.

I first interviewed Evelyn on August 12, 1980. She was a twenty-three-year-old, somewhat overweight young woman with a very troubled past. It seems that she felt she was always disappointing her boyfriends. They couldn't seem to explain what the problem was, but her relationships rarely lasted more than a few weeks. Evelyn never married but she did have a baby girl a year and a half old. She had no philosophical problems about having the baby, it was simply something she felt she had to do. Evelyn wanted to know through past life regression why she felt so strongly about wanting to have her child.

The father of Evelyn's daughter was a salesman named Merle. He was never informed of the pregnancy and to this day does not know of his daughter. Merle was also disappointed with Evelyn and had broken up with her just three weeks after they started dating. For some unknown reason, this short relationship with Merle had become important to Evelyn. It wasn't just that he was the father of the baby, according to Evelyn. There was more to it than that. She wanted to know what was behind this part of her life.

I regressed Evelyn back into her childhood. She reported some rather detailed scenes and I was very satisfied with this regression. She was given a past life regression conditioning tape and we set up an appointment for her past life regression.

Evelyn was very optimistic and cheerful when she arrived for her session. She had experienced a number of dreams since I last saw her that were highly suggestive of past life scenes. The induction went quickly and Evelyn entered into a deep hypnotic trance.

Dr. G.: Can you tell me what you see before you?
Evelyn: It's dark.
Dr. G.: Do you feel the presence of anyone else?
Evelyn: No. I just feel that I'm going to get hurt.
Dr. G.: Why do you feel that you are in danger?
Evelyn: I don't know. I'm just scared.
Dr. G.: Do you hear anything?
Evelyn: Um, noises.
Dr. G.: What kind of noises?
Evelyn: Animals.
Dr. G.: Do these noises bother you?
Evelyn: Yes.
Dr. G.: I want you to carry this scene to completion. Tell me what happens to you.
Evelyn: I don't like the animals. I can't see them. I'm running, running through the woods to my house. I can't think of anything other than getting home. I shouldn't have stayed in the woods so long. These berries that I came here to pick don't taste that good anyway. Wait a minute—I see my house. There it is. Oh, thank God, I'm home.

Evelyn was progressed forward to the following day. She lived in a small village in Switzerland in the early 1800s.

Dr. G.: How old are you?
Evelyn: Fourteen
Dr. G.: What is your name?
Evelyn: Lilly.
Dr. G.: What does your father do?
Evelyn: He works with his hands. He is a carpenter.
Dr. G.: Can you describe your house?

Evelyn: It's not a big house. It's nice.
Dr. G.:   Can you give me more details about the house?
Evelyn: It's simple. There's not many partitions but you know it separates into different rooms.
Dr. G.:   Do you have any brothers or sisters?
Evelyn: I don't have any sisters, but I do have a younger brother.
Dr. G.:   What is his name?
Evelyn: Derek.
Dr. G.:   What do you like to do most of all?
Evelyn: I like walking.
Dr. G.:   Do you have any friends?
Evelyn: I don't. I feel very alone. I don't know why.

Lilly was progressed five years into the future.

Dr. G.:   Can you tell me what you see now?
Evelyn: I'm sweeping.
Dr. G.:   Where are you sweeping?
Evelyn: It's my house. It's time for me to sweep up so I'm sweeping.
Dr. G.:   Can you see yourself?
Evelyn: Yes.
Dr. G.:   How old are you?
Evelyn: Nineteen.
Dr. G.:   Tell me what you look like?
Evelyn: I'm five feet four inches tall and very slim. My waist is so small [patient was giggling].
Dr. G.:   Who do you live with?
Evelyn: Will.
Dr. G.:   Who's Will?
Evelyn: He's my husband.
Dr. G.:   Can you describe him?
Evelyn: He's tall. He has deep blue eyes.
Dr. G.:   How long have you known Will?
Evelyn: A couple of years. I feel very comfortable around him.
Dr. G.:   What are you most looking forward to at this time?
Evelyn: Having a child.
Dr. G.:   Are you pregnant now?
Evelyn: No. Will and I have been talking about having a baby but we haven't had one yet.

Lilly was progressed to a very significant event that occurred between her and Will.

Dr. G.:   Can you tell me what you see?
Evelyn: I'm crying.
Dr. G.:   Why?
Evelyn: Because I'm a failure.
Dr. G.:   Why are you a failure?
Evelyn: I can't have children.
Dr. G.:   Who told you that?
Evelyn: My father and Will.
Dr. G.:   How does Will feel about your not being able to have children?
Evelyn: He tries to hide it but I see his disgust.
Dr. G.:   How about your father?
Evelyn: He wasn't supportive at all.
Dr. G.:   What about your mother?
Evelyn: She's there.
Dr.G.:   What is her attitude?
Evelyn: She's very meek. She means well but doesn't know what to say.

Lilly described a very frustrating life. As she grew older she became more and more sensitive about her inability to have children. All of her friends raised families. Lilly's parents didn't know how to relate to her. Will seemed to tolerate her, but there was no love between them. She tried everything to please him, but nothing worked. Will wanted children. He would not divorce her nor would he have affairs, but he was very disappointed in his wife's inability to bear him children.

I progressed Lilly to the last day of her life.

Dr. G.:   Did you ever have any children?
Evelyn: No.
Dr. G.:   Who is around you at this time?
Evelyn: Will's there.
Dr. G.:   Is there anyone else present?
Evelyn: No.
Dr. G.:   How old are you?
Evelyn: Fifty-four.

Lilly was progressed beyond her death to the "other side."

Dr. G.:   What sensations do you feel at this time?
Evelyn: I feel light.
Dr. G.:   What else do you feel?
Evelyn: Cold.
Dr. G.:   What do you see?
Evelyn: Colors. Many colors.
Dr. G.:   Do you see any people?
Evelyn: I see Will.
Dr. G.:   Is he still alive?
Evelyn: Yeah.
Dr. G.:   What is he doing?
Evelyn: He's pacing.
Dr. G.:   In this life as Lilly, what is it that you feel you didn't accomplish?
Evelyn: I couldn't give what I wanted to give.
Dr. G.:   Which was what?
Evelyn: A child, a child to Will. It meant so much to him.
Dr. G.:   What is it that you feel you did accomplish?
Evelyn: I was a good worker. I know that I was a good worker.
Dr. G.:   Did other people respect you for your work?
Evelyn: Yes, yes. Will was even proud of my work.

Lilly was taken up to the superconscious mind and asked some additional questions.

Dr. G.:   Who was Will in your life as Lilly? Is Will anyone you knew or now know as Evelyn?
Evelyn: Merle. Will is Merle.

This case illustrates some rather interesting principles of karma. First, Evelyn disappointed Will by not being able to have children. This was the aspect of their life together that brought about the most hardship. The karmic debt was then established. Failure to have children, coupled with Will's disappointment in her, left Evelyn with a rather severe karmic debt. Evelyn's subconscious mind felt that she was branded with a disappointing tendency. She felt that no matter what she did she would somehow disappoint any man that she was involved with.

This fear carried over to her present life. Every relationship she entered resulted in disappointment. It wasn't so much that she just met the wrong kind of man, although that was a factor, it was the way in which she projected herself—as a person who would disappoint you.

Evelyn is attractive, despite her being overweight. She tended to overcompensate for her self-image by acting seductive. She discussed with me how she would set out to seduce men, although in the back of her mind she knew that she was going to disappoint them. She continually tried to prove to herself that there was someone out there who would appreciate her. Clearly, she was going about this pursuit in the wrong way.

When Evelyn became pregnant, something changed. She was no longer the sterile Lilly. She was now fulfilling a nearly 200-year-old wish, a wish to have a child. This was one of the most important episodes in her present life. It is interesting to note that she never even considered abortion. The karmic lesson was well learned. That she was single made absolutely no difference. At least now she didn't disappoint herself. She proved to herself that she could, in fact, have a child.

The fact that Will (in Evelyn's life as Lilly) is Merle (in her present incarnation) is not as significant as it might be to Evelyn. Evelyn may have disappointed Merle in this life during their three-week affair, but a child resulted from this relationship. In their past life they were married for more than thirty-five years and no children resulted from the union. The karmic debt of fertility was paid. Merle simply had to father Evelyn's child. My only regret was that I was not able to work more with Evelyn on additional lives. I'm sure we would have traced back the origin of this karmic debt.

One last observation to make about Evelyn was her current weight problem. In her life as Lilly she was very slim and attractive. This present weight problem was probably caused by built-up frustrations during her life as Lilly. Lilly was a very hard worker, and that one quality pleased Will. Keeping herself slender and attractive and hardworking were, in Lilly's mind, the only ways she could hold on to Will.

Shortly after her pregnancy, Evelyn started to lose weight. Today, one year later, she is much thinner than she was when I originally saw her, yet I didn't work with her on weight control. I didn't have to. The pregnancy and the knowledge of her past life as Lilly was more than enough. She no longer needs to punish herself or feel frustrated. She has also reported to me that her relationships with men have changed. She now feels self-confident, no longer assuming that she will disappoint men.

Lilly has finally satisfied Will's 200-year-old wish. And Evelyn is well on her way to achieving happiness.

CHAPTER TEN

Hysterical Blindness
and a Past Life
in the London Slums

MANY PEOPLE ASK ME WHAT HYPNOSIS CAN REALLY DO.
If, according to recent statistics, modern medical
technology is only about 75 percent successful, can hypnosis
make up that additional 25 percent?

There are many syndromes that modern medicine can't cure.
Drugs can treat many symptoms temporarily, but such diseases
as ulcers, colitis, anxiety, and depression are not caused by
bacteria, viruses, or fungi. They can't be cured with medication
alone. They are psychosomatic in their origin, and the subconscious mind has a great deal to do with the elimination of these
disturbances.

But even more obviously in the realm of treatment through
hypnosis is a category of illness referred to as "hysterical disorders." Included in this category are hysterical paralysis, hysterical deafness, and hysterical blindness. These disorders have
absolutely no medical or organic cause. A complete physical
examination by a specialist would reveal no medical reason for
the patient's infirmity, yet the patient remains unable to function
in one of these areas.

The case that I am about to describe illustrates this principle
with respect to sight loss. An attractive twenty-five-year-old interior decorator was brought to my office early in January 1978
by her boyfriend. Her name was Judy, and Angelo was her male
companion. Angelo had called me earlier that day to make this
emergency appointment. It seemed that the week before Judy

had lost her sight without any warning and with no apparent cause.

Judy had never had problems with her eyes before and, in fact, didn't even wear glasses. She had been to an ophthalmologist affiliated with Johns Hopkins University and all of the tests turned out negative. In other words, there was no medical reason for Judy to be unable to see. I had personally spoken with her ophthalmologist and he verified these facts.

It wasn't easy to take a history from Judy since she was very upset and depressed. However, I finally found out that Judy lost her sight shortly after discovering Angelo taking amphetamine pills. She had been dating him for over a year but he had not informed her of his pill ingestion habit. Within five minutes after inadvertently seeing Angelo take these pills, Judy had screamed and lost her sight.

I asked her if she screamed because of some pain. She said that she just had an uncontrollable urge to scream but did not feel any form of pain. Judy was naturally anxious about whether or not I could help her. I explained to her and Angelo what I knew about hysterical blindness. I made no promises or guarantees, but told her I would do my best.

Inducing a hypnotic trance requires only that the patient hear the hypnotherapist, and since Judy's hearing was unimpaired, this presented no problem.

Judy entered into a good medium trance rather quickly, which surprised me, considering her depression and recent traumatic experience. I conditioned her for a simple age regression to be performed on her next visit. She left my office feeling relieved and more relaxed.

The second session consisted of a simple age regression. I instructed Judy's subconscious to search through its memory banks and relive a scene or scenes that were directly responsible for her current sight problems. She reviewed a number of childhood scenes, but nothing directly related to her present loss of sight.

During the next week I saw Judy two more times and performed a number of simple age regressions. Again nothing of significance surfaced. Past life regression was the only avenue we hadn't explored, so we decided to try it.

Judy was very willing, but Angelo didn't share her enthusiasm. I told them to discuss it and call me when they had made their decision. The next day Angelo called to schedule a past life regression. Judy told me she considered it her only real hope. If the ophthalmologist at Johns Hopkins couldn't find a medical cause, then the origin of her blindness must be psychological. Since she had been sightless for nearly three weeks, she was desperate. Angelo didn't think much of hypnosis, but he was willing to try anything to help Judy.

I induced Judy into a medium-level hypnotic trance and gave her subconscious mind the suggestion to return to the true origin of her present sight problems. For about five minutes she sat motionless in my recliner with her eyes closed. I could tell she was reviewing many scenes since her eyeballs were moving back and forth rapidly. (These rapid eye movements, or REMs, also indicate that a person is dreaming.)

Judy finally began to answer my questions in a high-pitched, childlike voice.

Dr. G.:   Can you tell me what you see now?
Judy: Everything I like (giggling).
Dr. G.:   Where are you?
Judy: I'm with my daddy.
Dr. G.:   And where are you both right now?
Judy: Daddy said I can have some candy. He said I can have three pieces. The shop is full of candy and stuff.
Dr. G.:   What kind of stuff?
Judy: Oh, you know. Food and stuff.
Dr. G.:   How long have you been in the shop?
Judy: We just got here. I can't make up my mind what to get (giggling).
Dr. G.:   What is your name?
Judy: Elsie. Do you want some candy too? (giggling)
Dr. G.:   No, thank you, Elsie. Where do you live?
Judy: In London, of course. Aren't you silly?
Dr. G.:   What is your father's name?
Judy: Daddy.
Dr. G.:   I mean what do other people call your daddy?
Judy: Mac.
Dr. G.:   Where is your mother?
Judy: She went away. (Her voice became soft.)
Dr. G.:   Where did she go?
Judy: I don't know. (Patient began crying.)
Dr. G.:   All right, Elsie, calm down. On the count of five all negative feelings about your mother not being here will disappear and you will feel happy again. One . . .

	two . . . three . . . four . . . five. What kind of work does your father do?
Judy:	He works in a place with machines, big machines. (Patient began giggling again.)
Dr. G.:	How old are you, Elsie?
Judy:	I'm six years old. (She sounded very proud.)

Elsie responded well to my questions. She quickly changed her emotional responses from that of crying to giggling when I gave her the appropriate instructions. Further questioning revealed the following past life.

Elsie lived in a very run-down apartment on the south side of London in 1887. Her father was a factory worker in a textile mill. Elsie's mother left her and Mac when Elsie was just three years old because of Mac's drinking. This was not a pleasant life for Elsie as she had no playmates and her father worked long hours. Even when he did have time for her, he was usually drunk.

It was surprising how much Elsie loved Mac, since he beat her often and spent very little time with her. The only real pleasure he provided was an occasional trip to the candy shop at the market. It was Elsie's short memory that allowed her to forget about Mac's faults and deal only with a present pleasurable experience.

I next progressed Elsie forward in time, asking her to remember the true cause, if any, of her present sight problem.

Dr. G.:	Where are you now, Elsie?
Judy:	I'm outside playing. (She sounded very sad.)
Dr. G.:	Is anything wrong?
:Judy:	No.
Dr. G.:	Come on now, Elsie, you can tell me. What is bothering you?
Judy:	Well, I don't have anyone to play with and everybody is in church.
Dr. G.:	Why aren't you in church?
Judy:	Daddy doesn't believe in going to church. He says it's a waste of time.
Dr. G.:	Is this Sunday?
Judy:	Yes. Can you play with me? (Patient began giggling again.)
Dr. G.:	I can't play with you, Elsie, but I would like to know

some things about your daddy. Would you mind telling me more about him?

Judy: Oh, okay. (Patient sounded bored.)

Dr. G.:   Where is he now?

Judy: He's in the house, probably in his room. He always spends Sundays in his room.

Dr. G.:   How old are you now, Elsie?

Judy: Eleven.

Dr. G.:   Does your daddy ever take you to the park or to the city on Sunday?

Judy: No, I can't remember the last time he took me anywhere.

Dr. G.:   Do you love your daddy?

Judy: Well, I, of course I do. (She hesitated a few seconds before answering this question.)

I next progressed Elsie forward, asking for the actual event that would explain her present sight problem. She had gone back into the apartment on this Sunday afternoon looking for her father.

Dr. G.:   Where are you now, Elsie?

Judy: I'm on the couch playing with my doll.

Dr. G.:   Where is your daddy?

Judy: He's in his room, I think.

Dr. G.:   What are you going to do now?

Judy: I'm going to sneak up on my daddy and scare him.

Elsie went to her father's room and quietly opened the door.

Dr. G.:   Can you see your daddy, Elsie?

Judy: Oh, God, what is my daddy doing? Daddy, Daddy, please don't do that! (Judy had a look of absolute horror on her face.)

Dr. G.:   What is your daddy doing?

Judy: He, he's sticking himself in the arm and he has a rubber band on his arm. (Patient sounded very excited.)

Dr. G.:   What is he doing now?

Judy: Daddy, Daddy, don't hurt me! No, no, I didn't mean to scare you. (Patient now was very upset.)

Dr. G.:   What is your daddy doing to you, Elsie?

| Judy: | He beat me, beat me bad. I hurt all over. (Patient was wincing.) |

Mac had severely beaten Elsie for walking in on him while he was in the process of injecting morphine into his arm. Elsie had never seen her father inject himself before. Apparently alcoholism wasn't Mac's only problem.

After he had beaten Elsie, Mac locked her in his closet for the rest of that day. Elsie was in a state of shock. She hadn't eaten all day and hurt from the beating. It wasn't until early the next morning that she was released from the closet.

It was necessary to give Judy (Elsie) many calming suggestions before bringing her out of the trance.

Dr. G.:	Judy, on the count of five, you will be back in the present, January 1978, and you will remember everything that you experienced and reexperienced. One . . . two . . . three . . . four . . . five, awaken.
Judy:	Wow, that was quite something! Dr. Goldberg, Dr. Goldberg, I can see you! You're very hazy but I can see you. (Patient was elated.)
Dr. G.:	Focus on my voice, Judy. When I snap my fingers, you will be able to see me clearly.

It took Judy about three minutes until she was able to see me clearly. We went into my reception room to join Angelo and explain to him what had happened.

When Judy saw Angelo take the amphetamine pill (an addictive drug) she associated this incident with watching Mac inject morphine (also an addictive drug). Judy was severely beaten by Mac for viewing something she wasn't supposed to see. Since Angelo hadn't told her about his taking amphetamines, when Judy accidentally happened in on him, her subconscious made the association of seeing something she wasn't supposed to see. Through the hypnotic regression, the cause of the blindness was removed and the symptom (blindness) disappeared.

This experience brought Judy and Angelo much closer together. They had not been getting along well of late, even before this hysterical blindness incident occurred. As a result of this regression, their feelings for each other grew stronger.

In addition to restoring Judy's sight, this past life regression had other unexpected benefits for her. For one thing, she reported that her claustrophobia had disappeared. It seemed that being locked in the closet caused Elsie, and later Judy, to become afraid of confined spaces. By reliving this past life, the true cause of Judy's claustrophobia was elicited and removed.

Another interesting fact was brought to my attention. Judy told me that she had quit her last job with a well-known interior decorating firm because she hadn't liked her boss. She hardly knew him and rarely saw him, but the few times she did see him he was either drinking or smoking. One day he had come into the office drunk from a lunch date and she had simply quit. It worried her that she couldn't explain why at the time, but he had made her feel so uncomfortable that she had had to leave. Clearly, Judy's former boss reminded her of Mac. The association that her subconscious mind made with his drinking compelled her to quit. Judy now understood what had motivated her behavior and was comfortable with her decision.

This was a most interesting and rewarding case. The fact that the cause of Judy's blindness was psychological made hypnotic regression the treatment of choice.

CHAPTER ELEVEN

Odontiatrophobia
and the Blacksmith

I RECEIVE MANY CALLS FROM PATIENTS TERRIFIED OF HAVING dental work performed on them. Negative conditioning is generally at fault. If a patient has a traumatic experience with a dentist as a child, a lasting negative impression is often left in the subconscious mind. This negative association of dentistry and a traumatic experience may affect the patient's attitude toward oral health care for the rest of his or her life.

When I received a telephone call from Miriam in September of 1978 I listened very carefully to her story. It seemed this fifty-one-year-old housewife has a tremendous fear of dentists. She hadn't been to a dentist in over ten years and she knew that she had many dental problems. What is especially interesting about Miriam's case is that her dental fear was related to other problems in her life. She had a low opinion of herself and felt that if she could somehow eliminate this phobia, her relationships with her husband, children, and friends would also improve. In fact, she felt her entire life would benefit from ridding herself of this fear. The technical term for a fear of dentists is *odontiatrophobia*.

When Miriam came to my hypnosis office for her first appointment, I discussed her dental history. It seemed that she could not remember a single traumatic incident involving herself and dentistry. Her interests in working with hypnosis weren't just to feel comfortable in my dental office, they were more

107

oriented to finding out why she had developed the dental phobia in the first place.

Miriam was an excellent hypnotic patient and I decided to use simple age regression to find out if there were some traumatic childhood incidents involving dentistry that were being repressed by her conscious mind proper. After three sessions of simple age regression, I found nothing to indicate a cause for her odontiatrophobia.

My next step was to explain the possibility of a past life cause to Miriam. She seemed quite interested in my explanation of karma and reincarnation and although she was somewhat skeptical, she seemed to trust me and was willing to try almost anything to get to the cause of her phobia. I gave her a past life regression conditioning tape and we made an appointment a few weeks hence.

Miriam seemed excited when she entered my office on that fall afternoon. As usual, she went into a deep trance quickly and was quite relaxed.

Dr. G.:   Can you tell me what you see at this moment?
Miriam: I'm, I'm standing in the middle of the street holding
          my right cheek.
Dr. G.:   Why are you holding your right cheek?
Miriam: It hurts. My damn tooth hurts.

Miriam is a very soft-spoken woman and in the four weeks that I had known her prior to this regression, she had never used any form of foul language. Now her voice dropped in pitch and her language became coarse. During most of this session she held her right cheek as if she were in severe pain, although consciously no such discomfort existed.

Dr. G.:   What are you going to do about your tooth?
Miriam: Well, first I'm gonna go to that there saloon (she
          pointed straight ahead with her left hand) and com-
          mence to drown this damn pain with some whiskey.
Dr. G.:   And then?
Miriam: And then I suppose I'll just have to have that damn
          tooth yanked.
Dr. G.:   Who will remove the tooth?
Miriam: Oh, Smitty, of course.

Miriam reported that she lived in a small town in Kansas in 1838. There were no dentists in her area so she had to go to the local blacksmith, Smitty, for an extraction. There was a physician in town but he did not perform any dentistry. It was not uncommon for blacksmiths and barbers to do dentistry at that time.

Dr. G.: What is your name?
Miriam: Anna.
Dr. G.: Anna, has Smitty ever taken out teeth from you before?
Miriam: Oh, sure he has. (Her voice sounded somewhat shaky now.)
Dr. G.: You don't sound very happy about the idea.
Miriam: I'm not. Damn it. Damn this tooth. Damn Smitty. (Anna's voice was loud and angry.)

I progressed Anna forward a few hours. She had gone into the saloon and drunk many glasses of whiskey to premedicate herself. We discovered that her husband had died a few years earlier, and she ran their small farm with just two hired hands. Anna was a very strong and resourceful woman in this life and had many friends. The only real problem area of her life was her teeth. She never took proper care of them and had many dental problems. Smitty had removed seven or eight teeth from her over the years, and every time he extracted one, Anna went through pure hell.

Dr. G.: Anna, on the count of five, I want you to move forward to the time Smitty will be removing your tooth. One . . . two . . . three . . . four . . . five. Can you tell me what you see now?
Miriam: Damn Smitty. His shop smells like horseshit. (Miriam had put her fingers up to her nose.)
Dr. G.: Where exactly are you now, Anna?
Miriam: I'm in the back of Smitty's blacksmith shop. It is right next to his horse stalls and it sure stinks something bad here.
Dr. G.: Where is Smitty?
Miriam: He is getting his apprentice, Paul, to help him.
Dr. G.: What is happening now?
Miriam: Paul went to get one of Smitty's pliers and now they're

both back. I'm sitting on this old wooden chair and
Paul is holding my head back.

Since there was no anesthesia at this time, all forms of dentistry, which mostly consisted of extractions, were performed
by physically restraining the patient.

Dr. G.:   What is happening now?
Miriam: Smitty is standing over me now with the pliers in his
          hand. (Her voice was very shaky again.)
Dr. G.:   Where is Paul?
Miriam: He is behind me holding my head back.
Dr. G.:   Continue on, Anna.
Miriam: Smitty puts those damn pliers in my mouth. I can taste
          the rust on them. (She grimaces and holds on very
          tightly to the arms of my recliner.)
Dr. G.:   What happens next?
Miriam: He puts the pliers on my back tooth. It hurts so bad
          now. The whiskey isn't working.
Dr. G.:   Go on, Anna.
Miriam: He yanks real hard and I try to turn my head but I
          can't. That Paul is so strong. (Her knuckles were beginning to turn white because she was holding onto
          my chair so tightly.) My tooth. Yeoow. Yeoow. Yeoow.

Anna screamed so loud it gave me a start. In a moment she
calmed down and sank back in the chair, exhausted. I let her
rest for about five minutes and then resumed the questioning.

Dr. G.:   Anna, are you all right?
Miriam: Oh, yes, I'm fine now. That Smitty is okay. He got
          that damned tooth with one yank. (She was very relieved now.)
Dr. G.:   Does your jaw hurt?
Miriam: No, not now. I'll be okay. I'm bleeding but I know it
          won't be long before that stops.
Dr. G.:   What are you going to do now?
Miriam: I'm going to stop back at the saloon and get me some
          more whiskey. Then I guess I'll go home and try to
          forget about today.

I progressed Anna throughout this day and the next day. Surprisingly, she didn't develop an infection from the dirty pliers.

Her resistance to disease was good. Anna was able to work on her farm the following day. She was quite a remarkable woman.

One of the interesting things I observed about this regression was that Miriam seemed to admire Anna. Anna's strength, assertiveness, frankness, and honesty were attractive qualities. After this session was over, I discussed my observations with Miriam. Miriam agreed that she found Anna a most unusual and admirable woman. Anna's self-confidence and ability to get along with people represented quite a contrast to Miriam.

Miriam was skeptical about whether she had actually lived before as Anna, but we decided that she would return to me for much-needed dental work. During her treatment I filled a number of teeth, performed two root canals, and crowned five additional teeth. Miriam showed very little apprehension and, throughout the entire treatment, was an excellent patient. What was even more interesting to observe were the other improvements in her life. Miriam was quickly becoming more self-confident and assertive. She reported to me a closer relationship with her husband and her children. Her friends and relatives also noted this behavioral change. Some asked her if she was taking some medication. Others asked her if she was seeing a psychiatrist. Miriam reported feeling like a different woman.

I may take credit for her dental improvement, but it was a combination of Miriam's understanding and her past life regression therapy that resulted in her other changes.

This case is one of my favorites not just because it illustrates removing a dental phobia, but because it illustrates the tremendous personality improvements that patients are able to make once they are presented with the true cause of their problem. Whether it is in this lifetime or another, reliving and letting go of repressed emotions and negative scenes will, more times than not, result in great changes in patients' lives. I am happy to say that Miriam is still a dental patient of mine and is doing just fine in all aspects of her life.

CHAPTER TWELVE

The 800-Year-Old Synchronicity

W HEN I APPEAR ON RADIO OR TELEVISION OR AM INTER-
viewed by a newspaper reporter, I am often asked to
relate my most interesting case. Although I find all of them
gratifying, one especially stands out in my memory, and it involves my favorite principle, *synchronicity*.

It is not uncommon for the same people to occur in several
of a patient's past lives. Group karma works just that way—a
husband and wife in one life may come back as a mother and
daughter or a brother and sister in another lifetime. An acquain-
tance in one life will often appear again in future lifetimes. This
phenomenon is well accepted. What is unusual about this particular case is the manner in which I investigated it.

Nearly five years ago, I received a call from a man who identified himself as Arnold. Arnold worked as an appliance salesman in a Baltimore department store and was calling me for
hypnotherapy at his wife's suggestion. In further conversation it
came out that Arnold was a very insecure man, and this was
negatively affecting his ability as a salesman.

Arnold proved to be an excellent hypnotic patient. After six
sessions, he began feeling better about himself. During these
sessions I gave Arnold many suggestions to improve his self-
image and assertiveness. The tape I recorded for him contained
these suggestions and helped him to believe more in himself.
Regression was not used at this time because I like to stabilize
the emotional level first. Once a solid emotional foundation is

established regression therapy is more efficiently carried out. Arnold expressed no interest in exploring regression at this time. His self-confidence improved and his sales record very much reflected this progress. He seemed troubled about something else; however, he was unwilling at this time to discuss it with me.

It is not my policy or purpose to pry, so I did not force the issue. I simply told Arnold that it was obvious something else was troubling him, and if he didn't feel comfortable discussing it with me, there was nothing else I could do for him. I instructed him to continue playing the cassette tape I recorded for him. This case was far from complete, but since the patient closed all avenues of communication, I had no choice. Arnold thanked me for my help and left my office for what I thought was to be his last session.

Two months passed before Arnold called me again. He wanted to see me immediately. I cleared some time that evening, and a very unusual journey began. Arnold seemed embarrassed as he told me the following facts out of trance.

People had always dominated him. Everyone from his mother, wife, boss, customers, his children, and just about anyone who had any contact with Arnold dominated him. It was not clear to me what he found especially embarrassing about relating this situation, and when I questioned him, he said he couldn't explain it. It was simply that this fear of being dominated was so strong and made him feel so inferior that he had a lot of trouble expressing it to anyone. In his eighteen years of marriage he had never even discussed this with his wife. Additional sessions were not very fruitful so I suggested the use of simple age regression. Arnold was now willing to try it. I like to obtain as thorough a history as possible out of trance. This relaxes the patient and gives specific paths to explore during actual hypnotic regressions.

When I had worked with Arnold initially, he had obtained a good level of hypnosis easily. Now, simple age regression was difficult for him and his level of trance was light. After some further conditioning, he was finally able to achieve a good medium trance level. We discovered that his childhood was fairly unremarkable, and there were many scenes of his being dominated and manipulated by people in his family as well as by his friends. I was, however, unsuccessful in eliciting a cause for this situation.

I suggested past life regression to Arnold. He was excited by the idea. The first few attempts resulted in very sketchy scenes, and none of them related to his problem. It was as if he were fighting me. One could deduce that subconsciously Arnold was afraid of my dominating him also. A series of four past life regressions made Arnold much more comfortable with the technique and more trusting of me.

Finally one afternoon in November, Arnold described a most unusual past life. This was a very long session and much time had been devoted to establishing the background of the scene.

Arnold's name was Thayer, and he lived in a small village in Bavaria in 1132. Bavaria was part of present-day Germany. He seemed very frightened about something as I questioned him.

Dr. G.:   Where are you?
Arnold: I'm under the table.
Dr. G.:   What are you doing under the table, Thayer?
Arnold: I'm eating my supper.
Dr. G.:   Why are you eating under the table instead of sitting down at the table and placing your food on top of the table?
Arnold: The chains are too short and anyway I'm not allowed to eat that way.
Dr. G.:   What chains?
Arnold: My hands and feet are chained to the table and the chains are very short.
Dr. G.:   Who chained you to the table?
Arnold: Gustave.
Dr. G.:   Who is Gustave?
Arnold: He is my master. I am his apprentice.

Thayer was an apprentice for a master guildsman by the name of Gustave. They worked with metal, mostly silver and gold. Drinking cups, plates, ornaments, and various other items for wealthy noblemen were produced by them. During the Middle Ages it was quite common to learn a particular trade by being an apprentice for many years to a master guildsman. What was becoming rather evident was that there was more to this relationship than merely a guildsman and his apprentice.

Dr. G.:   How long have you been chained to the table?
Arnold: Since we closed the shop.
Dr. G.:   Why are you chained this way?

Arnold: I am always chained after the shop is closed. Master Gustave doesn't want me to leave and this is the only way he knows to make sure I don't leave.

Dr. G.:   Why don't you just leave when he unchains you tomorrow?

Arnold: I can't do that. I was apprenticed to him by my father when I was thirteen.

Dr. G.:   How does Gustave treat you in general?

Arnold: He hates me. He beats me with a whip whenever I do anything wrong. I am afraid of him.

Dr. G.:   Has he always treated you this way?

Arnold: Yes. Ever since I can remember he has always beat me and treated me like this.

Dr. G.:   What happens when customers enter the shop? Does he mistreat you in front of other people?

Arnold: Oh, yes, all the time. There's nothing I can do about it. I think he gets great satisfaction out of humiliating me.

Dr. G.:   Is there anyone in particular that Gustave likes humiliating you in front of?

Arnold: Well, yes. There's this girl by the name of Clotilde. He likes to let her see me being treated this way.

Dr. G.:   Who is Clotilde?

Arnold: She is a very nice girl from a wealthy family and she likes me. She has bought many things from Master Gustave. He doesn't like it when she asks about me.

Dr. G.:   What does Gustave do when Clotilde asks about you?

Arnold: He yells at me and tells me I'm worthless. He makes fun of everything I do and say. Then after she leaves, he chains me to the table and beats me.

Dr. G.:   What else does he do to you?

Arnold: Well, he does these unnatural things to me. . . .

Arnold was very embarrassed about this particular question. He started to stutter and after about ten minutes he described a number of homosexual acts that Gustave subjected him to. Gustave had never married and he used Thayer (Arnold) to satisfy his every desire. Thayer was blamed for anything that went wrong. He was degraded by Gustave whenever the latter felt like abusing him. The hatred Thayer and Gustave felt for each other grew daily.

I progressed Thayer to a significant event in his life.

Dr. G.:   Can you tell me what is happening now, Thayer?

Arnold: I, I am scared.

Dr. G.:   Why are you afraid?

Arnold: Master Gustave, he is very angry with me.

Dr. G.:   Why is that unusual?

Arnold: It's not just his usual temper. It's more than that.

Dr. G.:   Why? What has happened since I last spoke with you?

Arnold: Clotilde has shown a great interest in me. She has asked Master Gustave to allow me to do some work at her family's house.

Dr. G.:   How did Gustave respond to that request?

Arnold: He almost lost his temper in front of Clotilde. Her family has given Master Gustave much business over the years, and this is the first time that he has acted this way in front of her. I just know that he is going to beat me tonight.

Dr. G.:   What did Gustave tell Clotilde?

Arnold: He said that I couldn't go to their home because of the tools that I would need, and he told Clotilde that I couldn't be trusted. Imagine, telling Clotilde that. I hate him so.

Dr. G.:   All right, Thayer. I want you to detach yourself from this scene and move forward to a resolution of this problem on the count of five. One . . . two . . . three . . . four . . . five.

Arnold: I'm being chained to the table again.

Dr. G.:   Is it dinnertime now?

Arnold: Yes; somehow I feel strange. It's as if I have some extra energy. Master Gustave tells me that he is going to abuse me tonight. He often tells me that before I eat to taunt me.

Dr. G.:   Tell me what happens next, Thayer.

Arnold: I don't let him chain me to the table. I'm arguing with him and he's laughing at me. Why does he laugh at me?

Dr. G.:   What do you do about it?

Arnold: I attack him as he tries to chain my leg to the table. The food gets thrown on the floor and Gustave is yelling at me. I fight with him and all I can think of is killing him. (Patient is very excited.)

Dr. G.:   Now calm down and slowly tell me what is happening.

Arnold: We are on the floor and I am reaching for his throat.
            I want to strangle him. We knocked over some tools
            and something is pressing against my leg.
Dr. G.:   What is it?
Arnold: It's a very sharp tool. I reached down with my left
            hand and brushed it aside but I shouldn't have done
            that.
Dr. G.:   Why not?
Arnold: Master Gustave, he pushed me off him and punched
            me in the face. I don't know what's happening now.
Dr. G.:   Focus your mind on this scene, Thayer. It's impor-
            tant.
Arnold: He threw me against the wall and cursed me. He said
            I was not worth the trouble I was causing.
Dr. G.:   What does Gustave do next?
Arnold: He picked up a knifelike tool. I know that it's very
            sharp. Oh, my God, he's stabbed me in my stomach.
            (Patient is very excited.) I'm bleeding and the pain is
            unbearable.
Dr. G.:   Relax, Thayer. Detach yourself from any pain or
            emotion and tell me what happens next.
Arnold: He stabbed me many times. I dropped to the floor
            and died. He killed me. That horrible fiend killed me.
Dr. G.:   How do you feel now?
Arnold: I feel as if I'm floating. I can see my body beneath
            me but I can't feel anything.

Since Arnold was upset by this scene, I allowed him to view
his death and to experience the complete detachment from all
discomfort that typically characterizes death scenes. He stayed
with this tranquil scene for about ten minutes. I then brought
him to the superconscious mind level and asked him about
Gustave and Clotilde. He reported to me that Clotilde was
his sister-in-law Margaret, with whom he gets along very well
today. Gustave was not yet involved in his present life.

After this fateful session, Arnold felt much better about himself. He finally realized why he was so afraid of people dominating him and why he seemed to allow other people to exert
their influence on him. What is interesting to note is that his
sister-in-law Margaret was one of the few people Arnold has
known who has not tried to dominate him. Margaret, as Clotilde, was the only bright spot in Thayer's life.

I saw Arnold a few more times to help him work out his

remaining doubts. He was not interested in finding out about other lifetimes in which he might have known Gustave. Arnold felt he had learned enough about his past.

During the next six months, Arnold kept in touch with me. He had made great progress in strengthening his self-image and no longer feared people or allowed them to dominate him. He received a promotion at the store and his relationship with his wife and children had also improved noticeably. I was gratified with the results.

A year and a half after my treatment of Arnold, I received a call from an attorney named Brian, who wanted to work out some psychological problems using hypnosis. Brian specialized in corporate law for a large Baltimore law firm. He was a very successful man in his late thirties, but he felt he had an undesirable tendency to manipulate people. Out of trance he described himself as a self-made man who used people time and time again. It is ironic that the ability to manipulate people, which some consider an asset to an attorney, should be this patient's chief complaint.

Brian's conscience was working overtime. He felt guilty about his actions. Insomnia was a nightly occurrence, along with a compulsive eating problem. I also learned that his hobby was collecting antiques, mostly metal objects such as silverware, drinking cups, jewelry, and so on. He didn't care much for antique furniture. I noted this in his chart for future reference.

Brian proved to be an excellent hypnotic patient. He attained a good trance level and was easy to work with. Some progress was made with his compulsive eating habits and insomnia, but I was not satisfied with the results. I suggested age regression, and after I had thoroughly explained the process to him, Brian agreed to try this technique.

Simple age regression was helpful but not to the extent that I had hoped. Brian relived a number of scenes concerning compulsive eating from his childhood and adolescence, though nothing of importance was discovered concerning his manipulative tendencies. He did report scenes in his adolescence and college years in which he used people for selfish purposes. Yet, I was not satisfied with this data because deeply rooted causes were not surfacing.

Brian couldn't understand my dissatisfaction. He felt he was making progress. I explained to him at this time the use of past life regression and asked him if he would consent to try it. He was skeptical about the concept of past lives but agreed nonetheless.

In late March I brought Brian back into a most interesting past life. He went into trance quickly and deeply and the following represents excerpts from this session:

Dr. G.:	What do you see now?
Brian:	I'm working in my shop.
Dr. G.:	What kind of shop is this?
Brian:	I'm some sort of metalworker—yes, I'm a master craftsman and I'm damn good at my work.
Dr. G.:	What year is this?
Brian:	1130.
Dr. G.:	What is your name?
Brian:	I'm called Gustave.
Dr. G.:	Can you describe your shop?
Brian:	Well, it's not a very big shop. I have many fine tools that I use in my work.
Dr. G.:	What specifically do you make?
Brian:	I mostly work with gold and silver. Noblemen commission me to make ornaments, jewelry, eating utensils, goblets, decorative containers, and other such objects.
Dr. G.:	Are you married?
Brian:	No, I don't have the time or patience for women.
Dr. G.:	What country do you live in?
Brian:	My land is called Bavaria.
Dr. G.:	Who is the leader of your land?
Brian:	King Henry.
Dr. G.:	Do you enjoy your work?
Brian:	Yes, I am the best at what I do and I like my craft.
Dr. G.:	Do you speak with the noblemen often?
Brian:	Only when they come into my shop.
Dr. G.:	What do they talk about?
Brian:	Oh, some damn nonsense about the election of the new Pope.
Dr. G.:	Can you tell me more about the situation?
Brian:	Well, not really. I don't get involved with other people's problems. I have enough of my own.
Dr. G.:	What have you heard lately about the Pope?
Brian:	The Pope died recently and there is some sort of fight going on as to who will be the next Pope.
Dr. G.:	What kind of fight?
Brian:	There were two Popes chosen and nobody knows who

is going to remain as Pope. In all my years I have never heard of such dealings. I don't like to think about those things.

An interesting historical note: in the year 1130, Lothair II was the Holy Roman Emperor, and his son-in-law, Henry the Proud, was Duke of Bavaria. Pope Honorius II died in 1130 and two elections were held. A small body of cardinals elected Innocent II while the majority of cardinals elected Analectus II. The latter controlled the Vatican and the castle of Saint Angelo. Innocent II was recognized by all of the kings north of the Alps and in Rome as the true Pope. He retired and went with Lothair to Germany until 1136 when Lothair reinstated him as the one and only Pope.

Dr. G.:   Is there anything about your work that you don't like?
Brian: It's my damn, incompetent apprentice.
Dr. G.:   Tell me about your apprentice.
Brian: There's not much to tell. I took this young lad into my shop and tried to make a craftsman out of him. But, he doesn't seem to be able to do the work.
Dr. G.:   What is his name?
Brian: Thayer.

At this point my skin began to crawl. However, my obligation was to my current patient, and it was important to continue this regression as if nothing unusual had happened. After all, Brian knew nothing of Arnold.

Dr. G.:   What exactly does Thayer do that bothers you?
Brian: He exists. That bothers me. I don't know what it is about him but I don't like him. I seem to want to hurt him. He is an incompetent and will never be the master craftsman that I am.

It was significant that Brian lacked this oversize ego in his present life. Although he was unquestionably independent and successful, he was almost soft-spoken and never exhibited such self-importance. In his life as Gustave, he was coarse, crude, cruel, and sadistic. His voice was deeper than Brian's and he spoke much more rapidly.

Dr. G.:   How do you treat Thayer?

Brian: Ha, ha! You ask a very interesting question. I am too
          kind to the lad. I feed him, clothe him, and beat him.
          I am a good provider.

Dr. G.:   You beat him?

Brian: You are offended? Of course I beat him. He deserves
          no better.

Dr. G.:   Do you enjoy beating him?

Brian: Yes. He does anything I ask and I ask a lot. He doesn't
          like what I ask of him, but I own him.

Dr. G.:   Tell me more of your life.

Brian: I work hard. I get up with the sun and work until the
          sun goes down. My work is fine. I am a great crafts-
          man. I am a master.

Gustave went on to describe the details of his life. He was a
very lonely and disturbed man. People bothered him. It wasn't
just Thayer whom he didn't like. He didn't like anyone. Cruelty
made him feel good. Thayer provided him with companionship
and someone on whom he could vent his frustrations.

Chaining Thayer to the table—which Arnold had described
to me from Thayer's point of view—was an example of Gustave's
cruelty. The chain was purposely made short to make it uncomfortable for Thayer. Even the simple act of eating became a
humiliation. Thayer was used, manipulated, dominated, and ut-
terly degraded by Gustave, nor was Gustave shy about describing the homosexual acts he committed with Thayer.

I next progressed Gustave to the year 1135.

Dr. G.:   How is your business these days?

Brian: Business is good thanks to my skill but not thanks to
          that good-for-nothing apprentice of mine. All he
          seems to care about is that damn girl.

Dr. G.:   What girl is that?

Brian: That Clotilde.

Dr. G.:   Who is Clotilde?

Brian: She is the daughter of a wealthy nobleman. Her fam-
          ily has been doing business with me for a long time.
          Imagine, that incompetent actually thinks that a no-
          bleman's daughter could actually love a commoner—
          and an incompetent one at that!

Dr. G.:   Why is that so impossible to imagine?

Brian: Look, I am a master craftsman. If I can't have a no-

blewoman such as Clotilde, I'll be damned if I'm
going to let Thayer have her. I will see to it that she
sees him for what he is.

Dr. G.:   And what is that?

Brian: A commoner. A possession of mine, and a rather
worthless one at that.

Dr. G.:   Wouldn't you like to be involved with someone like
Clotilde?

The response to that question can't be reported. I seemed to
have struck a nerve with that question. Apparently Gustave's
misanthropy and his homosexual tendencies grew out of his
frustration at not being able to socialize with the nobility. This
was a feudal society with a strict class system. Master guildsmen
were not allowed to marry or consort with noblewomen. To make
matters worse, Gustave was physically unattractive and crude.
These frustrations, among others, led to Gustave's attitude toward
Thayer and Clotilde. He used Thayer as his scapegoat.

I progressed Brian to the resolution of the situation between
Gustave and Thayer.

Dr. G.:   What is happening now?

Brian: I'm going to fix that Thayer once and for all.

Dr. G.:   What did he do now?

Brian: It's that Clotilde. She had the nerve to ask me to let
Thayer go to her house for some special work. Why
didn't she ask me to go? I am the master, the best.
He is just an apprentice!

Dr. G.:   Is that all that's bothering you?

Brian: No! I came very close to hurting that girl. She got me
very mad.

Dr. G.:   Have you ever acted that way before with her?

Brian: No. Of course not. It's Thayer's fault and I'm going
to fix him good.

Dr. G.:   What are you going to do to him?

Brian: I'm going to feed him very well tonight. Then I'm
going to give him the beating of his life.

Dr. G.:   Don't you think that Thayer will sense that something
is wrong?

Brian: I don't care. I just want to beat him until he begs for
mercy.

Dr. G.:   On the count of five, move forward to the actual confrontation with Thayer. One . . . two . . . three . . . four . . . five. What do you see now?

Brian: I'm chaining Thayer to the table. He looks a little strange after I tell him that this will be a night that he will long remember.

Dr. G.: What happens next?

Brian: He talks back to me and keeps moving his leg so I can't chain him to the table. That crazy fool jumps me and tries to knock me down.

Dr. G.: What do you do about it?

Brian: I laugh at the fool for his futile attempt to hurt mc. Then I pick him up and throw him on the table. He knocks over the nice meal I fixed for him. He will regret this night.

Dr. G.: Where are you now?

Brian: I'm standing by the table slapping the idiot. He reaches for my throat and tries to strangle me. Now I'm really mad.

Dr. G.: What happens next?

Brian: I pick him up again and throw him against the wall. My tools are there and I tease him with a very sharp knife. He curses me and I lose my temper. I stab him again and again. It feels good to rid myself of this incompetent. He is not worth any more trouble. I killed him and I am glad.

Dr. G.: Where did you stab Thayer?

Brian: First I stabbed him in his stomach and then I stabbed him in the neck.

I brought Brian back to the present after a few minutes. He seemed drained from the session, but he was very impressed by this experience. He didn't want to pursue additional regressions. Apparently he felt this one exposure was sufficient.

Over the next few months, Brian made considerable progress in controlling his manipulative and domineering tendencies. He has since sent numerous referrals to me. I never did tell him of the case of Arnold and his past life as Thayer. My professional ethics prevent me from revealing the details of another patient's case history.

I have already discussed the concept of synchronicity. Suffice it to say, my exposure to these two regressions was no coincidence. The odds must be billions to one against such a situation occurring. The correspondences were nothing short of startling.

All the names, dates, and events matched. The main difference occurs in the two accounts of the final fight between Thayer (Arnold) and Gustave (Brian). According to Thayer, he jumps Gustave, wrestles him to the floor, and is stabbed in the stomach repeatedly after Gustave throws him against the wall. In Gustave's version, he picks up Thayer and throws him against the wall and stabs him in the stomach repeatedly and then in the neck. The only discrepancy seems to be who first accosts whom, since if the stomach wounds killed Thayer, he would never know he had been stabbed in the neck!

Of course, I considered the possibility of fraud. But it seems clear to me that neither man had anything to gain from collusion. And if this was some sort of practical joke, I fail to see a motive. I had never discussed writing this book with either of them. In fact, it wasn't until October of 1980 that I even considered writing a book. And it was a year and a half between the two regressions. Finally, neither of them has ever contacted me with respect to publishing their cases. I can only think of this as an example of synchronicity.

Many people have asked me whether Arnold and Brian have ever met in this lifetime. The answer is that they have not met in this incarnation and I had no knowledge of their relationship prior to my regressing them. Furthermore, I have no intention of introducing them, for many reasons. First, if they were supposed to meet again to work out their karma, then they would have come into contact with each other long before they met me. Second, I do not attempt to play God with my patients. To introduce these two people, considering their past life history, would affect both of their karmic cycles. If this were meant to be, it would already be out of my control. Third, I would be concerned about Arnold's possible reaction to Brian, and vice versa. Considering the details of the regressions, both could be hostile and violent.

My involvement as the middleman may very well have been a test of my own karmic cycle. It was tempting to introduce these patients to each other. However, this may have done them both more harm than good, physically and psychologically. If they were meant to meet again in this life they would do so without my interference. Perhaps my knowledge of both Brian and Arnold did help me understand the effects they had on each other during the Middle Ages. I did not feel that they would have benefited at all from their meeting in this lifetime. Perhaps they will meet in this life but it won't be through me. My role in these two cases is complete. My task is to help the patient understand the root causes of his or her problems through the use of hypnotic regressions so that he or she is rid of mysterious compulsions and can lead a better existence in this lifetime.

Both Arnold's and Brian's lives have, in fact, been significantly improved as a result of hypnotherapy and especially past life regression. Arnold is less afraid and more self-confident; Brian informed me that he had successfully resisted two opportunities to manipulate a new lawyer in his firm. In addition, Brian's insomnia disappeared entirely, and he lost twenty-five pounds. Since neither of them showed any interest in exploring additional past lives, I can only guess that they did share additional lifetimes since the twelfth century and I hope they fulfilled their karmic obligations.

CHAPTER THIRTEEN

Anorexia Nervosa:
Self-Punishment for Her Last Life

ANOREXIA NERVOSA IS A VERY DANGEROUS SYNDROME. IT is characterized by a patient literally starving herself to death. The patient considers herself to be very much overweight even though, in reality, she is at her proper weight or slightly underweight. When she looks in the mirror she fantasizes that she sees an overweight figure. I have observed this neurosis in women of all ages and socioeconomic backgrounds. Most commonly it affects young, single women of middle-class backgrounds.

There was a case that was reported to me not long ago about a nineteen-year-old girl who read an article in a leading magazine stating that one can never be too rich or too thin. Since this young woman was from a lower middle-class family with little chance of becoming wealthy, she decided that her only hope was to lose weight quickly by starving herself. This sudden weight loss nearly killed her. After a number of hospitalizations and psychotherapy, she realized the futility and danger of her actions and fortunately came to her senses.

I do not treat many cases of anorexia nervosa, but the number of patients calling me with this problem has definitely increased over the past five years. One warm spring afternoon I received a telephone call from a woman by the name of Gina. Gina was a photographer by profession and she sounded in need of help.

It seemed that for the past three months she had literally been afraid to eat. Gina couldn't explain why, but she wanted to starve herself. Her appetite had all but disappeared and it took a great deal of effort to eat any kind of food. She was five feet six inches tall and now weighed only ninety-two pounds. Her weight had dropped from 120 pounds in just three months.

Gina arrived at my office the following day, immaculately dressed and, except for a rather emaciated figure, very attractive. She spoke almost in a whisper.

Gina described her problem, beginning when she started having a series of nightmares. At first she couldn't remember anything about her dreams but then memories began to surface. Most of the time she would see a very obese man in his thirties. The look on his face and his mere presence would frighten her. Gina didn't know what this meant, but she did know that she was afraid of this man.

My work with past life regression was well known to Gina, since two of her girlfriends had been regression patients of mine. She thought that these scenes could be indications of a past life. I agreed with her premise and began to explain the procedure involved in regressing to a past life.

I informed Gina that it might be difficult at first to go back to this lifetime since she had many negative responses to the scenes she saw in her dream state. Since we are in the alpha state (natural hypnosis) when we dream, it is not uncommon for people to have their own past life regressions while they sleep. Unfortunately, most of the scenes that are relived during the dream state are forgotten immediately upon awakening.

Gina was highly intelligent and, although she had little prior knowledge of karma or hypnosis, followed my explanations with ease. Yet when I asked her, out of trance, about past experiences with nightmares, she had a great deal of difficulty remembering the last time bad dreams had bothered her. She very rarely remembered her dreams, and when she did they were usually meaningless to her. Before the episode that brought her to my office, she had had occasional nightmares, but none of these had affected her the way these recent dreams had.

During Gina's second session, I used simple age regression to take her through various parts of her childhood. She reported scenes of little significance, but this was preparation for her past life regression. Gina was becoming more and more confident of her ability to relax with hypnosis and self-hypnosis. I always teach self-hypnosis to my patients for this very reason.

The third and fourth sessions were spent taking Gina through two past lives. The scenes and information that she reported to me were of little value as far as her anorexia nervosa was concerned. In one past life Gina was the wife of a Massachusetts farmer in the eighteenth century. She lived a full life and had no significant weight problems. The second life we explored showed Gina as a seamstress in Philadelphia during the 1850s. Again no weight problems emerged. It seemed that her subconscious mind was fighting me. I gave her some specific suggestions to allow her subconscious mind to relax any inhibitions concerning exploring past life scenes directly relating to her anorexia.

We were both surprised by what Gina reported during her fifth session. I induced Gina into a medium-level trance and directed her back into a past life that would explain the origin of her anorexia.

Dr. G.:   Can you tell me what you see?
Gina: I'm at the doctor's.
Dr. G.:   Why are you there? Are you ill?
Gina: No. I'm just getting weighed. My mom sent me here because of my weight.
Dr. G.:   What is wrong with your weight?
Gina: Well, it's high. (Gina's voice had become very deep and she spoke much slower than normal for her.)
Dr. G.:   What does the doctor tell you?
Gina: He tells me that I must lose thirty pounds.
Dr. G.:   How do you feel about that?
Gina: I want to tell him what he can do with those thirty pounds. (Patient very annoyed.)
Dr. G.:   What is your name?
Gina: Edward. Edward Laslow.
Dr. G.:   How old are you, Edward?
Gina: Call me Eddie. (Patient very demanding). I'm sixteen.
Dr. G.:   What year is this?
Gina: 1906.
Dr. G.:   Where do you live?
Gina: Chicago.

When I asked about her weight, Gina (Edward) squirmed in the recliner. It was as if seeing herself at that weight disgusted her. Further questioning revealed that Eddie had always been overweight, and his well-to-do parents had tried everything they could think of to help him lose weight.

Eddie was rather spoiled and was used to getting what he wanted. He was also quite cruel and got into many fights at school. He seemed to enjoy bullying other children, especially younger ones. As Gina described his activities, she would continue to squirm in my chair.

I next progressed Eddie ahead five years in time. The following information was uncovered over two forty-five minute sessions.

Dr. G.:   Where are you now, Eddie?
Gina: I'm working in one of my father's restaurants.
Dr. G.:   What kind of work do you do?
Gina: I'm assistant manager.
Dr. G.:   Do you like your job?
Gina: It's okay. But I'm going to like it better when I get to be manager.
Dr. G.:   Is that going to take long?
Gina: No. In fact, I'm going to see to it that I'm promoted real soon. (Gina had a very sinister look on her face.)
Dr. G.:   How are you going to do that?
Gina: One of the waitresses, Mary, is a real good friend of mine. I am going to arrange for a little show for my father's benefit.
Dr. G.:   What kind of show?
Gina: My father is a real prude. When he finds out that Mary is having an affair with Stan (the manager), he will most certainly fire Stan and I'll be made manager.
Dr. G.:   Why are you so certain your father will fire Stan?
Gina: Because Stan is a married man and, like I told you, my father is a real prude.

Eddie was a very shrewd operator. He had a great deal of influence on Mary since she owed him some money. It was not difficult for Eddie to talk her into staging an affair with Stan. One evening Mary was entertaining Stan at her apartment when they received an unexpected visitor—Eddie's father. Eddie had one of the waiters inform his father about the affair and the restaurateur went to question Mary about this accusation.

Upon entering Mary's apartment, Eddie's father became outraged at Stan and fired him immediately. The following day Eddie was appointed manager of the restaurant. This type of underhanded dealing was to become a trademark for Eddie.

Over the next ten years, Eddie developed quite a reputation. With his father dead, Eddie was now owner of four restaurants in Chicago. At one time he had a partner but this partnership broke up after it became evident that Eddie had cheated his partner out of fifty thousand dollars. Each time Gina described one of these unethical or illegal dealings, she wore a look of disgust.

I next progressed Eddie to the year 1926.

Dr. G.:   Eddie, where are you now?
Gina: I'm in my office counting the day's receipts. It's been a good day.
Dr. G.:   I trust the restaurant business has been good to you.
Gina: It's not just the restaurants. Ha, ha! (Patient was laughing now.)
Dr. G.:   What do you mean?
Gina: I run a separate business on the side.
Dr. G.:   What kind of business?
Gina: A speakeasy, what else?
Dr. G.:   How long have you been involved with speakeasies?
Gina: Oh, about five years now.
Dr. G.:   Who do you get your alcohol from?
Gina: Frankie.
Dr. G.:   Who is Frankie?
Gina: He has connections with the Capone mob. I like Frankie. He's my kind of guy.
Dr. G.:   Why is that?
Gina: Frankie kills people who get in his way. He is always straight with me and I like the way he handles his women.
Dr. G.:   How does he handle his women?
Gina: He beats them when they talk back to him. Now, that's the way to treat a dame.
Dr. G.:   Do you beat your women, Eddie?
Gina: Of course I do. I only hit my wife occasionally. But I beat my other women when they deserve it.

Eddie had many affairs and most of them ended violently. He had two different apartments in the city, which were inhabited by his two mistresses. A couple of his former girlfriends were killed by one of Frankie's men. One of these girls had tried to blackmail Eddie while the other had been unfaithful to him. If there was one thing Eddie couldn't tolerate, it was a woman going out on him.

It seems, in addition, that Eddie always rewarded himself with food. He would gorge himself with food after sex, after completing business deals, or after doing anything he found pleasurable. He even bragged to me about a food orgy he had in 1924 after successfully arranging the killing of a federal agent who was investigating his speakeasies.

Interestingly, Eddie would not allow his picture to be taken. He may have been afraid of its being used to identify him by the police, though he had no criminal record. My interpretation is that he didn't like seeing his obese figure. All of Eddie's girlfriends were thin and beautiful. His wife was also thin and very attractive. Eddie liked surrounding himself with beautiful objects and beautiful people.

I next progressed Eddie to the last day of his life.

Dr. G.:   Eddie, where are you now?
Gina: I'm in my office putting money into my safe.
Dr. G.:   What year is it?
Gina: It's 1928. Where have you been? (Patient quite nervous.)
Dr. G.:   Are you alone?
Gina: Of course I'm alone. Quiet, can you hear that?
Dr. G.:   No. What's happening?
Gina: It's Frankie. He came in through my private entrance.
Dr. G.:   Why is he here?
Gina: He's accusing me of skimming.
Dr. G.:   Have you been skimming money from Frankie and the mob?
Gina: Yes. Wait a minute, he's pulling a gun on me.
Dr. G.:   Where is Frankie now?
Gina: He's standing in front of my desk. He's telling me that he'll never have to worry about me skimming again. (Patient now very excited and begins to stutter.)
Dr. G.:   What's happening now, Eddie?
Gina: Frankie, please don't shoot! No, no, ohh! (Gina was motionless for about a minute.)

I progressed Gina forward after she died to find out exactly what happened. Frankie shot Eddie for cheating the mob out of hundreds of thousands of dollars. Gina seemed to be relieved when death finally came to Eddie. It was obviously an end to a most degrading life. I brought Gina back to the present.

We discussed this life in detail. She was very satisfied with her newfound knowledge. I am happy to report that during the next six weeks, she gained twenty-five pounds and maintained her weight at about 117 pounds. Her anorexia nervosa disappeared almost immediately and, to the best of my knowledge, has not recurred.

There were many interesting principles that Gina's life as Eddie illustrated. First, her viewing scenes of his past life in the dream state brought back the obesity and degeneracy of that incarnation. Gina couldn't deal with this so she decided to starve herself to prevent herself from becoming the obese Eddie Laslow. It was not just Eddie's obesity that horrified Gina. Eddie's complete lack of ethics or morality, his infidelity to his wife, and his criminal involvements all disgusted Gina.

Second, Eddie never allowed his picture to be taken. In this life Gina is a photographer and loves having her own picture taken. In fact, she once worked as a model.

Third, Gina had a fear of guns that she could never explain. Being shot to death by Frankie in her past life left Gina with this phobia, which disappeared shortly after this regression.

Finally, Gina's voice was naturally very soft, but when she spoke as Eddie Laslow, it became deeper and slower. In addition, she showed many facial changes and at times developed an almost sinister appearance when she spoke as Eddie.

Gina's life was greatly affected by her reliving her existence as Eddie Laslow. It may literally have saved her life.

CHAPTER FOURTEEN

On a Clear Day You Can See Tomorrow: Future Life Progression with Hypnosis

W HENEVER I MENTION PROGRESSION INTO FUTURE LIVES in an interview, I know many listeners scratch their heads in disbelief. The future seems to be forbidden territory. we are all taught that the past has occurred, the present is occurring, but the future has yet to occur. Then how could we possibly know it—by whatever means—in the present?

In Chapter 3, I discussed the concept of time. One has to think in abstract terms to understand it. Suppose, for example, that you are in a helicopter above a major highway. You look down and see that traffic is stopped because of an accident. At this time you could radio someone in a car five miles behind the scene of the accident and inform the driver of the upcoming traffic problem. Since you are in a helicopter above the traffic flow, you are actually detached from the scene itself. The car that you are warning is involved with the traffic flow. In a sense you are reading the future to this car. If the driver of that car keeps driving on that highway, he will be involved with the stopped traffic that you are now observing. The helicopter represents another plane, and on a different plane there is no time as we here on Earth (or on the highway, in this analogy) know it.

To continue the analogy, from the helicopter you could also see what the traffic flow is like behind the car that you are talking to. This would represent the past. The traffic ahead of the driver represents the future, and the traffic that the driver is experiencing now represents the present. You are, in effect, reading the past, present, and future from the helicopter. By leaving the earth plane or entering into a hypnotic trance, you can read the past or future without the restrictions that occur in the waking, or beta, state.

The actual experience of a progression is rather difficult to describe. I have personally conducted thousands of regressions, and hundreds of progressions. Most people are afraid of the future and don't want to be progressed. Also, I have regressed myself into past lives and progressed myself into future lives, so that I can speak of these phenomena from personal experience. In a regression, the scenes can unfold in a logical and orderly fashion. The patient can recall the past in great detail, and these episodes into the past are often most helpful to him or her in terms of understanding present karma and present behavioral problems. A progression, however, is far less stable. It is much more difficult to obtain information. I am attempting to see how a patient's karma will be manifested in the future when I perform progressions. This knowledge can greatly help a patient in his present life.

It seems that when an individual is progressed into the future, he or she may be quickly removed from a particular scene and transferred to another without any instructions from me. There is, of course, absolutely no danger to the patient, but the continuity of the scene may be lost. For example, the patient could be describing a scene in some futuristic city and the next thing we know, the city has disappeared and a desert scene has replaced it. The patient may then describe a third and completely different scene, and act as if nothing unusual has happened.

Unfortunately, there is no reference source that one can utilize to obtain additional information about our future. Psychics don't write books on this subject, if they do future life progressions at all. I know of no other therapist in the country who does progressions. People are as susceptible to progressions as they are to regressions. Progressions, however, do require more conditioning.

Our subconscious minds are programmed to think of the future as being mysterious and inaccessible. Thus, our minds would inhibit a free flow of information and instead present a constant change in scenes. Another possible explanation of the difficulty of extracting information about the future from the subconscious during hypnosis could be a physical one. The subconscious mind is pure energy. It is characterized by a certain electrical frequency and magnetic field. The future might affect this field and frequency in some way and thus result in this instability.

Karma would also be affected by individuals seeing into their future. Yet if we weren't supposed to know the future, progression simply wouldn't work. And in some exciting cases, there's no doubt that it does. Someday I expect science, probably quantum physics, to solve this mystery once and for all.

There have been numerous consistent observations made by my patients as to our future during their hypnotic progressions. Since people have reported similar observations independently in trance, I feel it my duty to report them.

As you will see in the cases that following, during the twenty-first century, world peace will finally become a reality. Peace will last for 300 years. Earth will undergo major geographical changes; scientific progress will be most evident. In the next century, hunger, greed, jealousy, prejudice, and other negative aspects of society seem to have been almost entirely eliminated.

During the twenty-second century, solar power will be incorporated into everyday life. Much advancement in medical science will be evident, especially in the fields of psychology and psychiatry. The life span of the average adult will be increased to about ninety years.

Technological advancements continue in the twenty-third century. Transportation systems become almost noiseless and very efficient; nuclear power is used extensively. Sophisticated computers and video equipment are household appliances. Advanced education is emphasized and readily available. Experiments in weather control are meeting with greater success. An average life span of 110 years also characterizes this century.

It is during the twenty-fourth century that humankind reverts to some of its earlier mistakes. International political problems recur; a small-scale nuclear war results in a reduction of the world's population; there are further geographical changes on the earth's surface.

The twenty-fifth century is characterized by man's ability to control the weather. Androids are used to perform all menial tasks; medicine makes more advances. A major nuclear war results in a tremendous decrease in the population of the world. However, mankind survives and civilization continues to prosper into at least the next century.

Underwater cities, the routine use of lasers in medicine, and sophisticated genetic engineering will characterize the twenty-sixth century. Information pills will keep citizens well informed, and one democratic form of world government will insure the rights of all. People will have much leisure time; the average life span will be over 125 years. Sickness and disease will be almost unknown; interplanetary travel will be a top priority and we will make contact with beings from other planets.

There seems to be an almost eerie stillness in the future, more peaceful, with a few exceptions, and more productive.

It is interesting to note patients' lack of emotion during future progressions. With rare exceptions, the scenes, no matter how horrible, are described with little reaction. Earthquakes, nuclear wars, accidental deaths, and so on, do not seem to bring out the same emotional response during progression as they do during past life regressions. The reason for this is unclear. Yet you will see it repeatedly in the cases that follow.

CHAPTER FIFTEEN

The Future Lives
of Our TV Personality

EARLY IN JANUARY 1981, HARRY MARTIN CALLED ME EX-
pressing interest in progressing into the future through
the use of hypnosis. He had done so well with past life regression that he wanted to see if it could work "in reverse." After
seeing himself as a self-made warehouse owner in the eighteenth
century, a nineteenth-century blind piano player, and an RAF
radio operator during World War II, Harry was ready for an
entirely different experience. I explained the theory concerning
the space-time continuum and he seemed very enthusiastic about
attempting a journey into the future.

At our first session, I wanted to establish the validity of this
technique. I decided to progress Harry just one week into the
future to the WBAL newsroom assignment board to see if he
could read news items about events that hadn't occurred yet.
This seemed to be a fair test of hypnotic progression and Harry
agreed to it wholeheartedly. My next step would be to progress
Harry into a future life. All of these sessions were tape-recorded
and I gave Harry a copy of these tapes.

On February 2, 1981, Harry began his first trip into the future. I progressed him one week forward, to February 9, 1981,
which was a Monday. The technique simply consisted of Harry's
reading either from the newsroom assignment board one hour
before air-time of his broadcast or his reading from the actual
script of that day's newscast. (The first fifteen minutes of "Hello
Baltimore" consisted of a news update.)

The following are exerpts from this February 2 session:

Dr. G.:   Tell me exactly what you see on the assignment board.
Harry: Plane, and the number 406.

When I asked Harry to read the newsscript about this item, this is what he reported:

Harry: State aviation officials are investigating the crash of a light plane this morning near route 406.

This item never made it on the air, but on February 9 a small plane did crash in Bowie, Maryland. This crash was investigated by state aviation officials.

Dr. G.:   What is the next item on the assignment board?
Harry: It's the name of a place, I think, but I can't make it out.
Dr. G.:   Can you spell it?
Harry: It's a long name. It's a very weird combination of consonants. It's the name of a man.
Dr. G.:   What letters can you make out?
Harry: ST W KI . . . it's a long Russian-type name.

On February 9 Stanislaw Kania, Poland's labor leader, was told that he might soon be fired unless he instructed his workers to return to work.

Dr. G.:   Move down to the next item that you will be reading on the air. Tell me what the script says.
Harry: This is an accident. It's on 695 (the Baltimore Beltway) between the Pikesville and Security Boulevard exits, but I don't know where.
Dr. G.:   What vehicles are involved in the accident?
Harry: One large vehicle and one small one. There were no deaths.

On February 9 a school bus on its way to Randallstown (between Pikesville and Security Boulevard) hit a car at 200 Embleton Road in Owings Mills (just north of Pikesville). No deaths were reported.

Dr. G.:   What is the next news item, Harry?

Harry: It has to do with Governor Hughes and the budget.

Dr. G.:   What about the budget?

Harry: Governor Hughes says he's holding the line this year
           on the budget. The legislature is going against him
           for some reason, saying that they don't have to hold
           the budget on some raise proposal.

On February 12, Governor Hughes vetoed a forty- to sixty-million-dollar raise for state employers. The Maryland Classified Employees Association (MCEA) had obtained the support of the State Legislature in voting for a salary raise.

Dr. G.:   What is the next news item?

Harry: It's something about Jerry Falwell.

Dr. G.:   What about Jerry Falwell?

Harry: It has something to do with Falwell's interview that
           appeared in *Penthouse*

On February 4 Jerry Falwell withdrew his lawsuit against *Penthouse* magazine. (Remember, this session was taking place on February 2.)

Harry's next progression session was the following Monday, February 9. There was much excitement and enthusiasm in his voice when he discussed last week's "hits." I was also stimulated and elated with the results of the last session.

Anyone can do what Harry accomplished. The hypnotic state allows the psychic component of the brain to be tapped. We all have this progression ability. Naturally, I do not use this technique to predict stock values or lottery numbers. First, I consider this an unethical use of our natural psychic abilities. Second, the dates are not always accurate. A progression of one week in the future may, in actuality, be three days or ten days hence.

I then progressed Harry to February 16 and again had him read the news items on the script that would be used on the air.

Dr. G.:   What news item appears next on the script?

Harry: A fire in the city.

Dr. G.:   What kind of building was involved?

Harry: A house fire; a row house.

Dr. G.:   Do you see the name of the person who owned the
           house?

Harry: I want to say Johnson. They don't own it; I think they
            just live there.
Dr. G.:   Anything else?
Harry: There are two little girls involved.
Dr. G.:   Are they hurt?
Harry: No, they escaped safely but somebody was hurt. I
            don't know who, though.
Dr. G.:   Can you see anything else?
Harry: I see two little girls being dangled from the second-
            story window of this row house. They're being res-
            cued by someone. They had ribbons in their hair.

On February 13 a child named Kenneth Blanda died in a
second-story fire on 540 Pulaski Street in the western part of
Baltimore City. A space heater had caused the fire. Patricia
Johnson, a neighbor, was interviewed about the fire. This fire
did occur in a row house.

What is especially interesting is that in four of the six "hits,"
the dates matched perfectly. With one of the misses the date was
five days before, and with the other it was three days before the
predicted date. I consulted with a professor of mathematics at a
local university and he stated that the odds were hundreds of
thousands to one against this type of thing happening by mere
chance. These hits don't *prove* progression but, in my opinion,
they lend significant credence to the theory.

The following chart summarizes Harry's progressions:

DATE OF SESSION	NEWS ITEM GIVEN IN TRANCE	ACTUAL NEWS ITEM THAT OCCURRED
February 2, 1981	State aviation officials investigating light plane crash—route 406.	February 9, 1981—A small plane crashed in Bowie, but this time didn't make it on the air.
	ST W KI—Long name with many consonants—possibly a Russian name.	February 9, 1981— Stanislaw Kania, Polish labor leader, may be fired.

Accident on 695 between Security Blvd. and Pikesville. NO DEATHS.	February 9, 1981—A school bus on its way to *Randallstown* hit a car at 200 Embleton Rd. (Owings Mills) NO DEATHS.
Harry Hughes (wants to hold the line on the budget) fights with State Legislature (wants to spend more dollars).	February 12, 1981— Harry Hughes wouldn't approve forty- to sixty-million-dollar raise for state employees. Maryland Classified Employees Assn. (MCEA) said salaries should be raised.
Jerry Falwell— *Penthouse* interview	February 4, 1981— Jerry Falwell withdrew his lawsuit concerning his interview that appeared in *Penthouse*.

February 9, 1981

Fire in the city—row house. The Johnsons live there. A neighbor helped rescue two children from the second story. One child was hurt.	February 13, 1981— Kenneth Blanda (a child) died in a second-story fire on 540 Pulaski St. in West Baltimore. A space heater caused the fire. Patricia Johnson, a neighbor, was interviewed about the fire.

On March 9, Harry came to my office for a progression into a future lifetime. He was excited about this adventure. I induced him into a medium trance and began questioning him. During this entire session, Harry spoke in a slow, almost monotonous voice, expressing no emotion whatsoever.

Dr. G.: What do you see before you?

Harry: A pyramid.

Dr. G.: Is this pyramid isolated or are there other structures around it?

Harry: It's isolated.
Dr. G.:   Where is this pyramid?
Harry: It's in the desert.
Dr. G.:   What is the purpose of this pyramid?
Harry: It has something to do with energy. It's getting energy
            from the sun.
Dr. G.:   Are there any other structures by the pyramid that are
            related to its energy functions?
Harry: There are pipes on the bottom of it.
Dr. G.:   Why are you there?
Harry: I'm just observing. It's like a tour.
Dr. G.:   How long have you been there?
Harry: I've just arrived.
Dr. G.:   How long are you going to be there?
Harry: Another hour and then we're going to leave.

I next progressed Harry to the tour itself.

Dr. G.:   What do you see now?
Harry: The pyramid is made of glass.
Dr. G.:   Are you inside the pyramid now?
Harry: Yes. There are living quarters in the far corners with
            plants and all sorts of supplies.
Dr. G.:   How tall is the pyramid?
Harry: Seventy feet high.
Dr. G.:   What is the source of energy for this pyramid other
            than the sun?
Harry: Nothing.
Dr. G.:   How many people live inside the pyramid?
Harry: Three hundred.
Dr. G.:   What is the purpose of this pyramid?
Harry: It's a self-sufficient structure. These 300 inhabitants
            are specially selected scientists.
Dr. G.:   What is the name of the pyramid?
Harry: Phobos.
Dr. G.:   Can you describe the leader of the tour?
Harry: A man wearing yellow coveralls leads us.
Dr. G.:   How many of you are on this tour?
Harry: There are ten of us.
Dr. G.:   Can you see any personal effects in this pyramid that
            would indicate that people are currently living here?
Harry: Yes. There are plants in various quarters.
Dr. G.:   What form of communication exists in the pyramid?

Harry: We don't speak. We think and our thoughts are trans-
             mitted as images. That is the purpose of this scientific
             team—to explore silent communication.
Dr. G.:   Can you see what the people on the tour are wearing?
Harry: We all wear a one-piece coverall suit of a certain color.
Dr. G.:   What kind of footwear do you have on?
Harry: It's a rubber ankle-high boot that's the same color as
             the suit.
Dr. G.:   Does the color of the suit have any meaning?
Harry: Yes. Each color signifies your function and rank on
             this project.
Dr. G.:   What is your color?
Harry: Beige.
Dr. G.:   What colors are the other people on the tour wearing?
Harry: We are all wearing beige. Red is the lowest color.
             Next is beige, orange, yellow, green, and violet. As
             we progress in our duties we move on to the higher
             colors.
Dr. G.:   What do the scientists in the pyramid do as you ob-
             serve them?
Harry: They just seem to be walking back and forth.
Dr. G.:   Do they make any sounds?
Harry: No.
Dr. G.:   What year is this?
Harry: 2153.

I next progressed Harry forward in time to when he would be
at work in his profession.

Dr. G.:   What do you see now?
Harry: I'm outside looking up at the glass pyramid.
Dr. G.:   Is this the same pyramid that you were in when I last
             spoke with you?
Harry: Yes.
Dr. G.:   What is your purpose in being outside now?
Harry: These glass panels have to be kept free of sand in
             order for the pyramid to operate properly. I inspect
             these panels. I make sure these panels are clean.
Dr. G.:   Do you now work and live in the pyramid?
Harry: Yes.
Dr. G.:   Do you have any way of noting down what needs to
             be replaced or corrected?
Harry: No. There's nothing like that. There is no writing.

Dr. G.:   How do you communicate problems with your super-
           visors?
Harry: You think about it and they will know it.
Dr. G.:   Are you the only inspector?
Harry: Yes.

This was Harry's first job in this future lifetime. He had very
little formal training for this inspector position. I next progressed Harry forward in time by ten years.

Dr. G.:   Where do you find yourself now?
Harry: I'm inspecting the irrigation system.
Dr. G.:   Has anything changed since I last spoke with you?
Harry: Yes. The pyramid is now being use for farming pur-
           poses.
Dr. G.:   Could you elaborate?
Harry: All of the plants are grown in water, not soil. The
           water has all the necessary nutrients in it.
Dr. G.:   What exactly do you do now?
Harry: I help monitor the ratio of various nutrients in the
           water so that the correct proportions are present.
Dr. G.:   Do you do this yourself?
Harry: No, the computer does this. I just double-check the
           computer.
Dr. G.:   What do you do if the computer is malfunctioning?
Harry: I repair it.
Dr. G.:   What color is your suit?
Harry: Yellow.

Apparently Harry had been promoted to a much more sophisticated position in the pyramid. I now progressed Harry to
the last day of his future life.

Dr. G.:   Where are you?
Harry: I'm reporting to the termination room.
Dr. G.:   Are you still in the pyramid?
Harry: Yes.
Dr. G.:   Why are you in the termination room?
Harry: It's my turn to change units.
Dr. G.:   Can you describe this procedure?
Harry: I lie down on a table and they put something on my
           fingers and you just go to sleep.
Dr. G.:   What does this do to you?

Harry:	It takes all of your energy out of you.
Dr. G.:	Why is this done?
Harry:	You can now be placed in a more appropriate unit. You don't grow old or grow up. You are just transferred.
Dr. G.:	Is this then a mechanical body?
Harry:	No. It's a totally biological unit.
Dr. G.:	What happens in between going from one unit to another?
Harry:	You are stored on tape.
Dr. G.:	Do you have a choice as to whether or not you will enter a certain unit?
Harry:	No.

Harry's voice and delivery in answering my questions were particularly interesting to me. I was also fascinated with Harry's report of the experiments in mental telepathy and the use of solar energy as the only energy source. The isolation of this future life was similiar to Harry's past life as Hap, the blind piano player. Even though he was born blind, Hap exhibited no remorse. As a twenty-second-century irrigation inspector Harry easily accepted his "termination." The eighteenth-century life as a warehouse owner and director of an import-export business required that he be an inspector and was also lonely work. This karmic lesson still needed to be learned 400 years later.

When Harry received his promotion to irrigation supervisor this reminded me of his start in newscasting as a radio personality. He was then promoted to television reporting. Today Harry is a well-organized television newscaster. He acquired this discipline from at least three previous lifetimes. As an RAF radio operator he was well trained in scientific discipline.

Assertiveness is a trait Harry Martin possesses today. It is a necessary quality for a television personality. Yet during the nineteenth, twentieth (as the RAF radio operator), and twenty-second centuries this characteristic was lacking. The karmic lesson was learned and didn't have to be repeated.

Harry's second future lifetime was revealed two weeks later. He came to my office on this spring afternoon feeling quite relaxed. I induced him into a medium trance and proceeded with the questioning.

Dr. G.:	What do you see?
Harry:	I see white curtains that look like lace in front of a window.

Dr. G.:   What else do you see?
Harry: I'm inside this room and I'm looking at my work.
Dr. G.:   What kind of work it that?
Harry: Silver plates. There are these silver plates on the wall.

Harry's answers were again almost mechanical without any
expression of emotion. His speech pattern was very slow and
his voice very deep. This was to continue throughout the session.

Dr. G.:   What is characteristic about these plates?
Harry: They have emblems on them but no writing.
Dr. G.:   Can you describe the furniture?
Harry: The design of the couch and chairs is cubical.
Dr. G.:   What is this place?
Harry: It's my home.
Dr. G.:   What is special about this particular day?
Harry: This is a rest day.
Dr. G.:   What kind of work do you do?
Harry: I'm a sort of craftsperson.
Dr. G.:   What do you construct?
Harry: Those plates. Those silver plates on the wall.
Dr. G.:   Who do you do these for?
Harry: People. People request my services.
Dr. G.:   Are there many craftsmen like you?
Harry: No. There are only a few of us who do this kind of
            work.
Dr. G.:   What do people call you?
Harry: Amygdala.
Dr. G.:   Is that your complete name?
Harry: Yes.
Dr. G.:   What year is this?
Harry: 2271.

I next progressed Amygdala forward in time by two years.

Dr. G.:   Can you tell me more about your work?
Harry: These plates are made of silver. They are a means of
            currency.
Dr. G.:   Are there other forms of currency?
Harry: Yes. You see, these silver plates are a way of holding
            massive amounts of wealth.

Dr. G.: The fact that you have some of these silver plates on your wall, does that mean that you are wealthy?

Harry: Yes.

Dr. G.: Why do people come to you for your work? Why don't they just store their own silver?

Harry: What happens is my making these plates increases the value of the metal.

Dr. G.: What kind of work do some of your clients do?

Harry: Law, and some of my people are in manufacturing and transportation.

Dr. G.: What kind of transportation are you referring to?

Harry: Molecular reassembly. This type of transportation is new but is being used more and more.

Dr. G.: Are there any other uses for molecular reassembly?

Harry: Sustenance. We have small units that help nourish us while we sleep.

Dr. G.: Could you describe your own molecular reassembly unit?

Harry: It's a platform, a round platform. There is a coordinate tracking system to set it.

Dr. G.: Do you need someone else to activate it?

Harry: No.

Dr. G.: When you do use it, how do you get reassembled?

Harry: It's programmed into the unit by the tracking system.

Dr. G.: Can you describe the last time you used the molecular reassembly unit for transporting yourself?

Harry: I recently went into the city for a meeting.

Dr. G.: Was anyone else present?

Harry: There were two other people. One is a man dressed in a gray suit made of very shiny material. (Patient paused.)

Dr. G.: And the woman, how was she dressed?

Harry: Oh, I'm really confused. (Patient exhibited emotions for the first time since the session began.)

Dr. G.: Why are you confused?

Harry: How did you know it was a woman?

Dr. G.: You said one of these two people was a male, so I assumed that the other was female. How was she dressed?

Harry: This other person in the room is not really a woman.

Dr. G.: Is she human?

Harry: Partially. She is part human and part machine.

Dr. G.: Can you describe her?

Harry: The top half of her body is of human form but the
           way she gets around is by machine. Her head is
           shaved. Her eyes are slanted and her skin is very pale.

It seemed the lower part of this being consisted of a mecha-
nized apparatus similar to a wheelchair.

Dr. G.:   Is there anyone else in the room?
Harry: No, just the computer.
Dr. G.:   What is the purpose of this meeting?
Harry: It has something to do with insurance.
Dr. G.:   Personal insurance or work-related insurance?
Harry: Work-related.
Dr. G.:   Can you read the policy right now?
Harry: There's no writing. You plug it in. (Patient sounded
           bored.)

I next progressed Amygdala to the time when he would return
home and review his policy.

Dr. G.:   What are you doing now?
Harry: I'm plugging the policy into the wall. The screen asks
           for my ID number so that only I can review it.
Dr. G.:   What specifically does it state?
Harry: Amygdala . . . insured against defects in workman-
           ship. Mars 1522.

Amygdala didn't know what Mars 1522 referred to. I returned
Harry to the present.
   In this life, Harry (Amygdala) showed more of his creative
potential as the silver craftsmen. This society seemed to value
silver more than any other metal and crime was almost unknown. In his present life, Harry is also quite creative. He is
currently writing a novel, plays the drums, and is much involved
with the production aspect of a news miniseries. As the nineteenth century piano player Hap, Harry was also showing his
creativity. The RAF radio operator died before he could leave
his mark on society. Harry's career as a television personality
is his way of contributing to the world. This twenty-third-
century life was the culmination of at least 400 years of creative
talent. The great wealth that Amygdala accumulated, in addition
to the recognition he was shown, were karmic paybacks for
centuries of hard work and dedication.

In the 1980s Harry is well on his way to "doing his thing." He has learned from his past and future lives the value of creativity and recognition. Now, as a media personality, he can put these lessons to use. Of the many benefits he received from hypnotherapy, Harry states that focusing his concentration, acquiring more discipline and energy, and the realization that maybe he should start loving life (taking time to smell the roses, and so on) were most significant. Developing a more open attitude toward hypnotherapy and a better understanding of himself must be added to these advantages. Perhaps the knowledge that there will still be a world in 300 years is enough to give us all an optimistic view of the future.

My reaction to Harry's progressions and regressions was one of satisfaction. Harry has previously stated positive changes in his behavior and attitude toward life. These positive results make me feel proud to be a hypnotherapist.

Most patients don't want to know about the future. That is unfortunate because of the tremendous therapeutic potential progression represents. Whether you believe in progression, regression, or hypnosis doesn't really matter. Anyone can obtain the benefits Harry Martin received through hypnotherapy.

CHAPTER SIXTEEN

Time Travel
via the Airwaves

I HAVE ALREADY DISCUSSED THE PAST AND FUTURE LIVES OF Harry Martin from WBAL-TV. These call letters were to come into my life again in 1982. Ken Manelis hosted an overnight talk show on WBAL radio. His producer called me in January of 1982 to schedule me for an interview the following month. On February 12, 1982, I met Ken Manelis and talked with him for five hours on the air about past life regression and future life progression.

Before the interview I hypnotized him so he could subjectively experience a hypnotic trance. Since he asked me to do this just ten minutes before the show began I didn't have the time to regress him. Ken was relaxed during the show. One characteristic commonly encountered after a trance is a feeling in one's fingers similar to that when your hand "falls asleep" and is now "waking up." This feeling of needles in your fingers (not painful, just a strange sensation) is what Ken described during the first hour of the show. I explained to him that the hypnotic state or trance lasts from thirty to sixty minutes after the trance is formally ended. There is no danger to this, as is exemplified by the decrease in car accident rates experienced by drivers in highway hypnosis. After his personal experience Ken was convinced of the accuracy of my statements.

The show went well but what was significant was that Ken expressed an interest in being regressed into a past life. I instinctively knew he was serious. The following week he contacted my office and made his first appointment.

On February 26, 1982, Ken Manelis began his journey through time. The first past life he described was that of Jake Miller. Jake was a tall, thin man who wore a black hat and had a shady past. The time was the late 1800s in Wyoming. He was involved in various con games swindling people out of their hard-earned money. One day he teamed up with an old man and convinced the townspeople that there was gold in the mountains. The old man and Jake sold gear and supplies to these would-be miners, knowing very well that there was no gold present. This scheme worked well for Jake but the old man and he decided to leave town before the miners discovered the truth about the status of gold in the mountains. Jake then ended up in San Francisco and went to work on the waterfront. Jake became an honest, hardworking man, starting all over in a new state. One day in 1906 a great earthquake ravaged the city, and Jake was killed when a wall of a building fell on him while he was helping firemen put out a fire.

What was intesting about this life was how Ken was initially quite skeptical about the concept of reincarnation. He thought these lives were all fantasy expressions. A check on the San Francisco Earthquake showed that it did indeed occur in 1906 and destroyed almost all the downtown business section of the city. Fires burned for days without stopping and five hundred people were killed. This shocked Ken and encouraged him to continue his explorations.

On March 12, Ken went down memory lane for a second time. This life was characterized by this radio personality living in a large Southern mansion in Virginia. His name was Pete Grant and his father was a very powerful general in the Confederate army. Pete was pressured to enter a military academy by his father. When he graduated Pete was a second lieutenant in the army.

He quickly became disillusioned with the South's cause and when his regiment was captured by Union soldiers, Pete joined the Union army. Pete liked being a Union soldier and received a medal for his valor in battle. After the war Pete married and raised a family. The key to this life was his ability to make his own decisions and to resist doing just what his father wanted.

Ken's interest remained quite high in continuing his search. He mentioned to me a fear of thunderstorms and lightning and

asked me if we could explore that next. I then guided Ken back
into two more past lives to relieve him of this fear.

In the early 1820s in Paris, Ken was a very successful businessman named Calvin. He had a daughter but his wife had died
of consumption a few years prior. Calvin didn't believe in banks
and thus kept all of his money and possessions in the house.
One night during an intense summer rain the house was hit by
a lightning bolt and burned to the ground. Calvin and his daughter escaped from the house but all of his wealth was destroyed.
They moved in with relatives but Calvin's spirit was broken and
he died a pauper.

In another life in the early 1900s Ken was a wealthy male
named Royston who lived in London. During a Sunday afternoon party Royston and his girlfriend, Marie, went for a ride in
a field. A thunderstorm ensued and Marie asked Royston to
return her to the house. Royston felt the storm was romantic and
insisted they stay awhile. A few minutes later a lightning bolt
struck Marie and knocked her unconscious. Royston brought
her back to the house in his carriage but upon arrival back at the
party discovers she is dead. The guests were shocked, and Royston was thoroughly embarrassed. He felt so guilty, he took his
own life with a gun out of deep despair.

These two lives seemed to have done the trick because by the
time Ken experienced his first thunderstorm of the spring his
fear was gone. He now expressed a great interest in progressing
into a future life and I was more than happy to accommodate
him.

For Ken's first future life progression, he chose the end of the
twenty-first century, where he was a male college student by
the name of Scott. He lived in an underground city in Arizona.
The city was underground because of the threat of a nuclear
war. This war never manifested itself during Scott's lifetime.

Dr. G.:   Scott, are there people living above the ground?
Ken: Yes. We live underground because my family is very
           wealthy and we can afford to.
Dr. G.:   How would you describe this city?
Ken: Well, it's very science-oriented. Conveyor belts trans-
           port us around the city. Computers are everywhere
           and most of my courses are taught by computers.

This society was indeed very technological. Scott was supposed to study science but he didn't like it and dropped out of

school. Later he worked as a repairman for a robot manufac-
turer. He was trained on the job and enjoyed it. I next progressed
Ken to the age of twenty-five.

Dr. G.:   Where are you now, Scott?
Ken: I am meeting Susan for lunch.
Dr. G.:   Who is Susan?
Ken: She is my fiancée.
Dr. G.:   What kind of work does she do?
Ken: She is a teacher.

Scott hated living underground. Scott and Susan married and
moved above ground. Scott's parents disowned him and Susan
was able to secure a teaching position above ground and Scott
began to sell solar homes.

Dr. G.:   How are things going for you now, Scott?
Ken: Everything is great. I'm happy. Susan is happy. We
           have two children and I'm making lots of money.
Dr. G.:   Do you have any long-term goals now.
Ken: Yes, I do. I would like some of the poor people above
           ground to experience the underground city. I want
           to see more intermingling of the cultures.
Dr.G.:   Do others feel that way, too?
Ken: Yes, but lack of money prevents them from experi-
           encing the underground city.
Dr. G.:   Since you hated the underground city why do you
           concern yourself with it now?
Ken: Life has been good to my family and myself and I
           would like to return the favor. I also want to see my
           parents again to show them that I made it in life.
Dr. G.:   Let's move to the culmination of this project on the
           count of five. One . . . two . . . three . . . four . . .
           five. What has happened, Scott?
Ken: We had many problems. The wealthy people didn't
           like the influx of the poor people. The poor people
           didn't appreciate the snobbish attitude of the rich.
Dr. G.:   And your family life?
Ken: Susan and I work together well but all of these prob-
           lems caused a great deal of strain on our relationship.

Dr. G.:   Does she still teach?
Ken: No, she works as a social worker. She doesn't regret
            giving up teaching.

I progressed Scott forward another five years and found out
that he had sold his solar home business and retired. His relationship with Susan had improved and he was financially secure.
Scott's parents had eventually accepted him and apologized for
their previous behavior. Years later when Scott's parents died he
inherited their estate. Scott and Susan spent most of their time
traveling. At the age of fifty-seven Scott died while mountain-
climbing in Europe.

When I brought Ken to the superconscious mind level and
asked him what he learned as Scott he stated that he learned to
share and to be a family man. He felt bad about not being able
to bring the surface people together with those who lived underground. This life was quite an improvement over Jake Miller
and the con games he ran in the early part of his lifetime.

The last future life we explored was a most unusual lifetime.
My instructions to Ken were to move to a future lifetime that
would represent the culmination of his professional life. He described being on an asteroid during the early part of the twenty-
fourth century. He was in charge of a shuttle service that brought
tourists to a rest area. Large vertical neon tubes served as mark-
ers for the landing pad. Ken's name was Xarva and he supervised a crew of technicians.

This asteroid was owned and run by the government (The
League of One) of Earth.

Dr. G.:   Xarva, how did you end up on this asteroid?
Ken: For many years I worked for the League's space center
            as a chief technician. One unfortunate day I badly hurt
            my leg in an accident on a launching pad. My injury
            was permanent and the government offered me this
            assignment in lieu of retirement. Since I liked to be
            active I accepted the position.
Dr. G.:   Do you have a family on Earth?
Ken: No, I live alone.
Dr. G.:   Are you happy here?
Ken: Let's just say that I'm content. I have plenty to do and
            still have the time to tinker with some pet projects.
Dr. G.:   What kind of projects?
Ken: I am a kind of amateur inventor.

Dr. G.:   Have you invented anything yet?
Ken: Not yet, but I am working on a communications de-
           vice that will enable communication with beings from
           another planet.

Xarva stayed on this asteroid for many years and then returned to Earth to retire. He lived in Florida and at the age of
eighty invented a device that led to communications with extra-
terrestials.

Dr. G.:   What happened to this invention?
Ken: The League took over the application of my invention.
           I received complete credit for it and was well re-
           warded professionally and financially.
Dr. G.:   Did you continue to work for the League?
Ken: Yes. I was placed in charge of this project.
Dr. G.:   Aren't you a bit old for this position?
Ken: Heavens no; people work until they are well over 100
           years old.
Dr. G.:   What kind of communications do you receive from
           outer space?
Ken: At first we just received strange noises. Later on we
           realized that it may be an alien language.
Dr. G.:   How did you translate it?
Ken: We used our most sophisticated computers to finally
           make some sense out of it.
Dr. G.:   What were the messages you received?
Ken: They kept warning us to stop polluting the universe.
Dr. G.:   In what way did they mean pollution?
Ken: We did have a small-scale nuclear war a few years
           back. Additionally, we sent space probes out and
           dumped out nuclear wastes in space.
Dr. G.:   Were these warnings in the form of a threat?
Ken: Not at first, but when we kept ignoring the messages
           the warnings became downright threats.
Dr. G.:   Did you try to convince the government to heed these
           warnings?
Ken: I most certainly did, but nobody would listen to me.
           I tried everything but all I obtained for my trouble
           was forced retirement.

Xarva was frustrated and depressed. He left the government
somewhat disgraced. He was now about 100 years old and

burned out. One night he died in his sleep—at least he thought he died. What happened next was quite strange, definitely not a typical death experience: Xarva's soul was actually beamed out of his body and transferred through outer space to another galaxy. The aliens who did this seemed very angry and disappointed in Xarva.

Dr. G.: What do these aliens look like?

Ken: They are pure light and all communication is telepathic.

Dr. G.: Why are they upset with you?

Ken: They said I was selected to open communications between our galaxies and they expected me to convince the government to heed their warnings.

Dr. G.: Didn't you inform them of your efforts?

Ken: Sure, I did, but you try to convince a green ball of light that you tried your best. These things were not very understanding.

Dr. G.: What did they do next?

Ken: They sent me to another planet to monitor the activities of a rapidly evolving culture. This was considered a punishment.

Dr. G.: How did you make out?

Ken: Actually, quite well. I worked very hard and telepathically advised this society what the aliens instructed me to say. They progressed very nicely and I actually enjoyed it as much as a beam of light can enjoy anything.

Dr. G.: Then what happened?

Ken: As a reward for my efforts I was to accompany a representative of their people to Earth. This sounded really strange.

Dr. G.: And then . . . ?

Ken: We arrived on Earth and these aliens somehow got their message across to the League.

Dr. G.: What happened to you?

Ken: The League found alternative methods of disposing of the waste material. I was somehow transported back into my body again and woke up from this hibernation. The next thing I knew I was being treated like a hero by the League. The aliens saw to it that I received full credit for this diplomatic action.

So ended the most unusual progression I ever conducted. Xarva lived out the rest of his life in peace and was professionally respected. He died happy at the age of 144. Ken saw that he would achieve a form of greatness in about 400 years.

What became an added fringe benefit to this story is that Ken was so moved by the regressions and progressions that he played these sessions on the air at WBAL radio during his show from midnight to 5:00 A.M. Monday through Friday. His audience loved it. Al Burke, the general manager of WBAL radio at that time, heard some of these regressions and asked me if I would be interested in hosting my own weekly show on WBAL radio.

I readily agreed and for eight months I hosted a five-hour weekly show on Saturday evenings from midnight to 5:00 A.M. on WBAL radio called "Insights into Parapsychology." Every week I presented guests covering the entire field of parapsychology from UFOs to ghost-hunters to bigfoot to out-of-body experiences. I conducted live past life regressions occasionally on the air. It was truly an example of time travel via the airways. Listeners from Bermuda to Canada heard the show and I very much enjoyed the role of talk show host.

CHAPTER SEVENTEEN

Marsha:
A Career Woman of the Future

NANCY, A THIRTY-FOUR-YEAR-OLD WAITRESS IN A SMALL
Baltimore restaurant, first came to me for a past life
regression. In one of her past lives she was a cleaning woman
in a Madrid hotel during the nineteenth century. She worked
very hard to put her son (her daughter in this life) through school.
One night she was raped and suffered much indignation from
the hotel manager (her former husband in this life). Another
past life regression revealed Nancy as a beggar in Italy during
the fourteenth century. After a number of additional successful
regressions, we discussed the idea of progression. She was very
interested and I arranged to progress her into a future lifetime
at her next appointment.

Nancy had no background in parapsychology. She had never
read books on the topic. She had little formal education. Her
interests in this field began when she saw me interviewed on
television. She had been divorced for seven years and had been
the victim of much harassment from her former husband, yet
she was not bitter. Rather, she was always pleasant and cooperative.

On a Wednesday afternoon at the end of October, this personable young woman began her trip into the twenty-third
century. Nancy entered into a hypnotic trance quickly. In a matter of minutes she was in a deep trance and ready to respond to
my questions. When I instructed her, she went right into a future

life, as if it were something she did every day. This is what we discovered from these taped sessions.

Dr. G.:   What do you see at this moment?
Nancy: I, I'm not sure. I seem to be floating. I can't make anything out.
Dr. G.:   Focus on my voice. On the count of three you will no longer be floating. One . . . two . . . three. Now can you tell me what you see?
Nancy: I'm on my way to the Ministry.
Dr. G.:   What Ministry is that?
Nancy: The Ministry of Peace, of course. My training is almost complete and I'm very excited about my career.
Dr. G.:   What year is this?
Nancy: Why, it's 2206.
Dr. G.:   What is your name?
Nancy: Marsha.
Dr. G.:   How long have you been with the Ministry?
Nancy: Four years. In a few months I will be given my first assignment. I'm so excited. This is what I've wanted to do ever since I was a child.

Marsha's voice was childlike as she described this scene. Yet her vocabulary was sophisticated and she seemed to express more emotions than she did as Nancy.

Dr. G.:   How old are you, Marsha?
Nancy: I'm twenty-four.
Dr. G.:   What nation is the Ministry of Peace associated with?
Nancy: Why, we are a member of the Western Federation of Nations. You must be new to our country.
Dr. G.:   How do your parents feel about your work?
Nancy: Oh, they are very proud of me. I am an only child and my parents want me to do what I want.
Dr. G.:   What are you parents' names and what do they do?
Nancy: My mother's name is Lani and she is a housewife now. She used to be an architect. My father's name is Howard and he is a nuclear engineer.
Dr. G.:   Who trains you at the Ministry of Peace?
Nancy: Most of our training is done by the simulators (a self-teaching videocassette). We go along with the diplomats after certain phases of our training are complete.

We must first pass some rather comprehensive examinations.

In a calm, monotone voice, Nancy (Marsha) described an ultra-modern city. The sidewalks moved along as if one were on a conveyor belt or an escalator that moved horizontally. Most of the buildings were white and very tall. The streets were immaculately clean and smooth, almost marblelike. There was very little noise to distract people. The two major forms of transportation were the monorail above ground and a kind of subway. There were no cars permitted inside the city limits. Thus, there was virtually no pollution and no vehicle accidents. Even the monorail, subway, and moving sidewalks operated with only the slightest amount of noise. It seemed that this society had conquered noise as well as air pollution.

The average life span was about 110 years. Mandatory retirement was set at age eighty-five.

The lack of stability that I have previously alluded to during progressions was illustrated by the next conversation. Since this information was reported haphazardly and out of sequence, I have pieced together the story of this twenty-third-century career woman.

Dr. G.: Marsha, can you tell me more about your work?
Nancy: As I mentioned before, I work for the Ministry of Peace in the Diplomatic Corps. In a few months my training will be completed and if I pass my exams, I will be given my first assignment. I am very—

All of a sudden she stopped talking and remained motionless and relaxed in her chair.

Dr. G.: Marsha, where are you now?
Nancy: I'm in the jungle. It's so hot and humid.
Dr. G.: Where is this jungle located?
Nancy: It's in Brazil, not far from the Amazon River. I'm with the Diplomatic Corps on assignment.
Dr. G.: What year is this?
Nancy: 2207.

Nancy had progressed herself forward one year in time. She was sweating even though my therapy room was about 70 degrees. At this time Marsha was on assignment in Brazil. It seemed that weather experiments conducted by the Western Federation had accidentally created a small earthquake, which had destroyed a number of small towns in this area, and the Western Federation had sent Marsha and two other diplomats to work out the details of the financial assistance and to smooth things out politically. Marsha didn't know much about these experiments but it seemed that the Federation was attempting to regulate the weather through the use of high-pitched sound. Brazil was a member of the Western Federation, along with North America, the rest of South America, Central America, Western Europe, Africa, and the Middle East.

Dr. G.:   Marsha, can you tell me what is happening now?
Nancy: My superior is working out the details of the mission with the Brazilian representative. I am filming the disaster site.
Dr. G.:   Why are you meeting in the jungle instead of in an embassy?
Nancy: Federation regulations require us to investigate the site of the catastrophe. We must bring back videotapes of the affected area.
Dr. G.:   Is this your first assignment?
Nancy: Oh, heavens no. I've been on six other assignments in the past nine months.
Dr. G.:   What is happening now?
Nancy: I seem to be . . . I'm at my desk writing up reports of the Brazilian catastrophe.

Apparently, Marsha departed from the jungle scene and returned to the Ministry of Peace. She had progressed herself two weeks forward in time. I next progressed Marsha forward to a scene outside of the Ministry.

Dr. G.:   What is the weather like outside?
Nancy: It is sunny and warm. The S.D.'s are going to have to work overtime today.
Dr. G.:   What are S.D.'s?
Nancy: Why, they're solar discs, of course. It's really quite pretty to see them move like that.

Further questioning revealed that these solar discs were large structures that slowly rotated in wide arcs. They were responsible for heating and cooling the city as well as providing other

energy needs. I then progressed Marsha to her living quarters.
She lived in an apartment in the city.

Dr. G.:   Marsha, can you describe your apartment to me?
Nancy: Well, I live on the ninth elevation. What exactly do
          you want to know?
Dr. G.:   How is your food prepared?
Nancy: My apartment is fully equipped with an omni-
          regulator.
Dr. G.:   What is an omni-regulator?
Nancy: It is a self-regulating cooking unit that prepares all
          forms of consumables to my preprogrammed specifi-
          cations.
Dr. G.:   How do you communicate with other people from
          your apartment?
Nancy: I use my view-phone.
Dr. G.:   What does the view-phone do?
Nancy: It is a device that I speak into. There is a small screen
          attached to it that allows me to see the person calling
          me. We use devices of this type at the Ministry for
          security purposes, only these are far more complex.
Dr. G.:   Can you describe anything else in your apartment that
          operates by mechanical devices?
Nancy: The doors and windows are equipped with electronic
          devices that control their opening and closing. These
          devices are programmed to respond to certain words.
          By repeating these words or phrases I can open or
          close them without getting up.
Dr. G.:   Can you tell me more about your work at the Minis-
          try?
Nancy: I am not cleared to discuss that many aspects of my
          position, but I will try to be as informative as possible.
Dr. G.:   Didn't you say that your Ministry is part of the West-
          ern Federation of Nations?
Nancy: That's correct.
Dr. G.:   What other great nations exist at this time?
Nancy: There are no great nations, just the Alliance.
Dr. G.:   What is the Alliance?
Nancy: The Eastern Alliance includes all those countries that
          aren't a member of the Western Federation of Nations.

Russia, China, India, Japan, Southeast Asia, New Zealand,
Australia, and some smaller islands, along with parts of Eastern

Europe were included in the Eastern Alliance. However, there didn't seem to be any ill feeling between the Western Federation and the Eastern Alliance. The main differences were philosophical. There hadn't been any wars in over 100 years. Marsha was then progressed to the year 2221.

Dr. G.:   What do you see now?
Nancy: I'm in my office. My work schedule is very congested.
Dr. G.:   Why is that?
Nancy: There are many problems with the Eastern Alliance.
Dr. G.:   What specifically is the problem?
Nancy: The Ministry received a request from India to act as an arbitrator in a local border dispute. The problem arose when the message was misplaced by one of our computer banks and no response was sent. The Indian delegation then sent a similar request to the Eastern Alliance. Last week our computer gave us the message and we immediately sent a team down to India. Now there are two groups of arbitrators, and there is no protocol to decide who should stay and who should leave.
Dr. G.:   Why wouldn't India have gone to the Eastern Alliance first?
Nancy   India is not happy with the Alliance and has been trying to join the Federation for years.
Dr. G.:   What is your present position with the Ministry?
Nancy: I'm head of the Arbitration Division of Section C-311.
Dr. G.:   What does that entail?
Nancy: I am a supervisor over forty-seven arbitrators. These arbitrators handle small negotiations, which I assign to them. If there are problems or if there is an unusual situation, then I might handle it myself.
Dr. G.:   Then, you mostly stay in the Ministry rather than being out in the field?
Nancy: That's correct. I prefer to go out on missions every now and then as a change of pace.
Dr. G.:   Are you married now?
Nancy: No. I have devoted my life to the Ministry. I love my work.
Dr. G.:   Do you date often?
Nancy: Not very often. I am not seeing anyone at this time, but that doesn't bother me.
Dr. G.:   What do you like to do when you are not working?

Nancy: I get a great deal of satisfaction from my vegetations (plants).

As I was questioning Marsha, she suddenly transported herself to a large meeting room in the Ministry of Peace. It seemed that she was going over her notes alone in this large room. This was just a few hours ahead in time from her last answer to my question concerning her outside interests. This particular hypnotic session was rather long (about an hour and a half), and the frequency of switching scenes became less of a problem during the last half hour of this trance. I began questioning her about her interests again.

Dr. G.: Do you ever go to the theater?
Nancy: Yes, but not very often.
Dr. G.: What plays are currently running in New York?
Nancy: New York? I don't understand. Where is New York?
Dr. G.   Isn't there a city called New York that is known for its theater?
Nancy: Oh, you must be referring to New City. There was such a place called New York, but that city was destroyed by the great earthquake over 150 years ago. The city was completely destroyed and it took many years to rebuild it. It was renamed New City. I haven't heard the name New York mentioned since I was in school many years ago studying history.
Dr. G.: Is New City still a theater center?
Nancy: Well, not really. After it was rebuilt, if I can remember my history, theater became more universal and no single city became the permanent seat or main contributor to this field. New City functioned just like any other city.
Dr. G.: Were there any other cities that were destroyed by the great earthquake?
Nancy: Yes, a number of smaller cities were also destroyed. San Francisco and Los Angeles were leveled just before New York collapsed. It seemed funny to me that both San Francisco and Los Angeles retained their names when they were rebuilt, but New York was renamed New City.

When Marsha spoke of the great earthquake, she showed complete emotional detachment. This destruction apparently had little meaning to her. What had occurred in the past was almost forgotten. The only things that seemed important to Marsha were her activities at the Ministry and her vegetations.

I next progressed Marsha to the year 2235, in which she was fifty-three years old. She described a very full life, being active in athletics and community affairs. She seemed to function like a twentieth-century woman in her late twenties or early thirties. Her vegetations were still important to her. There were no wars or other catastrophes to report during the past fourteen years, and the Eastern Alliance got along famously with the Western Federation. Marsha had become head of the entire Arbitration Division of the Ministry of Peace, not just Section C-311. It was not unusual for women to attain high governmental positions. As a result, there was apparently no feminist movement or any other kind of movement; there simply wasn't a need. Humankind had apparently learned to live peacefully; prejudice, jealously, greed, hunger, and fear were all but extinct. When problems did occur, they were handled quickly and efficiently.

Television, computers, and other electronic marvels were commonplace. People were informed about current events constantly; sickness was a rare phenomenon. What I found most interesting was the lack of psychological problems. Citizens of the twenty-third century didn't seem to get anxious or depressed. Tranquilizers were not needed. Communication problems rarely manifested themselves. This had a direct effect on politics (making Marsha's job much easier).

When I brought Nancy back to the present, she felt relaxed and good about her experiences. She found them difficult to accept, but gradually she admitted the possibility of a future life as Marsha.

There were a number of interesting elements in this session. First, Nancy's voice deepened and her speech slowed considerably when she spoke as Marsha. Most notably, her vocabulary increased tremendously. Nancy was shocked by the command she had of language in trance. Third, she behaved more confidently as Marsha. Marsha was very proud of her achievements and talked about little else outside of Ministry affairs. Nancy, on the other hand, never talked about her job as a waitress and spent many hours with her friends and her daughter. Nancy was married at the age of seventeen, but Marsha never married.

Clearly, there were great differences between Nancy and Marsha—perhaps owing in part to the improved social status of women in this future society.

Nancy's position in society during her past lives was rather low on the socioeconomic scale. As a waitress in this life she hadn't made much progress in her station in life. By viewing her future as a successful career woman with the Ministry of Peace, Nancy sensed that she not only could, but would, improve her professional status. As Marsha, she accepted a very responsible position and devoted her life to the Ministry. I noted how proud she acted after seeing this future life.

Karma was at work here as well. The close relationship that existed between Nancy and her daughter was exemplified during the nineteenth century in Madrid when Nancy worked hard as a cleaning woman to put her son (her daughter in this life) through school. In addition, the degradation showed her by the manager of this hotel in Spain (her ex-husband in her present life) carried over as harassment by him even after their divorce in this life. The lessons of a close family life were learned and, as Marsha, she no longer required a close family unit to achieve her goals. Her career dominated her life in the twenty-third century.

CHAPTER EIGHTEEN

From Soothsayer
to Keeper of Knowledge

I N ORDER TO PROGRESS INTO A FUTURE LIFE IT IS USUALLY necessary to regress into several past lives first. The reasons for this are somewhat unclear but my clinical experience leads me to propose the theory that most people simply create too many blocks, related to what society tells us we can and cannot do. During our developmental years we are told that the future cannot be predicted or perceived. Our culture informs us that only charlatans or evil people delve into the future.

Thus the blocks are implanted and only clinical experience and knowledge can chip away at these mountains of inhibitions. Since basically all of my patients present themselves with an array of self-defeating sequences (SDSs), it is critical to remove these blocks before any long-lasting progress can be achieved.

Good examples of self-defeating sequences are procrastination, lateness, compulsive spending, alcoholism, overeating, impatience, etc. One tends to create difficulties in one's life (and lives) that prevent one from achieving desired goals, whether personal or professional. The self-image (how we perceive ourselves, not how others perceive us) is lowered. The first step in hypnotherapy is to improve this self-image. If you build a house on quicksand, it won't be around to benefit by appreciation. I have already discussed the use of cassette tapes personally recorded by myself for my patients to help establish a sound and strong psychological foundation from which patients can more

fully understand their karmic purpose and make strides toward
fulfilling their karma.

Past life regression and future life progression therapy is the
only type of the more than 250 therapies recognized in the United
States that utilizes the dream level for cleansing, reprogramming, and goal attainment. Recent medical studies have shown
that we spend about three hours every night in rapid eye movement (REM) dream levels. This is an alpha level intertwined
with the unconscious (theta and delta) levels of sleep. Thus my
therapy helps patients become their own therapists with nightly
self-induced hypnotic sessions utilizing dream levels for past life
regressions, future life progressions, superconscious mind taps
(to receive information from their Masters and Guides), cleansing, and reprogramming.

Emily's case is interesting because it illustrates many of the
previously mentioned principles. We will explore her past lives
from Achmud the soothsayer in ancient Egypt to Sequestra the
300-year-old keeper of knowledge in the thirty-sixth century.
Emily came to me in the summer of 1981 with the chief complaint of ulcerative colitis. This gastrointestinal disorder is described as a chronic, nonspecific inflammatory and ulcerative
disease of the colon, characterized most often by bloody diar-
rhea. This disease most frequently begins between the ages of
fifteen and forty. The cause is unknown. This syndrome is most
uncomfortable, as it consists of an increased need to defecate,
mild lower abdominal cramps, and the appearance of blood and
mucus in the stools. It is not uncommon for a patient to have
ten to twenty bowel movements in a day, often accompanied by
severe cramps. A great concern is the possibility of colon cancer. By the fourth decade of the disease the chances are 70
percent that the patient will develop colorectal cancer. Nearly
one-third of all patients with extensive ulcerative colitis ulti-
mately require surgery. As you can see by this description this
disease is no picnic for the patient.

Emily was forty-one years old when she came to my office
and she had given up on the corticosteroids she had been given
since she had had no relief from these symptoms during the past
thirteen years. Today, Emily no longer suffers from ulcerative
colitis. She can drive for hours and not have to worry about
searching for a restroom every fifteen to thirty minutes.

Since we know stress brings on colitis attacks, tracing the
source of the stress and reprogramming it out literally solves the

problem. Emily went back into a number of past lives to remove these stresses.

In ancient Egypt, Emily was a young male boy named Achmud. Achmud's father was the chief scribe for the pharaoh. The boy didn't like his father's work and wanted to be a builder. Occasionally, Achmud's father would take him to a temple to visit with the priests. Every time Achmud entered the temple he would shake and feel tingling sensations all over his body.

One day on a construction site Achmud annoyed a master builder and the builder struck Achmud. After hitting his head on a table, Achmud became blind in his right eye. But an interesting thing happened: He could now see into the future.

The priests found out about this talent and recruited Achmud for the priesthood. After years of rigorous training, Achmud was ordained as a priest. Later, as an adviser to the pharaoh, Achmud alienated the monarch with forecasts of his death. The pharaoh ordered Achmud to leave the city so Achmud returned home to work with his brother, Housad.

Achmud and Housad worked together utilizing the former's psychic talents but this irritated the local authorities. One politician asked Achmud to predict the future solely for him. When Achmud refused, soldiers tied both brothers to stakes in the desert and left them to die. Achmud screamed when his stomach yearned for food and eventually he and his brother died of exposure. Hence the origin of Emily's intestinal problems.

During the Middle Ages in England, Emily was a man named Alfred. His father was a wealthy landowner who greatly favored Alfred's older brother, Jeremy. Their father was a cruel man and very selfish. Jeremy was more assertive than Alfred but kind to his younger brother. Later on Jeremy and his father went off to war, leaving Alfred behind. Both were killed and Alfred took over the estate since his mother had died much earlier and there were no other family members. Alfred couldn't take the pressures of running the estate, collecting taxes, supervising the workers, and others. He suffered many episodes of stomach pains and insomnia. Eventually he died of a fever, leaving no heirs.

During the sixteenth century in Holland, Emily was again a male named Stefan. Stefan was a big man with an enormous appetite who was married to Maria. When she died during childbirth Stefan abandoned the life he knew and went to sea. The captain he worked under was a tyrant and later Stefan organized a mutiny and killed him. Stefan then became a pirate. After numerous raids, Stefan's ship was sunk and he and his first mate,

Otto, escaped to a small island, where they manufactured rum. Eventually Stefan became an alcoholic and developed an ulcer, dying in terrible pain one night from the ulcer.

In another lifetime, in the early 1800s, Emily was a Seminole Indian named Osciola. Osciola was part-white and a very rebellious sort who led raids on white settlers in Florida. After white soldiers finally defeated his people, Osciola was imprisoned and his people were driven west. Osciola escaped and helped some of his tribe to elude this forced migration. He was eventually captured again and starved to death in prison, refusing to eat on principle. His many hours of suffering, especially with stomach and intestinal pain, were finally relieved by crossing into spirit.

It wasn't until the late nineteenth century that Emily uncovered a past life as a female. Ingrid lived in Germany and was married to Anson. They farmed and Anson worked as a forester. One day a snow avalanche hit her house and clogged her chimney. Ingrid almost suffocated but was saved by her neighbors. They brought her to a hospital where her legs were found to be paralyzed. This paralysis was purely psychosomatic, however; she was afraid Anson would leave her and this syndrome was merely her way of keeping him close to her. One day, after Anson told her he loved her, Ingrid's legs began to move and she quickly regained complete use of her legs. Shortly thereafter she left the hospital cured. Ingrid lived for many years and died of natural causes. It is interesting to note that part of the psychological profile of a patient with ulcerative colitis is the need for attention (i.e., secondary gain).

By this stage in our hypnotherapy Emily's colitis symptoms had disappeared. Intestinal and stomach pain and problems were exhibited during most of these lives. Indeed, stress was always paramount. After each lifetime I brought Emily to the superconscious mind level and had her cleanse away the stress carryovers. Emily was most satisfied with her results and she asked me whether there was such a thing as future lives.

During the next four weeks Emily lived her life free of colitis symptoms. She had family responsibilities and she and her husband did some traveling. Thus, it was over a month later when I saw Emily again. She now wanted to explore future lives, "if they really exist."

Since in four out of five of her past lives Emily was male, I didn't know what to expect for her future lives. Like a good clinician I approached the progression aspect of her therapy objectively and fully explained the theory behind what we were about to delve into through hypnosis.

Emily was not very educated, so I had to keep my explanations simple. I began explaining the concept of frequencies. These are at least five major frequencies or probable futures to choose from. If you do nothing, your present frequency will be your future frequency. However, if you are able to perceive all of your major options (frequencies), you can then choose your most ideal future and can be programmed for your choice. This ideal frequency will then become your reality (i.e., your future has now changed from the frequency you were on to this more positive choice). The other frequencies are the equivalent of parallel universes.

Emily scratched her head a few times during this discussion but she actually began to comprehend it. I informed her that future lives work the same way. The principles of regression, progression, parallel universes, and so on, are all well documented by quantum physics through rather complicated mathematical equations. In addition, there are intricate laboratory experiments conducted by quantum physicists to demonstrate the space-time continuum.

Another way of looking at this concept is what I call the tree branch effect. If you can imagine the various branches of a tree representing the outcome of a series of choices, then you are well on your way to understanding this concept. Suppose you made a choice and the choice you made led to the choices based on your previous choice. In other words, had you chosen the opposite alternative initially you could have faced a totally different series of succeeding selections. This tree branch effect can grow rather complicated after a series of choices are made. One favorable aspect of this theory is that we are really in control of our lives, not merely a victim of karma. By working out one's karma (wisdom erases negative karma) we can improve upon the quality of our choices and our task is simplified.

Self-defeating sequences (SDSs) represent blocks that we create ourselves that prevent us from achieving a desired goal. Examples of SDS are procrastination, alcoholism, drug addictions, smoking, overeating, sexual dysfunction, depression, lateness, and impatience, among others. The purpose of past life regression therapy is to identify, confront, and remove these SDSs so patients can not only go on with their lives but continue to erase negative karma. In addition the lessons learned (wisdom) will add positive karma, which will automatically negate some of the negative karma. Thus, patients will progress toward the ultimate goal of fulfilling all of their karmic lessons and then rise above the karmic cycle to the higher planes (heaven, nirvana, or whatever you want to call it).

The various past lives Emily experienced showed patterns of guilt, victimization, insecurity, rebelliousness, and lowered self-esteem, and these blocks carried over into her current life as internalized day-to-day stresses, eventually manifesting as ulcerative colitis. By confronting and processing out these blocks from the superconscious mind level (the highest level of the subconscious mind) the causes were removed and the symptoms naturally disappeared.

In the year 2984 Emily found herself living in a subterranean city named Tera. Her name was Alexandra and her occupation was a botanist. Tera was located in the state of New Georgia (after the major nuclear war during the twenty-fifth century many states in what we refer to as the United States today were renamed). This was a very difficult progression to conduct because Emily was very emotional by nature and as her mind perceived some of our future society's mistakes she would cry and be quite saddened.

The League of One that we saw in the twenty-sixth century was replaced by the Atlantic and Pacific federations, during the twenty-eighth century. Alexandra worked for the Atlantic Federation. Both Federations were friendly toward each other and there was free exchange of scientific data. Interestingly, each federation prided itself on being the best so a form of nationalism existed. Emily (as Alexandra) described this as a friendly and healthy rivalry. It was equivalent to someone today rooting for a favorite football team in the Superbowl.

Dr. G.:   Alexandra, can you tell me about your day-to-day activities.

Emily: Well, I don't exactly know what you want me to tell you.

Dr. G.:   For example, where do you live in Tera?

Emily: My quarters consist of a small but functional apartment, naturally blue in color.

Dr. G.:   Why do you say naturally blue in color?

Emily: Whenever I am being briefed or programmed for a new project or debriefed after I have completed a project, the blue color is utilized to clear my mind.

Dr. G.:   I thought you stated that there was a free exchange of

	scientific data between the Atlantic and Pacific federations. So why the debriefing?
Emily:	The debriefing is performed merely to remove the clutter from our mind from previous projects so we can devote our full energies to the next one. All data recorded and tested are sent to computer banks and both federations have free access to these banks.
Dr. G.:	Do you have a family?
Emily:	I live alone. We don't have families, as you call it.

Alexandra went on to describe a process of selection of offspring made entirely by the government. Test-tube babies, as was described during the twenty-sixth century, were carried to a further extreme. Sperm and egg banks were set up and genetics was monitored by the use of lasers and radiation. This was a rather cold system but it did result in physically superior people with long life expectancies and peak performance efficiencies. The problem with this system was that there was no way to control the emotional status of the child. Some of Tera's citizens would develop emotional problems and the only system that proved effective, to a certain degree, was that of color programming. This entailed utilizing a form of hypnosis, aided by certain chemicals placed in the water supply to maintain the programming.

Dr. G	Do you socialize with others much?
Emily:	Our meals are eaten together by sectors. We do communicate socially but I am only interested in my work.
Dr. G.:	Tell me more about the color programming.
Emily:	In my apartment there is a monitor that flashes certain colors. Each color combination represents a schedule of what I am supposed to be doing at a certain time. Blue is always used to reinforce this reminder.
Dr. G.:	How else is blue used?
Emily:	There are certain periods of the day that I rest and the monitor programs me to brief or debrief from my projects. It also allays certain tensions I might be experiencing at that time.
Dr. G.:	Why are you living in a subterranean city?
Emily:	The surface is quite habitable but we do have a food shortage. We are developing new strains of vegetation to feed our people. The last nuclear war (twenty-fifth century) very much destroyed our basic crops.
Dr. G.:	How many people are there on the planet today?

Emily: Oh, there are about 1¼ billion people, but our pop-
            ulation is growing very rapidly and it is our job to
            provide food for them.

I then progressed Alexandra forward to an important event
in her professional life. She was now fifty-five years old.

Dr. G.:   What has happened since I last spoke to you?
Emily: (Very emotional) Oh, my, oh, my—why did I have to
            be so stupid?
Dr. G.:   What happened?
Emily: I disobeyed my orders and continued working on a
            method I developed to increase the size and quality
            of certain plants. My method was a failure and be-
            cause I wasted so much time and resources on it they
            are sending me to the surface.
Dr. G.:   What will you do on the surface?
Emily: I will now be assigned and retrained to work in the
            weather control ministry.

I progressed Alexandra five years forward in time.

Dr. G.:   What are your job functions now?
Emily: After going through a rather extensive retraining pro-
            gram I supervise the solar discs in Sector 834HR.
Dr. G.:   What about your training as a botanist? Don't you
            miss that?
Emily: Oh, yes, I occasionally think of the old days but my
            new programming has helped me orient to my new
            duties.

It appears the blue color method she discussed earlier was
utilized in her debriefing and comprehensive retraining programming to work with the solar discs.

Dr. G.:   What do you do when you are not working?
Emily: Oh, I spend my spare time with my best friend.
Dr. G.:   And who is that?
Emily: Mara K2. She is an android, but we do have fun to-
            gether.
Dr. G.:   What about men?
Emily: Oh, haven't I told you? I'm going to unite with Azram.

Azram was Alexandra's fiancé. The term *unite* meant marry. Alexandra seemed emotionally more stable now and beyond regrets about her demotion from Tera. The karmic pattern of rebelliousness had reared its ugly head again in this life and this lesson was finally learned.

After this future life progression, Emily was becoming more and more fascinated by the prospect of the future. She had learned and benefited quite a bit from her past life explorations but something was different about the progressions. First, her voice inflection changed. Second, her vocabulary became far more sophisticated in the future. Third, she seemed to be more emotionally stable and productive. Alexandra had her ups and downs but Emily respected what she represented and accomplished, and this gave her a new lease on life.

The prospect of going even further in time interested Emily and she asked me to conduct one more future life progression. As you will recall when I earlier discussed progressions I mentioned that they can be very unstable and sporadic. Such was the case during Emily's future life as Sequestra during the thirty-sixth century.

I progressed Emily forward in time to a future life that would illustrate the culmination of her karmic achievements. She reported a series of fragmented scenes that would soon tie together illustrating a rather significant lifetime.

Dr. G.:   What are you perceiving now, Sequestra?
Emily: I hear voices chanting . . . There is a man, Jason, whom I know. Don't . . . don't jump. Oh, heavens, he jumped off a building and fell to his death.
Dr. G.:   Who was Jason?
Emily: Jason was the head of the Aracatha. Actually, he still is.
Dr. G.:   I don't understand. Just a moment ago you said he killed himself.
Emily: Well, its true the physical body died but Jason is pure energy and he will just have to find another body.
Dr. G.:   What is the Aracatha?
Emily: The Aracatha is a religious group that leads our people. They are pure energy in form of light.

You may remember the past life regression I conducted with Bob (Bob and the light people), which may illustrate that the ultimate form of evolution is pure energy.

Dr. G.	What is the name of your land, Sequestra?
Emily:	I live on Phonican, a planet in the Andromeda system.
Dr. G.:	What is your opinion of the Aracatha?
Emily:	I have two opinions of them. My opinion when I am being monitored is quite different from that when I am not monitored.
Dr. G.:	What is your opinion of the Aracatha when you are not being monitored?
Emily:	I despise them, but I do not fear them. They are cruel and enslave my people through mind control.
Dr. G.:	How is this mind control accomplished?
Dr. G.:	The Aracatha uses high-pitched sounds to interfere with our brain physiology. They then program us to do their bidding.
Dr. G.:	How is it that you are not completely enslaved by them?
Emily:	Since I have a body I am useful to them because they want to occasionally have use of a body. In addition I am the "Keeper of Knowledge" so they must not risk irreversible damage to my mind.
Dr. G.	What does "Keeper of Knowledge" mean?
Emily:	Over the last thousand years or more there is chosen one person to carry the knowledge of our civilization. It's a very complicated process requiring some manipulation and neurosurgery. I was the one chosen by my people to receive this information.
Dr. G.:	Why can't the Aracatha just force you to give them this information?
Emily:	Their techniques are characterized by certain unpredictable side effects. If they accidentally harm my brain's functioning the information they seek will be lost forever.
Dr. G.:	Was the suicide by Jason an example of such side effects?
Emily:	Yes, Don't worry about Jason. His energy will just leave the body and he will rejoin the rest of the Aracatha.
Dr. G.:	Why do you refer to Jason as a he? Isn't he just energy?
Emily:	Yes, but Jason only wants to inhabit the body of a male. Therefore, I refer to his presence as a he.
Dr. G.:	Tell me more about yourself.
Emily:	I am six feet seven inches tall and my body is practi-

cally perfect, as are those of my people. I am 159 years old.

Dr. G.: Tell me about your parents.

Emily: My mother left Phonican when I was a child, so I really only knew my father.

Dr. G.: What did he do?

Emily: He was guardian of the animals before the Aracatha killed him for attempting to lead a rebellion. I guess I have inherited his rebelliousness.

Dr. G.: How did the Aracatha find out about your father's activities?

Emily: There are tall metal rods on the top of most buildings. These rods scan the thought patterns of our people and allow the Aracatha to read our minds. My father developed a helmet made of some unusual metal that appeared to block this scanning. It worked well but one day a minute crack formed in the center and the Aracatha's rods successfully scanned his mind.

Dr. G.: How can you avoid this fate?

Emily: Before my father was taken prisoner he built dozens of functioning helmets and instructed some of my people in how to make more of them.

Dr. G.: Are you wearing such a helmet now?

Emily: Of course. I wear it most of the time, except when I know the Aracatha are around.

Dr. G.: How can you tell when they are around?

Emily: Oh, that's easy. We have badges that inform us of a change in energy fields and they work quite well. Whenever the Aracatha arrive they affect the energy fields so much that any child can sense their presence.

Dr. G.: Why don't your people just constantly wear these helmets and fight the Aracatha?

Emily: Our sun is dying and we don't have the technology to transport all of our people to another planet. We depend upon the Aracatha for their superior knowledge to help us survive. It's a very sad situation.

Dr. G.: Indeed it is. What do the Aracatha demand of your people?

Emily: Complete obedience. We are slaves to them. They want to perfect the technique of taking over a body and I am the only one who can help them.

Dr. G.: Is there some kind of organized movement against the Aracatha?

Emily: Yes, and I am the leader of this movement. We meet
            in the underground tunnels (this was a nuclear-
            powered subway system). The Aracatha's brainwash-
            ing signals are ineffective down there.

   As I progressed Sequestra forward in time it became clear to
me that this, indeed, was a significant lifetime. Emily for the
first time in any of her lives had some control over her destiny.
She was no longer a small pawn on a large chessboard but a
leader of her people. Emily as Sequestra spoke in an assertive
voice and her bodily movements reflected a confidence that I
had not previously observed in her behavior, Sequestra was 202
years old when I next spoke to her.

Dr. G.:   Sequestra, what has transpired since I last spoke to
            you?
Emily: Quite a bit has happened. My people were trans-
            ported from Phonican to Phibus (a smaller planet in
            the Andromeda system not far away from Phonican).
Dr. G.:   Why the move; and did you join your people?
Emily: There were too many earthquakes and other problems
            with our planet. Yes, I did join my people but unfor-
            tunately the Aracatha are still enslaving us. They
            helped us to prepare Phibus for our occupation.
Dr. G.:   How many people are on Phibus now?
Emily: We are small in numbers—just a few thousand. Many
            millions were killed or died during the earthquakes
            and the move.
Dr. G.:   What about the resistance movement?
Emily: Oh, we pretty much stayed intact. There is a nucleus
            of a few hundred of us and I am still their leader.
Dr.G: How do the Aracatha treat you now?
Emily: Well, they became very angry with me when I in-
            formed them that our sun was dying and that in the
            distant future they would have to transport our people
            great distances to a new planet.
Dr. G.:   What did they do to you?
Emily: They ostracized me and labeled me some sort of fa-
            natic. Then they placed me in a glass cage for all to
            mock.
Dr. G.:   How long were you in this cage?
Emily: Oh, just a few weeks and everything returned to nor-
            mal. What they didn't know was that I mastered the

technique of leaving my body, so this confinement was very easy to take.

Over the next few years the Aracatha gave Sequestra more and more responsibilities. She was taken to Lexicon II (a space station) to attend a very important meeting. It seemed that Gorad (a small moon not far from Phibus) was colonized but in great need of supervision. The Aracatha felt that Gorad would be the ideal location for a research facility that would finally allow them to have free access to a body. Because of Sequestra's unique makeup and her being the Keeper of Knowledge, she was appointed governor of Gorad. She was allowed to bring anyone she wanted to Gorad to help her. Sequestra then had all of the members of the resistance movement transported to Gorad. Sequestra made sure the helmets were transported (disguised as laser testing shields) to Gorad also. I then progressed Sequestra to the age of 275.

Dr. G.: What has happened since I last spoke to you?

Emily: I have my own building and a laboratory to supervise the Aracatha's research. My assistant, Arcon the Acadian, is most amusing. He coordinates the studies of the body's makeup to eliminate the emotional problems the Aracatha have when they enter the body.

Dr. G.: But, Sequestra, it sounds like you are helping your enemies. Have you been brainwashed to do this.

Emily: All is not as it appears. The Aracatha surgically implanted a diode in my brain during biogenesis (a two-hour daily sleep period). But what they didn't know is that my knowledge of all things makes me resistant to such a procedure.

Dr. G.: Then, why do you need to wear the helmet to avoid brainwashing.

Emily: The helmet is necessary because I cannot continually resist the frequency changes generated by the different sounds. However, a surgical procedure is easily bypassed by my own neurotransfer system.

Apparently, Sequestra was treated as a young girl to resist surgical attempts at brainwashing. She had certain brain pathways altered to allow a natural bypass system to be activated whenever any surgery was performed on her. This also helped Sequestra to resist brainwashing via the metal rods but she could not maintain this form of resistance for long periods of time.

Dr. G.:   I still don't understand how your helping this research
          is going to help you rid your people of the Aracatha.

Emily: The answer is surprisingly simple. Gorad is the ideal
          location for this project. I have within me the knowledge
          to complete this assignment. You see my knowledge
          extends far beyond our technology to include many se-
          crets of the universe. The karmic cycle is our only
          salvation. There are sixteen members of the Aracatha
          and their goal is to occupy a human body at will. When
          I assist in the perfection of the technique I know each
          member of the Aracatha will immediately play with
          their new toy. They will all enter a body and play.

Dr. G.:   Suppose they choose your body and others of your
          fellow rebels?

Emily: They won't because only a certain genetic type of
          body will fulfill their needs and mine and those of my
          resistance group fail to meet these standards. What
          we have been working on for years is genetic engi-
          neering to create an ideal body that will have stabi-
          lized emotions. We have just perfected that body type.

Dr. G.:   What, then, is your plan?

Emily: When one of the Aracatha enter into one of these
          bodies they will feel fine. The emotions will be sta-
          bilized and they will rejoice. Then all sixteen of these
          fools will enter a body and then I will use a resonance
          frequency device to trap them in the body. They will
          then live out a lifetime, incurring karmic debts (since
          they are such wicked forces), and their karmic cycle
          will begin.

Dr. G.:   But when the body dies won't they be pure light again,
          and can't they keep your people enslaved?

Emily: No, you see, once they have established a karmic cy-
          cle they must reincarnate again and again before they
          can free themselves of this system.

Dr. G.:   And since their psychological profile is to use and
          manipulate others it will take thousands of years, at
          least, for them to return as pure energy.

Emily: Exactly, my plan is foolproof. The only part I don't
          like is that our genetically and emotionally perfect
          research bodies will house those fiends.

Dr. G.:   How close are you to completing this project?

Emily: Very close. In another year we will be ready.

I progressed Sequestra forward to the completion of this project. She was nearly three hundred years old and still going strong. Jason himself decided to be the first to try the new body. He did and it worked fine. He was able to come and go as he pleased and he reported his success to the other fifteen members of the Aracatha. One by one, each member tested a body (there were sixteen bodies). They only stayed in the body a few hours at a time at first. Later on days would go by before the Aracatha would leave the body. Sequestra was very patient, she knew she had to wait until all sixteen members were in their respective bodies at the same time in order to effect her plan. She also had to wait until their guard dropped to trap the Aracatha in the body. The necessary apparatus was set up and ready but had to be kept hidden at all times.

While the Aracatha occupied their respective bodies they had already begun to illustrate the genius of Sequestra's plan. They participated in unusual sexual practices, murdered some of Sequestra's people for sport, and, all in all, incurred some heavy karmic debts. Another three years passed before the ideal opportunity presented itself. When it did Sequestra and her people were ready. They waited until all sixteen members of the Aracatha were in their bodies; then a banquet was held in their honor. Each of the Aracatha was drugged and taken to the research facility, where Sequestra and Arcon operated the trapping device and accomplished the deed. Sequestra and her people rejoiced.

The Aracatha were trapped in the body and could not escape. They were exiled to a small asteroid to live out the rest of their lives. Occasionally, Sequestra would receive reports of their activities. True to form, they were incurring more and more karmic debts but could in no way harm Sequestra or her people any longer. Sequestra remained as leader of Gorad. She would return to Phibus now and then but preferred to spend most of her time on Gorad.

Emily had now learned quite a lot about her karmic cycle. She perceived herself as a woman almost 1600 years from now who would lead a major rebellion successfully against truly negative entities. She utilized the principles of karma to outwit her enemies and to eliminate much of her own negative karma. She learned to deal with frustration, cruelty, and inhumanity while at the same time still retaining her composure and her goals.

Emily truly benefited from the progression aspect of my therapy. She now is free of colitis and has a new lease on life.

CHAPTER NINETEEN

Zeku:
A Case of Genetic Engineering

PROGRESSIONS INTO FUTURE LIFETIMES ARE CHARACTER-
ized by two unusual events. The first is that the patient
will usually regress into a past life before progressing forward
into a future life. The second is the lack of stability of scenes I
have already described. It doesn't seem to matter whether these
are positive, negative, or neutral scenes; they will appear and
disappear suddenly. During this time the patient remains very
relaxed. Many scenes appear cloudy and background sounds are
evident to the patient and sometimes distracting. High-pitched
sounds and repetitious thumping noises are commonly reported,
but they disappear quickly.

Larry was a skeptic about hypnosis in general. He called me
in 1977 to inquire about my hypnosis practice. A friend of his
wife's had been regressed by me into a number of past lives,
and Larry had been arguing with her about it for over a year.
He made it quite clear to me that he thought this entire field was
pure fantasy, without any scientific substance. Larry was artic-
ulate about his skepticism and he ended the conversation by
asking me if I would consider regressing him under these conditions.

I like challenges. The idea of successfully regressing Larry
appealed to me, not because I thought it would alter his opinion
much, but because I like difficult cases. Larry came across to
me as a very logical thinker. His professional calling involved

the management of many employees in a large Baltimore corporation. His work was very high-pressured, and he was a very unemotional man. When I asked him why he bothered to argue so much with his wife's friend, he stated that he didn't like illogical and unscientific philosophies.

The argumentative and hypercritical characteristics illustrated by Larry are far from ideal for hypnosis, but I accepted the challenge. In April I regressed Larry back into his childhood. I was happily surprised to find that Larry was an excellent hypnotic patient. To show him the positive effects of hypnosis, I gave him some motivational suggestions to help him in his high-pressured job. These suggestions worked quickly and well. It didn't take Larry long to see the benefits and validity of hypnosis, but he was still skeptical about past lives.

We began Larry's journey into his previous lives in early May. The first two past life regressions were sketchy, but Larry's interest was increasing and his skepticism was diminishing. After two additional past life regressions, he was warming considerably to the idea. There were many karmic lessons that were applicable to his present life, and his recognition of their significance resulted in some major improvements in his personal and professional life. One of these regressions dealt with Larry in a past life as a merchant in England during the sixteenth century. He was argumentative, stubborn, and narrow-minded in that life and this resulted in an early and violent death. One day he argued with a customer so strongly that this shopper strangled Larry. Now he no longer felt so argumentative.

It was at this time that I brought up the concept of progression into future lives. He expressed great interest in going into the future; an appointment for his progression was made. Larry was one of my first progression patients. The challenge of this new technique, combined with Larry's skeptical stance, greatly appealed to me.

On a very warm June afternoon, we began Larry's progression. At first he regressed into a past life. It was a different life than we had explored in previous sessions. I gave him the appropriate suggestions to detach himself from this scene and to go into the future. He reported a most unusual existence.

Dr. G.:   What do you see at this time?
Larry: The decompression chamber.
Dr. G.:   What is the decompression chamber used for?

Larry: They are using it to help the divers rest.
Dr. G.:   Who are the divers?
Larry: Builders. The new city under the ocean is being built,
          and these divers must spend some time in the decom-
          pression chamber before they can resume normal
          functioning.
Dr. G.:   What is your name?
Larry: Zeku.
Dr. G.:   What year is this?
Larry: 2542.
Dr. G.:   How old are you, Zeku?
Larry: Fourteen.

Zeku was the son of a scientist who headed a team of technicians in charge of construction of an underwater city. The
scientist's name was Lus-Lu, and to say he was Zeku's father
requires some explaining. Genetics had made some rather significant advances in this civilization. It seems that the egg of the
mother was removed by a special surgical technique and placed
in a test tube of some kind. The sperm of the proposed father
was then analyzed for genetic content and compared to that of
the egg. Any undesirable genetic qualities were then altered or
removed from the sperm or the ovum by the use of very fine
lasers and some form of radiation treatment.

After the appropriate alterations were made, the egg was then
placed back in the mother's uterus and the pregnancy continued
as usual. It was not illegal to have children without scientific
intervention, but most people chose this method to avoid having
intellectually or physically inferior offspring.

The scene quickly changed and Zeku next found himself in a
desert environment. It was very difficult to obtain information
until after the patient regained his orientation to the scene.

Dr. G.:   Why are you in the desert?
Larry: It's so hot. I don't like it. My father wants me to
          become a scientist but I don't want to do this type of
          work. I'm here with the Weather Control Team to re-
          build the thermal transformer.
Dr. G.:   What does a thermal transformer do?
Larry: It regulates the weather. The humidity as well as the
          ground temperature are controlled by the transformer.
          It malfunctioned and my team was sent to repair it.

It seemed that Zeku was twenty years old now and he was training to be part of a Weather Control Team. This civilization had discovered a way to control the weather by setting up a series of thermal transformers all around the world. The average temperature was set between 70 and 75 degrees Fahrenheit all year round. Zeku was not doing very well in his studies and wanted to leave the Weather Control Team. Lus-Lu wouldn't permit him to quit, so Zeku unhappily went on this assignment.

I couldn't get much information about the form of government that existed at this time. It appears there were no separate nations, just one society. The entire population of the world was fewer than one billion people since two major events. One was a major geographical alteration of the earth's surface by earthquakes, tidal waves, and other natural disasters. Much land was submerged and many of our present-day nations were completely destroyed. A second factor was a small-scale nuclear war, which occurred in the twenty-fourth century, and a much larger war in the twenty-fifth century, which destroyed much of the world's population. Buildings weren't primarily affected, but human life was terminated in great numbers. Peace was finally achieved and now the world functioned harmoniously for technological advancement and education.

Zeku didn't seem to care much about anything. Unlike Larry, he had no great interest in current events but just wanted to be left alone. I next progressed Zeku to the age of twenty-four.

Dr. G.:   Zeku, do you have a girlfriend?
Larry: Yes. I see a great deal of Kara.
Dr. G.:   What kind of work does Kara do?
Larry: She works for the Nuclear Sanitation Team. Her job is to monitor the water supply and to test certain foods for radiation poisoning.

As a result of the twenty-fifth century nuclear war, much radiation-contamination still remained and presented certain dangers to the public. The government, known as The League of One, consisted of various specialty teams, each with specific functions to perform. Zeku's team required extensive traveling, separating him too often from Kara, so he decided to quit his job and was reassigned to a form of maintenance supervisor at a spaceport. These spaceports represented transportation centers much like our airports and train stations. The difference here was the type of transportation that existed. You could be beamed from one place to another, which consisted of disassembling the molecules of your body and reassembling them at the other transportation center at your destination. (Harry Martin's progression into the future also mentioned this.) Another mode of transportation was some sort of nuclear-powered mini-jet aircraft. These small crafts transported twenty-five to fifty people to various small cities. The third form of transportation was a very large nuclear-powered aircraft that carried between 150 and 500 people to major cities only.

Dr. G.:   Zeku, what does your job consist of?
Larry: I monitor the operation of Transportation Depot R-16.
Dr.G.:   Who takes care of the daily maintenance tasks?
Larry: D-7164 and E-431.
Dr. G.:   What are D-7164 and E-431?
Larry: They are androids constructed and programmed for performing all of the specific cleaning and organizational tasks.
Dr. G.:   Are there other uses for androids?
Larry: Yes. Androids perform all of the menial tasks. The League assigns millions of these androids all over the world to perform all types of lifting, cleaning, general maintenance, and very specific functions. They accompany all of the teams on every kind of assignment.
Dr. G.:   Do you like your present assignment?
Larry: It's all right. I can spend more time with Kara and I don't have to be in a laboratory day after day.

Zeku's mother died and he and his father saw very little of each other. Zeku described many technological advancements of his civilization. It seemed that mental telepathy was being developed as a form of communication. A pill of some kind was created to place a person in a psychic state (probably some form of chemically induced hypnosis) that allowed for a free exchange of thoughts. This was an experimental technique, but according to Zeku, much progress was being made.

Farming had undergone tremendous change. Very large forms of vegetation were developed by geneticists, resulting in fruits the size of cars. Lasers were used to divide and process the foodstuffs. Education was a part of everyday life. The average worker spent only three six-hour days working. The rest of the time was for leisure. Many vacations were taken each year and life seemed to be rather easy. The average life span was over 125 years.

As a result of the nuclear war of the twenty-fifth century, mutants existed. These mutants were treated with very fine laser beams, though these treatments weren't always successful.

An information pill containing all the new scientific achievements, new items of general interest, and all of the latest advancements was available daily. A type of indestructible plastic was used extensively in construction of vehicles, buildings, and machinery.

Much research was being done on interplanetary and intergalactic travel. This society had made contact with other planets, but the time it took to reach these planets was still enormous. The molecular-beaming procedure that I referred to earlier was only used for relatively short distances. Even with nuclear-powered engines and travel at the speed of light, it still took many years to reach other galaxies.

I next progressed Zeku to a very significant event in his life. He was now twenty-seven years old.

Dr. G.:   Where are you now?

Larry: I am working at R-16 but I am worried.

Dr. G.:   What are you worried about?

Larry: There have been problems with some of the molecular transport units.

Dr. G.:   What specifically is the problem?

Larry: There have been additional time lapses between transport sites. It is unsafe to be disassembled for longer than five minutes.

Dr. G.:   Who is responsible for their proper functioning?

Larry: I am. If I can't repair them soon, some people are going to get hurt.

Dr. G.:   Why don't you just shut them down for repair?

Larry: I can't do that without the proper authority. Since these units work properly most of the time and since this malfunction is not consistent or predictable, I could get into trouble for shutting them down.

Dr. G.:   Why is that?

Larry: These units are used by many people every day and I must keep them operational.

Dr. G.:   Is that the only reason you're worried?

Larry: No. My supervisor, Deui, will probably transfer me

	if I can't solve this problem. He has already trans-
	ferred Treva and Graf and I know that I'm next to go.
	If he transfers me, I won't be able to see Kara often.
Dr. G.:	So, what are you going to do?
Larry:	I'm going to stay here tonight and work on all of these
	units until they work perfectly.
Dr. G.:	Are you going to do this alone?
Larry:	Yes. The android units are shut off after the normal
	workday ends.

Zeku described a scene in which he was busy at work on the molecular transport units. It was very difficult for him to work without the aid of the androids, and he seemed very stressed and tense.

Dr. G.:	What is happening now, Zeku?
Larry:	I think I solved the malfunction problem. There seems
	to be a defective circuit by the main power unit, and
	I'm going to repair it quickly and test all of the units.
Dr. G.:	Did you repair the defective circuit?
Larry:	I'm working on the circuit now. I'm very tired but I
	know I'm right. I've attached the new circuit and . . .

There was silence for the next minute or so. I found out what had happened shortly. It seemed that in the process of replacing the defective circuit, Zeku had accidentally activated the transport unit. His molecules were disassembled and never reassembled. He died a painless death. He reported the usual sensations of floating and freedom from all discomforts that patients describe in regression following their death.

I brought Larry back to the present and discussed the event with him. It was a rather long session and I felt somewhat drained after it was over. Larry felt drained himself, but he was immensely happy with the experience. I don't know whether he fully accepted the idea of progression, but he now thought it worthy of consideration.

In his past lives, Larry was argumentative and stubborn. This resulted in a violent death during the sixteenth century in England. Presently, this tendency toward disagreement caused him marital problems and personality conflicts with his employees. Overcoming this negative trait improved Larry's personal and professional lives.

Larry has always been interested in current events and logical scientific thought processes. He expressed his interest in progression even though he was initially skeptical about hypnosis. As Zeku, he didn't care for science or much of anything else, except Kara. Zeku showed a lack of responsibility but when it came to the molecular transport unit's repair he accepted this challenge well. The pressure he was under was similar to Larry's environment in his twentieth-century position as a manager of large numbers of employees. Even though it resulted in his death Zeku accepted a great responsibility. Larry also accepted a great responsibility when he gave up his argumentative trait. The karmic lesson was learned and probably won't have to be dealt with again.

CHAPTER TWENTY

From Greece to Moonan

A T THE END OF JULY OF 1987, A VERY INTERESTING COL-
lege student called my office for an appointment. She
had seen me on the Phil Donahue show a few weeks prior and
was interested in exploring past and future lives. She had heard
of past life regressions before, but when I discussed the concept
of progressing patients into future lives she grew intent on following through with her time quest. She also enjoyed my comments about my personal belief in reincarnation. I had
mentioned on the show that my car tags read Karma-2 and the
names of my three dogs are Karma, Phoenix, and Alpha.

Françesca was an attractive and personable twenty-year-old
junior in a local university. Her major was business and she
confessed to me that she thought I would not see her because of
her lack of a serious problem. While it is true that I prioritize
my time with patients who have real problems such as overeating, smoking, insomnia, phobias, mood swings, compulsions,
and the like, I always allot some time for patients with existential
difficulties. An existential difficulty is characterized by not
knowing why we are here. What is my karmic purpose? Why
do I keep making the same mistakes over and over again? Such
questions are asked by patients with existential deficiencies.

Francesca had an existential need. She wanted to know why
she was here, what she was, and who she would be. I discussed
thoroughly with her the basis of my therapy. She was most interested in the comments I made about dreaming. It was sur-

prising to her to hear that a large part of my therapy was aimed
at utilizing the REM dream levels at night for cleansing and
reprogramming. She had heard of REM (rapid eye movement)
alpha levels before but she wasn't aware that recent medical
studies showed that we go through three hours of these every
night.

Since the beta level (which includes defense mechanisms
and willpower) doesn't function at this time, this is a perfect opportunity to train the alpha level to do the one thing it
does best: cleansing. Sleep studies have shown that without
REM we experience fatigue, restlessness, hallucinations, and
eventually, death. Yes, we cannot survive without our natural
alpha levels to "de-stress" and relax us. The purpose of the
dream level is to cleanse away our anxieties. The problem is we
tend to worry so much that right before we go to sleep we program anxiety and subsequently nightmares into our dream levels.

Properly guided through the use of hypnosis, anyone can be
trained to reprogram the subconscious and more efficiently use
this cleansing alpha level. Therefore, we can obtain the equivalent of three hours of free therapy every night. Not bad for a
natural level.

Francesca found this fascinating and couldn't wait to begin.
So in early August I guided her through her first past life experience. Her first stop was ancient Greece. Her name was Cassandra and she attended a school of philosophy. She had no real
goals but knew what she didn't want. She didn't want to get
married, especially at the ripe old age of sixteen. Her father had
arranged for Cassandra to be married to the son of a wealthy
landowner. Cassandra chose to run away from home instead.
She ran away to a temple and stayed with some of her friends
from the philosophy school. Eventually she returned home but
was not forced to marry. She later met a boy and married him.
At the age of twenty-four she and her husband and most of her
village were killed when their village was attacked. Although
this may not appear to be much of a life, Francesca now perceived the mechanism of time travel through hypnosis.

Francesca's next lifetime was in Ireland in the early part of
the sixteenth century. Her name was Katie and she married Sean
at an early age. She didn't really love Sean but getting married
was the thing to do in her village. Sean and Katie lived on a
farm. Katie was fairly happy during the early years of her marriage; however after her miscarriage Sean changed. He wanted

a son badly, and Katie's inability to give him this child caused Sean to drink and lose his temper often. He began to beat Katie regularly. Katie didn't know what to do; she couldn't leave but she also couldn't stay. Shortly after these beatings began, though, Sean argued with a neighbor over some cows and was killed. Katie lived out the rest of her life alone and quite bitter.

By this time Francesca was confused. What did this all mean? In Greece she hadn't wanted to be part of an arranged marriage. She had asserted herself and avoided that alternative. But after only a few years of marriage and happiness, she was killed in a raid on her village. In Ireland she married someone she didn't love and paid the price. Physical and verbal abuse along with lonely years of solitude had followed. Was her karmic lesson that you can't have your cake and eat it, too? It took a future life progression to shed light on this question.

On a hot August afternoon Francesca began her journey forward in time. She had a hard time orienting to a future life—not an uncommon situation, especially during the first future life progression. Finally, she settled on a future life during the latter part of the twenty-seventh century. Her name was Tia and she was living in the City of Colton, located in Asia (as we term it today). Her father worked as an astronomer for the League of One and her mother was an artist. She was an only child and was currently attending a university, majoring in anthropology.

Tia sounded quite excited about her academic pursuits. She liked anthropology because it gave her an opportunity to help mold the future. What society advanced to during the twenty-seventh century was related to helping the evolution of less developed civilizations on different planets. Apparently, extra-terrestrial contact had occurred and we were involved in facilitating this contact. Most contact required years of travel to other galaxies. Anthropologists were used to help guide the evolution of more primitive cultures with minimal interference. Tia wanted to be a part of this work.

Dr. G.:	What is it about your field that attracts you so?
Francesca:	Imagine helping an entire culture to develop and to avoid making the mistakes we made.
Dr. G.:	Don't you run into cultures that are more advanced than Earth's?
Francesca:	Yes, but we haven't been doing this for a very long time. When we come across a more advanced society we are trained to present our planet's purpose

and to seek futher direction from them so as not to alienate these people. When we come across a less advanced society we help them advance and take care of their needs.

Dr. G.: Have you graduated from school yet?

Francesca: No, but I will very shortly.

I next progressed Tia beyond her graduation. She reported being happy and working for the government as an anthropologist.

Dr. G.: Tia, tell me about your life at this time.

Francesca: I have only been out of school a short time now. Since I graduated at the top of my class I was placed on a special project.

Dr. G.: What project is this?

Francesca: A small asteroid was discovered off Mars. This asteroid surprisingly has an atmosphere, gravitational pull, and inhabitants.

Tia informed me that it was not uncommon to come across situations similar to this. Normally an asteroid would just be a large rock floating in space with no gravity or atmosphere. But other more advanced planets conducted various experiments and were successful in creating artificial atmospherelike conditions along with gravitational pulls, magnetic fields, and the like. They also experimented with placing plant and animal life on these planetlike asteroids. These asteroids's size placed them more in the range of our moon, so they became veritable planets in a sense.

The problem was that after these asteroids were developed their civilizations were left to develop by themselves because the aliens who developed them initially did so for experimental purposes to test various techniques for application on a larger scale. The League felt it was its responsibility to oversee these experimental planets.

Dr. G.: What are your plans now?

Francesca: I have been assigned to Moonan.

Dr. G.: What is Moonan?

Francesca: Moonan is the name the League has given to the asteroid off Mars.

Dr. G.:   When will you leave for Moonan?
Francesca: Very soon.

Later Tia was progressed to her arrival on Moonan. She went as a member of a team. This was her first real assignment and she worked directly under Nahill (chief anthropologist). Their arrival on Moonan was unobserved by the primitive inhabitants. The League had developed a kind of invisibility shield to prevent direct observation of their space vehicles by other societies, especially for this type of assignment. After establishing a base far away from the inhabitants, Tia and her team set out to explore Moonan. A number of months passed and I resumed my questioning.

Dr. G.   What is Moonan like?
Francesca: Interestingly, it reminds me of Earth. The atmo-
               sphere is very similar and the coastline is most
               beautiful.
Dr. G.:   There are bodies of water on this asteroid?
Francesca: Yes. As I said, it looks like Earth.
Dr. G.:   What about the people?
Francesca: We have found only two groups of people. They
               are quite human in appearance but in our months
               here we have observed major differences in their
               psychological makeup.
Dr. G.:   Can you be specific?
Francesca: This is a small asteroid and we have observed only
               one land mass inhabited by humans. Those living
               inland are called Hecow. They are barbaric, prim-
               itive people who are very materialistic and war-
               like. The Saleans live along the coast. They are
               more spiritual people who are peaceful.
Dr. G.:   Is there any contact between the two groups?
Francesca: Very little. The Hecow in the past would attack
               the Saleans but this hasn't happened in a long time.
Dr. G.:   Why not?
Francesca: The Saleans simply don't have anything the Hecow
               want. The Saleans are very simple people and the
               Hecow are too obsessed with heroic accomplish-
               ments, and defeating the Saleans would not be
               considered heroic.
Dr. G.:   So what can you do to help them?
Francesca: Our task is very complicated and difficult. On the
               one hand we must help the Saleans become more

self-sufficient. Also, we need to cut down the aggressive tendencies and materialism of the Hecow. On the other hand, we don't want to just interfere with their cultures.

Dr. G.: Is there anything about the physical environment that you observed that can assist you in your project?

Francesca: It takes the Hecow quite a long time to come down from the mountains to the coast. So it is going to be physically difficult to have the two groups work together.

Dr. G.: Is that necessary?

Francesca: Yes, they must perceive each other's environments and learn from each other.

Dr. G.: Are there any dangerous animals present?

Francesca: No, just small game and some unusual creatures.

Dr. G.: What do you mean by unusual?

Francesca: There are flying lizards here. They are not very big but they have wings and they fly. That I call strange.

Dr. G.: Anything else?

Francesca: Not really. The plant life supports the animal life and there is plenty of food to go around.

Dr. G.: What is your next step?

Francesca: We have made contact with the Saleans.

Dr. G.: How did they accept you?

Francesca: There were surprisingly no problems with them. We let them introduce us to their culture. They are very peaceful people. Most of their day is spent meditating. They are very religious, worshipping the God of Light.

Dr. G.: How did you learn their language?

Francesca: We don't have to worry about that. The League equips all of us with a thought transference coordinator.

Dr. G.: What is that?

Francesca: It's a small metal box that we carry. It projects our thoughts by mental telepathy to the recipient. It also translates our thoughts to any language so it is always understood by the receiver.

Dr. G.: What else did you learn?

Francesca: The Saleans are much more advanced than we suspected.

Dr. G.:	In what way?
Francesca:	To look at their life-style you wouldn't think much of it. But the meditation they do is much more than that.
Dr. G.:	What do you mean, much more?
Francesca:	They practice a form of astral projection. They leave their bodies and travel around Moonan in groups.
Dr. G.:	You mean the souls travel around Moonan all day long?
Francesca:	Yes, exactly.
Dr. G.:	Isn't that unusual for this type of culture?
Francesca:	Actually, no. It is not uncommon for primitive people who have their basic needs met to seek out spiritual practices.
Dr. G.:	But astral projection is a very advanced technique.
Francesca:	That it is.
Dr. G.:	So this isn't that unexpected?
Francesca:	Not really. Remember, we do not know the original species used on this experimental planet. Their predecessors probably were very expert in astral travel.

It was somewhat difficult for Tia's people to communicate with the Saleans, since they spent so much time out of the body.

Dr. G.:	How did you work with the Saleans, then?
Francesca:	We struggled for a while but then came upon a rather simple solution.
Dr. G.:	And what was that?
Francesca:	We simply astrally projected along with them.
Dr. G.:	Just like that?
Francesca:	Yes. It was that simple. They instructed us in the art of astral travel and we joined them in another dimension.
Dr. G.:	Could you communicate effectively at this level and do your job?
Francesca:	At first it was very strange but as we became accustomed to it we became more comfortable with leaving the body.
Dr. G.:	If they could leave their body at will, doesn't this suggest that maybe they didn't need your help?
Francesca:	They are primitive people and the Hecow repre-

sent a serious threat to them. We must help them
communicate and coexist in peace.

During the next few months Tia's group communicated freely
with the Saleans. They found out that the Saleans didn't fear the
Hecow. It was their philosophy to "live and let live." If the
Hecow attacked them and killed their people then it was just
"meant to be." The Saleans really were quite primitive. They
responded well to the project's specialists and developed more
efficient techniques of farming, irrigation, construction, and so
forth.

The next phase of this project consisted of meeting with the
Hecow. Tia was frightened by the very prospect. The rest of her
team weren't thrilled with the idea either. The Saleans had
painted a pretty horrible picture of the Hecow.

Indeed, the Hecow were true barbarians. They hunted for
sport as well as for food. Killing was respected and there were
no inhibitions demonstrated by these inhabitants of the mountains. I progressed Tia forward to their working with the Hecow.

Dr. G.:   How did the attempts with the Hecow turn out?
Francesca: All is not well.
Dr. G.:   What do you mean?
Francesca: At first the Hecow attacked our group and nearly
                killed one of our people.
Dr. G.:   How did you protect yourselves?
Francesca: We always work in groups. Our weapons can stun
                and immobilize without hurting.
Dr. G.:   Did the Hecow think you were some kind of evil
                spirits?
Francesca: Yes, in a way. They didn't respond well to our
                initial attempts. We kept on trying.
Dr. G.:   Did they inquire as to your working with the Sa-
                leans?
Francesca: Yes. And in fact, that was our first breakthrough.
Dr. G.:   I don't understand.
Francesca: The Hecow have large egos. They were very jeal-
                ous of the Saleans learning things that they them-
                selves weren't given.
Dr. G.:   So, did that stimulate their interest?
Francesca: Yes. It did. They became quick students. How-
                ever, I have a bad feeling.
Dr. G.:   What do you mean?

Francesca:	I don't trust them. I feel they are going to use the knowledge we give them against the Saleans in some way.
Dr. G.:	How could bettering themselves affect the Saleans?
Francesca:	It can't really. I just don't like the profile they represent. I have read about other cases like this and I just have a bad feeling.
Dr. G.:	Have you discussed this with Nahill?
Francesca:	Not at first, but later I did.
Dr. G.:	What was his reaction?
Francesca:	He really surprised me. He feels the same way and has communicated his concern to the others.
Dr. G.:	Does this mean an end to the project?
Francesca:	No, just the exercising of extra caution.

The Hecow did quite well assimilating the techniques and information Tia's group gave them. At no time did they threaten the project participants again. Still, a growing feeling of concern was felt by each member of the team.

Another interesting factor that became apparent was Tia's growing affection for Nahill. Nahill was a good deal older than Tia but they became quite close. This added to Tia's restlessness. She just couldn't wait for this project to be completed so she could return home. This experience would lead to other choice assignments. Furthermore, she was hoping to expand her relationship with Nahill.

I progressed Tia forward to a significant development in the Hecow part of the project. What she reported confirmed her suspicions and those of the rest of her team.

Dr. G.:	What has occurred since I last spoke with you, Tia?
Francesca:	Things have gotten somewhat out of hand.
Dr. G.:	In what way?
Francesca:	The Hecow became quite jealous of us working with the Saleans first.
Dr. G.:	What did they do?
Francesca:	They sent a small party down the mountain to observe the Saleans.
Dr. G.:	What did they find out?
Francesca:	They noticed that the Saleans were progressing at a more rapid rate, and they became very jealous.

	They thought the Saleans would somehow use their superior skills to attack the Hecow.
Dr. G.:	But that's ridiculous. The Saleans are peaceful.
Francesca:	Of course it is. But the Hecow won't listen to reason.
Dr. G.:	Didn't your people try to explain that the Saleans are incapable of such barbaric actions?
Francesca:	We tried many times, but when the scouting party returned to the Hecow capital they began making plans for war.
Dr. G.:	War?
Francesca:	Yes, war.
Dr. G.:	Why would the Hecow want to declare war on the Saleans?
Francesca:	The Hecow are so insecure in their thought processes and so obsessed with paranoia that they felt the only solution was to wipe out the Saleans before the Saleans killed off the Hecow.
Dr. G.:	And you call this ''somewhat out of hand?''
Francesca:	I guess I'm prone to understatement.
Dr. G.:	Didn't your people attempt to negotiate a settlement?
Francesca:	The Hecow attacked our camp and it was all we could do to escape with our lives. Had we stayed longer we might have killed some of the Hecow in self-defense and that is totally against our code.
Dr. G.:	What about the safety of the Saleans?
Francesca:	Nahill instructed us to return to the coast and warn the Saleans. We instructed them to defend themselves against the Hecow.
Dr. G.:	Isn't that overstepping your bounds just a bit?
Francesca:	Yes, it is, but what can we do? We have already irreversibly interfered with this ''planet'' and now we are at the point of no return.
Dr. G.:	How did the Saleans respond to your warnings and offer of help?
Francesca:	That's another part of the problem. You see, the Saleans don't believe in violence or war. They just meditate, astrally project, and hope for the best.
Dr. G.:	They are going to be massacred.
Francesca:	You're telling me!
Dr. G.:	Nahill seems to be in charge. What does he recommend?

Francesca: He is our group leader. He doesn't know what to
              do, and frankly, I'm scared.

A lot of discussions took place within Tia's group. Nobody
could come up with a viable solution. The mission was becoming a total failure. The Hecow hadn't attacked the Saleans in
many years. Now, just months after Tia's group had arrived, the
Hecow were planning to exterminate the Saleans. I progressed
Tia to a resolution of this problem.

Dr. G.:   Where are you now?
Francesca: I am in a meeting with Nahill and the others. We
              are desperately trying to solve this mess.
Dr. G.:   What does the group come up with?
Francesca: Nothing. Absolutely nothing. The only solution
              we could think of was to equip the Saleans with
              some of our weapons (set on stun) for protection.
Dr. G.:   But the Saleans won't use the weapons because
              they don't believe in warfare.
Francesca: That's correct. We are stumped.
Dr. G.:   Move to the resolution of this problem.
Francesca: Nahill is a genius.
Dr. G.:   What did he do?
Francesca: He figured out a solution at the last minute.
Dr. G.:   Please tell me what he came up with.
Francesca: The Saleans spend most of their time astrally pro-
              jecting.
Dr. G.:   So.
Francesca: So, Nahill suggested that they project themselves
              on the same plane as the Hecow when the latter
              sleep. We know that when we sleep and are in the
              REM (rapid eye movement) stage we leave the
              body and go to the astral plane while the body
              sleeps. The Saleans informed Nahill of this and
              that they would occasionally run into a Hecow soul
              during their own REM stage.
Dr. G.:   So.
Francesca: So, Nahill's solution was to have the Saleans con-
              tact these Hecow souls and educate them as to the
              true nature of the Salean life-style.
Dr. G.:   How long would this reprogramming take?
Francesca: Since the Saleans are so adept at astral travel one
              night would be sufficient.

Dr. G.:   One night?
Francesca: Yes, one night.

So now all that needed to be done was to convince the Saleans to help educate the Hecow during their dream level. I progressed Tia forward to the all-important night of this astral negotiation.

Dr. G: How is the plan going?
Francesca: Everything is arranged. The Saleans were very co-
               operative and saw this as an opportunity to expand
               their level of awareness.
Dr. G.:   When is the Hecow attack scheduled?
Francesca: The best we can figure is about two days.
Dr. G.:   You don't have much time.
Francesca: Tonight the Saleans will meet with the Hecow on
               the astral plane.

This was a most interesting solution to an age-old problem. Tia went on to describe how she and the team accompanied the Saleans (astrally) on this trip. They all astrally projected together. By this time Tia and the team were rather proficient at astral travel. It hadn't taken them long to orient to this different dimension.

The meeting of the souls went quite well. The Hecow on the astral plane acted quite different from their physical-plane counterparts. What seemed like an eternity in actuality took only a few moments of Moonan time, since on the astral plane all time is simultaneous.

Dr. G.:   What finally happened?
Francesca: The following day the Hecow came down from the
               mountain for their mission of peace. They were a
               different people. They met with the Saleans with
               open arms and all were satisfied.
Dr. G.:   Does that end the project?
Francesca: Basically, yes. We will stay on for a month or so
               to supervise them. I have a very good feeling about
               this now.
Dr. G.:   You were quite lucky.
Francesca: Don't give me the credit. It's Nahill who should
               be thanked.

The project team did remain on Moonan for about one month. Their work was complete and they returned home to Earth. What was interesting about the result of this project was the team's report. They were very honest about the events that transpired. Instead of being disciplined for incompetence, their superiors rewarded them. The astral travel technique was later used in other projects and Nahill, Tia, and the rest of the team were highly regarded in the scientific community.

Tia did continue to see Nahill on Earth. They were assigned to work together as a permanent team. More than that, they became romantically involved and were married.

As the years went by Tia became a university professor and she and Nahill raised two children. She remained well respected in the academic and scientific communities throughout her life.

Francesca was most satisfied by the future life progression. As a business major she had no real interest in science and additionally, she could not see herself today doing any of the things Tia did. Even so, the future life progression seemed to add meaning and purpose to Francesca's life. She saw that she would choose a good man in Nahill and have a happy and productive life. This was quite different from the lifetimes of Cassandra and Katie.

This type of case is also very satisfying for me to supervise. Working out problems such as habits, phobias, mood swings, etc. is an important part of my role as a hypnotherapist; however, there is more to life than just the elimination of problems. There are existential needs that also must be met. This global overview of our perspective is exactly what the karmic cycle is all about. Francesca found her purpose in life. You can, too.

CHAPTER TWENTY-ONE

A Future Life Under Glass

W HEN JANET CALLED MY OFFICE IN 1984, SHE SOUNDED almost hysterical. She had been upset for weeks about losing a long-term relationship with her boyfriend, Mike. I gave Janet an appointment later that day and when she arrived at my office I could tell she had been crying quite a bit that day.

It seems that she had been dating Mike for two years and he was constantly "cheating" on her. When I asked Janet about why she kept seeing him she merely informed me that she was in love with him and wanted to be with him, no matter what happened.

It was obvious to me that she had a very dependent personality and that Mike had taken advantage of her. The first thing I did was to record a personalized cassette tape for her and to explain the need to remove the causes of her dilemma. She agreed to the treatment recommendation and we began therapy.

Janet was a thirty-one-year-old dietitian, somewhat overweight, and always disheveled. Her clothes were wrinkled and her hair looked like she had just come out of a windstorm. She had a very low self-image and a history of failure in previous attempts at psychotherapy. This was her first attempt at hypnotherapy. She had been referred to my office by a good friend at the hospital that employed her.

Her case is interesting in many respects. Janet was not a very good hypnotic subject in that her trance depth was very light and she continually interrupted my inductions with skeptical questions. After a few sessions of hypnotherapy she began to feel better emotionally and became a more cooperative patient. However, her trance depth was still very light. This illustrates how one doesn't have to reach a deep level of trance to experience regression and progression therapy. In addition, quality results can still be attained from such light levels.

Janet's pattern in relationships was rather self-defeating. She was attracted to men who didn't want to "take care" of her. She had trouble saying no to men sexually because she was afraid they wouldn't be interested in her for her other qualities. This is another example of a self-defeating sequence (SDS).

In a past life in England in 1693 Janet was a woman named Tabatha. She lived with her mother and stepfather. Her stepfather beat Tabatha and tried to rape her one night. Tabatha's mother prevented this from happening by knocking her husband unconscious with some firewood. Tabatha's only outlet was in practicing black magic, which she did rather well. She cast a spell on her stepfather and he committed murder one night in response to this spell. Before the authorities could catch him he returned home and confronted Tabatha with this spell. She admitted it and he beat and raped her. She then killed him with a knife and contacted the authorities.

The authorities later suspected her of being a witch and watched her very closely. She was careful but eventually she was tried as a witch and burned at the stake. Her stepfather in that life was Mike and her mother was her best friend, Joan. Janet, as Tabatha, incurred many karmic debts in that life involving Mike.

In another past life during the Middle Ages in France, Janet was a woman named Giselle. She was engaged to a man named Sebastian. This marriage was arranged by her father. Giselle did not like Sebastian at all. He was overweight and not very physically appealing. In addition, he had very poor manners and a speech impediment. Giselle's father had insisted on this marriage because their financial status had deteriorated over the years and Sebastian's family was rather wealthy.

Marc entered Giselle's life about three years after her marriage to Sebastian. Marc was a wealthy landowner who was married to Isabelle. He was attracted to Giselle and she to him. They had an affair and this gave Giselle something to look forward to. A few years went by and everyone was happy, except Isabelle. Isabelle wanted a child but nothing seemed to work for her. Giselle hated Isabelle and was very jealous of her for being married to Marc, for Giselle very much wanted to be Marc's wife.

Giselle discussed her frustrations with Marc and he seemed to sympathize with her needs. She suggested a plan for Marc to dispose of Isabelle and marry her. Marc at first was horrified by this idea but later agreed to it. They planned to murder Isabelle one day when she took a ride on her horse in the mountains. Giselle wanted to be there when it happened.

One fine day Isabelle was riding her horse and Giselle and Marc were waiting for her behind a rock. The plan was for Marc to take a long pole and knock Isabelle off her horse and throw her off the mountain. At the last minute Marc backed out of the plan. Giselle was so upset that she took the pole and executed the plan. At the very last possible moment, though, Isabelle's horse lurched forward and Giselle fell off the mountain to her death. Marc then escaped undetected and never discussed the incident with his wife.

Janet's tendency for violence still remained as a rather large karmic debt. Additionally, Marc is her ex-lover in this life and Isabelle is Marc's ex-wife. The reason why Janet's boyfriend finally ended their relationship was because he went back with his ex-wife. Sebastian is Janet's current father, whom she dislikes very much.

The stage was now set for a future life progression. Janet felt better emotionally as a result of these two past life experiences, coupled with the cleansing conducted at the superconscious mind level. I explained the procedures and concepts involved in going forward in time and she seemed quite motivated to complete the cycle.

In the year 3015 Janet was a female named Melodea. She lived on a small moon in the Shyron system, many light-years from Earth. This moon was similar to our moon, so in order to function efficiently, Melodea's people built a glass enclosure to their city. This wasn't like the glass we are familiar with. This glass was indestructible yet lightweight and, of course, transparent. There were many chambers to this enclosure so their small space vehicles could come and go without endangering the inhabitants. The planet Melodea was originally from was uninhabitable because of nuclear wars, so her people had left and occupied moons such as this one. There were about 100,000 people on this moon and they all lived in the city under glass.

The buildings within the city were round and conical in shape. They were constructed of a very lightweight metal that was also quite durable. Transportation within the city was characterized by a moving conveyorlike belt and an overhead monorail system. There were space vehicles capable of traveling rather large distances to other moons and planets.

Melodea was twenty years old when I first spoke with her. She lived at home with her parents, two brothers, and two sisters. She worked as a travel agent and very much enjoyed her work.

Dr. G.:	Tell me about your life, Mclodea.
Janet:	I am saddened today.
Dr. G.:	What happened?
Janet:	My grandfather died yesterday and I just came back from viewing his body. The rings were beautiful. (She began crying.)
Dr. G.:	What do you mean by the rings?
Janet:	When we die there are two large crystal rings placed around our bodies. They cleanse our aura and allow for a smooth transition to the other dimension.
Dr. G.:	Were you very close with your grandfather?
Janet:	Yes. My grandmother died a few years ago and I miss them both.

I next progressed Melodea forward by eight years.

Dr. G.:	What has happened since I last spoke to you?
Janet:	I now have my own apartment. Also I have gone back to school and I now have a degree in medical technology.
Dr. G.:	I thought you really enjoyed being a travel agent?
Janet:	I did, but it became too phony and I need more challenge in my life. Also I like the medical field.
Dr. G.:	Do you date anyone at this time?
Janet:	Yes, I see Romor.
Dr. G.:	What kind of work does he do?
Janet:	He is a doctor, a laser surgeon, specifically.
Dr. G.:	How long have you been seeing him?
Janet:	On and off for nearly three years, but we have become very seriously involved lately.
Dr. G.:	How does your family feel about Romor?
Janet:	They think he's wonderful and so do I.
Dr. G.:	What kind of medical facilities do you have?
Janet:	Our hospitals are all located in the center of the city.

It takes very little time to get to them no matter where you may be. We have many mobile units to stabilize patients until they can be brought in to our main facility.

Dr. G.: Does that mean you don't work far from Romor?

Janet: Yes, we work in the same facility. That is how I met him.

Dr. G.: Before you met Romor and since you have been seeing him, has jealousy ever been a problem with you?

Janet: Absolutely not. I have always had a tendency to trust people, especially men. In fact, my family tells me I'm too trusting.

Apparently, Janet overcame her previous jealousy and insecurity problems by the thirty-first century. She seemed to be a very well adjusted and highly motivated young woman with her future in front of her.

Dr. G.: How does Romor treat you?

Janet: He is very kind and considerate. It's amazing how he can be so dedicated and serious at the facility yet at the same be so attentive and sensitive with me.

Dr. G.: This sounds like more than just a casual relationship.

Janet: It is to me. My problem is in convincing Romor to take me seriously.

I next progressed Melodea to a significant event in her relationship with Romor, if any. She described a rather elaborate wedding ceremony. All of her family and his relatives attended. They were the happiest couple in this city under the glass.

Dr. G.: Tell me what has happened since I last spoke to you.

Janet: Our marriage is beautiful. I cannot begin to describe how happy we are.

Dr. G.: Are you still working?

Janet: Yes. I have no intentions of giving up my profession. Romor actually encourages me to continue with my work.

Dr. G.: Does it cause any problems, being in the same facility?

Janet: No, not at all. We work in separate departments but we sometimes have lunch together. Romor does work

Dr. G.:   longer hours than I and many times he cannot be dis-
          turbed for hours at a time.
Dr. G.:   Has Romor changed at all since the wedding?
Janet: No, he is still just as sweet and sensitive as ever.

I then progressed Melodea forward to an event that would
significantly affect her relationship with Romor, if any such event
was to occur.

Dr. G.:   What's going on in your life now, Melodea?
Janet: I don't know. Something is not right.
Dr. G.:   What do you mean?
Janet: Well, a number of our inhabitants have died at a rel-
          atively young age. We normally live to be well over
          150 years old. A virus is the cause.
Dr. G.:   Are you worried about this virus infecting you and
          Romor?
Janet: Not really; it's just that he has been so distant lately
          and he has been coming home late a lot.
Dr. G.:   Do you suspect he may be seeing another woman?
Janet: Of course not (in a matter-of-fact tone). I know Ro-
          mor a lot better than that.
Dr. G.:   Have you spoken to him about your concern?
Janet: Yes, I have. He doesn't seem to want to talk about it.
          He is so preoccupied lately.

After some additional questioning I was able to elicit some
very interesting facts. Disease, for the most part, was rare in
this city. The virus was of such an unusual strain that it quickly
compromised the immune systems of its victims. Nobody could
understand why this virus affected such a small percentage of
the population. Most new strains of viruses affected much greater
numbers of people. An example today would be a new flu strain
introduced into a country. This would spread like wildfire.
Melodea's fellow citizens seem to be immune to it at first.

However, lately many more people began falling victim to its
effects. This virus caused the death of its host in less than two
days. This quite worried the city's elders. They organized a
special research team and recruited Romor. Since he was one
of the best surgeons in the city and since he had done quite a bit
of research on viruses before, he was a logical choice.

Romor readily accepted this assignment and became part of
the government's secret project. This project had to be kept

secret because of the fear of panic. There was no way this moon could be evacuated in a short period of time and the recent cases of death by the virus made the government act quickly. Romor was under strict orders not to discuss this project with anyone, and that included Melodea. Melodea was aware that Romor was involved in some secret project but she had difficulty in accepting not being a part of it.

Dr. G.:	Has Romor told you anything of his work?
Janet:	No, and this frustrates me.
Dr. G.:	Has this affected your marriage?
Janet:	Yes and no. Romor is still attentive and considerate but his preoccupation with his work is affecting his health.
Dr. G.:	Is he aware of this?
Janet:	Yes, but he thinks the project must take priority.
Dr. G.:	What can you do about this?
Janet:	Nothing.

I then progressed Melodea forward to any significant event in reference to this project and her relationship with Romor.

Dr. G.:	You look upset. What happened?
Janet:	I don't believe it. I just don't believe this could happen.
Dr. G.:	What happened?
Janet:	Well, Romor was instructed by the government to scan through the medical records of our people to find a human subject for a serum to fight the virus.
Dr. G.:	I thought this was a secret project.
Janet:	It is. Romor could only find a handful of our people who were ideal for this experiment.
Dr. G.:	Why only a handful?
Janet:	There were many other candidates but most of them had left our city or were in key positions within our system.
Dr. G.:	Please continue.
Janet:	Out of all of the candidates the only logical choice for this experiment was me. I didn't hold a key position and my medical profile was perfect for this test.
Dr. G.:	So is this why he told you about this experiment?
Janet:	Yes. The funny thing is that he is right. By approach-

ing other people he would run the risk of a panic. He knows that I will tell nobody about this.

Dr. G.: Do you find this a cold decision on Romor's part?

Janet: Yes, I guess it is. I really don't hold it against Romor. He is just doing his job. What I can't believe is that the only way I can see more of my husband is to be a guinea pig in one of his experiments.

Dr. G.: How has this affected your marriage?

Janet: Actually, it has brought us closer together. Romor can speak openly to me about the project and we have definitely grown closer.

Dr. G.: Tell me more about this project.

Janet: This project is top secret and has been in operation for about two years. Romor has been involved since the very beginning. At first, animal tests were made to try to find a serum. However, there was much failure and these animals died.

Dr. G.: When did the animal tests succeed?

Janet: It has only been within the last six months or so that the animal tests have been successful. So now a human test is in order and I am to be that test.

Dr. G.: Are you afraid of the experiment?

Janet: Not really . . . well, maybe a little afraid. There is something that bothers me more.

Dr. G.: What is that?

Janet: If this serum should prove successful, then it will be mass-produced and Romor will be away from me again and our relationship will suffer even more.

Dr. G.: If it is successful, won't they turn the production and distribution over to others?

Janet: Yes, but Romor will have to be available for problems. There are always problems.

What is interesting to note about this facet of Melodea's personality and growth is the complete elimination of jealousy and insecurity problems she exhibited in the past. Apparently, she worked out these in prior future lives. Her concern about Romor was quite natural and normal. She didn't want him to work too hard for too long a period of time for health reasons. This really wasn't selfish but a truly caring and loving quality that Melodea was sharing. I next progressed her to the time of her involvement in this project.

Dr. G.:   Tell me about your role in this experiment.

Janet: At first I had to go through all kinds of tests. Blood
          tests, tissue specimens, brain scans, and other pro-
          cedures that I don't care to mention. These tests were
          necessary to prepare me for the inoculations.

Dr. G.:   And where was Romor during all this?

Janet: Oh, he was there all the time. If he wasn't sticking
          me with something he was by my side giving me emo-
          tional support.

Dr. G.:   Was he also supervising the actual details of the pro-
          cedure?

Janet: Yes, of course. When he is not running tests and con-
          sulting with others, Romor is very attentive to me.

Dr. G.:   What are your responsibilities on this project?

Janet: As I stated before, I am the human guinea pig. After
          certain preliminary tests were run I was inoculated
          with the experimental serum.

Dr. G.:   Then what?

Janet: Then I was observed. I was relieved of my regular job
          functions and I stay in this room twenty-four hours a
          day.

Dr. G.:   Who observes you?

Janet: A staff is always present. Romor is there all day and
          part of the evening. He performs various tests on me
          and comforts me throughout the day.

Dr. G.:   I take it, then, that you cannot leave the facility.

Janet: That's correct. It's really not that bad. My room is
          comfortable and Romor has seen to it that my per-
          sonal effects were brought here, so it's like my home
          away from home.

Dr. G.:   Do you have any side effects from the serum?

Janet: Just drowsiness. All I want to do is sleep all day and
          night.

Dr. G.:   What is Romor's attitude like at this time?

Janet: He is wonderful. He is a fine clinician and most sup-
          portive to me emotionally.

Dr. G.:   Is he impatient with you about the results of this drug?

Janet: No, he is very kind and patient.

I then progressed Melodea to an important development in
this test. She reported continued drowsiness, but then a most
unusual event occurred.

Dr. G.:   What has happened since we last talked?
Janet: Where am I?
Dr. G.:   What's going on?
Janet: I'm floating.
Dr. G.:   Have you died or crossed over?
Janet: No.
Dr. G.:   Where are you?
Janet: I must have left my body but I can see a silver cord.

Melodea went into a coma and almost died. When she spoke to me she was having a near-death experience. Remember, Janet in my therapy was perfectly safe. No matter what a patient is reliving in a past or future life there is absolutely no danger to them emotionally, physically, psychologically, or spiritually. Melodea reported the classic core scenario of a near-death experience (NDE)—moving through a tunnel, hearing strange sounds, seeing colors, feeling the presence of a departed loved one, etc.

A special team was brought in to revive Melodea, but she still remained in a coma. Romor was at her side day and night for days on end. It was quite something to speak to a patient from the perspective of an NDE. Melodea accommodated to this level rather quickly and we were able to continue with the questioning.

Dr. G.:   What is going on now?
Janet: Everyone is panicking. Since I'm the ideal candidate
           for this serum and since I am nearly dead from it,
           they don't know what to do. I am their only hope.

I then progressed her to a resolution of this difficulty one way or another.

Dr. G.:   Where are you now?
Janet: I'm still floating—wait, I feel something strange.
Dr. G.:   What is it?
Janet: I don't know. It's like . . . oh . . . oh . . . oh

Melodea was quickly reentering her body and slowly regained consciousness. In a few hours, she was fine. The crisis was over.

Dr. G.: Aren't things still as bad as you described?

Janet: No. For some reason my response to the serum was only temporary. I'm still being monitored.

Dr. G.: What I mean is since the serum almost killed you doesn't that mean it's unsafe for use in inoculating your people against the virus?

Janet: At first, I thought that, too. But, apparently, the dosage is being adjusted and they are still optimistic about its potential.

Dr. G.: You mean Romor is going to subject you to this serum again?

Janet: He wanted to choose someone else but I insisted that he use me. It is too late to get anyone else.

The dosage was adjusted and despite Romor's objections Melodea was inoculated again with the serum.

Dr. G.: How do you feel now?

Janet: I'm fine.

Dr. G.: How long has it been since this second injection?

Janet: Over two weeks.

Dr. G.: How long will they wait before they can consider this a success?

Janet: Just one more week.

Another week went by and Melodea exhibited absolutely no side effects. The serum worked and her people were saved.

Dr. G.: What happened next?

Janet: The serum was quickly mass-produced and given to all the inhabitants of the city.

Dr. G.: Did it work?

Janet: Yes, and quite well.

Dr. G.: Did the people find out about this crisis eventually?

Janet: The government ordered everyone to be inoculated. This did initiate questions. I'm sure many people guessed that something was wrong but there was no panic.

Dr. G.: And were there other deaths from the virus?

Janet: There were none after the inoculations were given.

Dr. G.: What about your relationship with Romor?

Janet: Surprisingly enough, it was not that greatly affected.

Romor did have to work some late hours but not that many. We are very close.

Dr. G.: Did this experience teach you something?

Janet: It sure did (very happy)! I guess I really didn't understand my relationship with Romor.

Dr. G.: Or how he really felt about you?

Janet: Exactly.

Dr. G.: And after this incident?

Janet: What do you mean?

Dr. G.: Did you have any other problems with Romor or this virus situation?

Janet: No, we were all immunized and never had to worry about the virus again. As far as Romor and me, we were never happier.

Dr. G.: What about your career as a medical technologist?

Janet: I went back to work soon after I was released from the facility.

So ends the future life progression in the city under glass. To a certain extent Melodea wanted Romor to "take care" of her, as Janet had wanted in this life. But the difference was one of degree. Melodea was a very confident, assertive, and independent woman who could take care of herself. By the thirty-first century Janet had eliminated a lot of karma. Mike was gone from her karmic cycle (from her superconscious level Melodea informed me that she didn't know Romor in her current life as Janet). Janet as Melodea will no longer be the jealous and insecure woman she was in days gone by.

An interesting effect occurred after this future life progression. Janet became much more self-confident and became involved with a man who was totally unlike his predecessors. Janet thus began to establish a pattern much more akin to the one that would characterize Melodea in 1100 years. The future life progression, in my opinion, had more of a therapeutic benefit for Janet than her past life experiences.

CHAPTER TWENTY-TWO

A Contaminated Future Life

A COMPULSION IS DEFINED AS A REPETITIVE AND SEEM-ingly purposeful behavior that is performed according to certain rules or in a stereotyped fashion. The behavior is not an end in itself but is designed to produce or prevent some future event or situation. The activity is quite excessive and not connected in a realistic way with what it is designed to produce or prevent. The individual generally recognizes the senselessness of the behavior and does not derive pleasure from carrying out the activity, although it provides a release of tension.

With this background you can now appreciate Pete's predicament. Pete called me in August of 1984. He was a clinical psychologist and had a hand-washing compulsion. He knew very well the definition of a compulsion but could not help himself. Pete had spent years in therapy with no results. He would constantly wash his hands, day and night. He changed his clothes two to three times a day to "remove the dirt."

Pete was a truly pleasant man. I could see him relating rather well to his patients. He was always neatly dressed, well groomed, and soft-spoken. Under no circumstances could he treat a patient with a compulsion. It was just too close to home and he would refer them out. There were many interruptions in his practice since he would wash his hands at least once during a session, usually after shaking hands with the patient.

Pete's biggest fear was of being contaminated. There was absolutely no logic to his concern. He felt that if he didn't go

215

through his daily rituals that he would somehow be contaminated and wouldn't be able to function. Another unusual aspect of his psychological profile was the number 8. This number haunted him. He was born in August (the eighth month). Every time he obtained a telephone number or a new address the number 8 was always well represented. His grandmother had died in August and there were many other deaths in his family during the eighth month of the year.

As a result, Pete always exhibited a form of anxiety and depression every August. His first call to my office to set up his initial session occurred at the end of August. Another strange occurrence was the name Teresa. This is not a particularly common name but one that Pete associated with negativity. A girl he dated in graduate school rather cruelly ended their relationship just prior to his oral exam for his doctorate. Her name was Teresa. Throughout his growing up years the name Teresa would send chills down Pete's spine. He could not explain why.

Pete recovered from the Teresa who had ended their relationship, but the name still haunted him. He had one car accident in his life and it happened about ten years ago and the woman involved was hospitalized with numerous injuries. Her first name was Teresa and there were two 8s on the license plate. In addition, this automobile accident took place late one August evening.

By the time Pete actually entered my office in September of 1984 he was desperate. He just had to rid himself of this compulsion once and for all. It was causing him to lose sleep, and additionally, it was certainly not helping his therapy practice. Many people are given a poor impression by a psychologist who washes his hand immediately after greeting you.

Pete proved to be an average hypnotic patient. By that I mean his trance depth fit into the light-medium range. The majority of the population can easily attain this level. As I have mentioned before, one does not need to reach a deep level of hypnosis to regress into past lives or progress into a future lifetime. In Pete's case this was more than sufficient for his explorations.

Pete's first past life helped explain a lot about his current symptoms. The year was 1888 (note the presence of the number 8) and the city was Paris. Pete was a female singer named Marie Duvall. Marie was very successful on the stage, but her morals left something to be desired. She was a prostitute for years before she became known for her musical and acting talents.

Even after achieving a name on the stage Marie still used her body to get what she wanted. She was very ambitious and aggressive (a complete opposite of Pete today). Pete cringed at the thought of what Marie did and represented. She was vain, selfish, cruel, and ruthless. She slept with men indiscriminately just to get what she wanted from them. She was never satisfied; she always had to have more.

Pete would comment to me during these sessions about how "dirty" Marie was. She would have sex with one man and without washing herself sleep with another during her prostitute days. One of the events that truly saddened Marie was the death of a lover. She became infatuated with a man who worked for the government. He was powerful and Marie couldn't get enough of him. She loved power. One day he was killed by a German agent.

The French government knew about their affair and convinced Marie to work for them. She readily agreed because revenge was a part of her personality. She acted occasionally as a spy for the French government and only wanted assignments against Germany. One night she was sleeping with a German agent and her assignment was complete. She obtained the needed information but decided to kill him herself. In a series of violent thrusts Marie stabbed the German agent to death. Her naked body was covered with his blood. She stood and laughed about this. It was at least an hour before she washed herself off. During this scene Pete was cringing in the chair. He couldn't stand the sight of Marie standing there drenched in blood laughing about a murder she had just committed.

Shortly thereafter Marie informed the French government she could no longer work for them. She continued with her life, satisfied that her lover's death was avenged. As the years went by she began to have nightmares about that murder. Feelings of guilt flooded her mind. She didn't know what to do.

Although she was not a religious woman, Marie felt a trip to a convent outside the city would be the solution. She wanted to confess her sins, especially the murder. When she arrived at the convent the sister in charge spent a great deal of time listening to her story. At the end of all this she told Marie that they could not absolve her of her sins. The date was August 8 and the nun was named Sister Teresa.

When Pete came out of that trance he was made aware of a number of facts. First, the number 8 had played a rather prominent role in Marie's life. Second, a person with the name Teresa had finally emerged as a possible source of his anxiety. Last but not least, a source of his hand-washing compulsion reared its head. (You will note that I say *a* source and not *the* source. Pete's case was far too complicated to be explained by one past life regression.) One interesting aside on this life was Marie's failure to find peace with Sister Teresa. Perhaps that was the main reason Pete chose psychology as a profession: now he could help people when he himself couldn't obtain that needed aid 100 years ago.

The rest of Marie's life was inconsequential to Pete's condition so we left her alone and explored another life. In an African life Pete was a female and a mother. Her husband was killed in a war and she was left to raise her baby daughter. Loneliness was a definite problem but, even more significant, a plague annihilated her baby daughter and most of her village. She survived a good many years but lived in constant fear for her life and always blamed herself for the death of her daughter, even though there was nothing she could have done to prevent it. Eventually this woman died. The key point in this life was the plague and the blame she projected onto herself. Here we have another cause-effect relationship with the current compulsion.

For Pete's third trip back in time he described a life in England during the fifteenth century. This time Pete was a male named James. James was a nobleman and spent most of his time in the king's court. He had an older brother, Robert, who was also at the king's side. Later the king became sexually involved with James and his brother. Pete again began to cringe when he described this homosexual relationship. He called it "sick" and "dirty."

As time passed a power struggle developed between James and his brother. Since both were lovers of the king they received special treatment and favors. Robert was older and was thus given more power and authority. This angered James and a battle of wits ensued between the brothers for power and position.

James (Pete) lost this battle and was banished from England. He grew depressed and, in France, planned his next move. He returned with some men and murdered Robert. The king was furious and had James beheaded.

Pete cringed in my recliner as he perceived his death. He described the blade as being "filthy with the blood of its previous victims." Here again we can see cause-effect relationships to explain Pete's current compulsion. Do not ignore the guilt he felt from violence (killing his brother) and his homosexual relationship with the king. Sex, violence, guilt, and a dirty blade were the karmic carryovers from this English life.

The stage was set for the most significant life relating to Pete's present-day compulsion. As I stated elsewhere in this book since all time is simultaneous the cause of a present-day problem could very well rest in a future lifetime. Although all of the lives we explored were causative, they were not the only or most significant factors. In Pete's case, the most significant life turned out to be a future life.

By this stage in our hypnotherapy Pete was beginning to show marked progress in sleeping better and in the lessening of the frequency and intensity of his compulsive symptoms. He was eager to continue his therapy and most probably expected to regress to another past life during his next session. Such was not the case. Pete traveled forward instead to the latter part of the twenty-first century.

Dr. G.:   What is your name?
Pete: Ben. Ben Kingsley.
Dr. G.:   Where do you find yourself?
Pete: I am in school and I like what I'm studying.
Dr. G.:   What is it that you are studying?
Pete: It's a science course and I like the work.

Ben was in a high school physics course. He had a natural talent for science and loved putting things together, taking them apart, and calculating the probability of various experiments.

Dr. G.:   Where do you live, Ben?
Pete: Tulsa. Tulsa, Oklahoma.
Dr. G.:   What year is this?
Pete: 2074.
Dr. G.:   Tell me about your family.
Pete: What do you want to know?
Dr. G.:   What does your father do?
Pete: He is a psychiatrist.
Dr. G.:   And your mother?
Pete: She works as an architect.
Dr. G.:   Any brothers or sisters?
Pete: I have one brother, Roger, and one sister, Tenina.
Dr. G.:   Are they older than you?
Pete: No, they are both younger.
Dr. G.:   What do you want to do with your life?

Pete: I want to go to college and do something in the sci-
           entific field. I don't know exactly which field yet.

As I continued questioning Ben I found out that he was a very
conscientious young adult. He didn't seem to have any bad habits. He was a good student and got along well with his family.
Ben exhibited a great deal of respect for his father and mother.
He admired their dedication to their respective careers but, at
the same time, did not feel neglected. Ben was kind and helpful
to his younger brother and sister.

Ben was progressed beyond his high school years to any relevant advanced education or occupation. He described going to
college and majoring in physics.

Dr. G.:   How do you like school?
Pete: I love it.
Dr. G.:   What is your major?
Pete: Now I'm concentrating in nuclear physics.
Dr. G.:   With what goal?
Pete: When I graduate I want to work as a technician in a
           nuclear power plant.
Dr. G.:   With your skills, why not become a nuclear physicist?
Pete: I couldn't do that.
Dr. G.:   Why not?
Pete: Because I'm not cut out for that kind of responsibility.
Dr. G.:   Don't you think you could handle the training?
Pete: I'm sure I could but, you see, I get a little nervous
           sometimes when things don't go well.
Dr. G.:   What do you mean by a little nervous?
Pete: Well, every once in a while when I get nervous and
           frustrated I develop a panicky feeling.
Dr. G.:   What do you do?
Pete: I lose my temper sometimes and don't think too clearly
           for a few minutes.
Dr.G.:   This sounds like a real problem. Have you told your
           father about this?
Pete: Yes, he knows about it.
Dr. G.:   Has he done anything about it?
Pete: I am seeing one of his colleagues, a Dr. Margolis.
Dr. G.:   What does Dr. Margolis tell you about your condi-
           tion?
Pete: He tells me it's not very serious but that I should keep

my stress levels down and to avoid repeated confrontations.

Dr. G.: Doesn't that preclude a career as a nuclear plant technician?

Pete: It would if it was found out but that won't be a problem.

Dr. G.: How so?

Pete: Dr. Margolis is a very good friend of my father. He owes Dad a big favor. Also, he is well aware of my academic record.

Dr. G.: By that you mean he will keep your therapy off the record.

Pete: That's correct.

Dr. G.: Is there anything else about yourself that might surface as a problem in your chosen profession?

Pete: Nothing that I can think of.

I was looking for some carryover of Pete's compulsion but found none. Ben was only occasionally out of control with these temper episodes and nobody seemed to be concerned. No one except me, that is.

None of Pete's characteristics seemed to have expressed themselves in Ben. If anything, he was quite the opposite of Pete's present-day personality. I next progressed Ben to a significant event in his college career.

Dr. G.: Where are you now, Ben?

Pete: I'm meeting Gail.

Dr. G.: Who is Gail?

Pete: She is my fiancée.

Dr. G.: Does she know about your temper episodes?

Pete: No. I don't know why you keep stressing those rare behaviors. When Gail is around I am calm and in complete control.

Ben was quite right. When he was with Gail he was a different person. He was calm, confident, yet sensitive to her needs. Even if things weren't going well for Ben, Gail's presence made it easier to take. She was obviously the best thing that had ever happened to him.

Dr. G.: How are things going with Dr. Margolis's treatment?

Pete: Okay, I guess.

Dr. G.:   What does he do when you see him?
Pete: He uses a form of biofeedback with me.
Dr. G.:   Does he put you on any medication?
Pete: Only occasionally. He only prescribes drugs when I
           report a series of episodes.
Dr. G.:   Have you done that recently.
Pete: No. I have been doing fine lately.

Ben was correct: he had been feeling better. Gail had moved
in with him and Ben felt on top of the world. Dr. Margolis was
pleased and monitored Ben once a month. Gail had no idea that
Ben was seeing Dr. Margolis. She had her own career as a
computer programmer and kept quite busy.

Gail never saw Ben at his worst. He studied in the library and
when he got frustrated in the lab it was usually when he was
alone. Ben's father was proud of his son and felt everything was
progressing nicely.

Ben was a very happy man. He graduated from college and
married Gail. His family was proud of him and he was well on
his way to achieving his lifelong goals. I next progressed Ben to
his working environment.

Dr. G.:   Tell me about your work.
Pete: I absolutely love it. I work as a technician in the nu-
           clear plant outside of Tulsa.
Dr. G.:   So you have remained in Tulsa.
Pete: Yes. I am a junior technician and I am supervised by
           Ralph.
Dr. G.:   How do you get along with Ralph?
Pete: We have a good working relationship. He is an excel-
           lent teacher and we have become good friends.
Dr. G.:   Do you ever get upset at work?
Pete: Sometimes I feel a little frustrated at the vast com-
           plexities of the plant, but I don't really get upset.
Dr. G.:   How about at home?
Pete: No, Gail and I love each other.
Dr. G.:   Do you still see Dr. Margolis?
Pete: Just three or four times a year. He says I am doing
           fine.
Dr. G.:   Then, why does he keep seeing you at all?
Pete: My father wants to make sure that I am really all right.
           Since Dr. Margolis's therapy is strictly off the record

Dad feels responsible for my psychological well-being.

As I progressed Ben forward in time he reported a true love for his life. Although his family life was important, he was truly dedicated to his job. I perceived a little too much dedication. Ben had an obsessive-compulsive personality, but that is not uncommon among scientifically trained people. What I was concerned with was the excessive workaholic traits he was exhibiting, coupled with a high-strung nature that was potentially explosive and dangerous.

None of my concerns manifested themselves during my questioning of Ben. I then progressed him forward five years.

Dr. G.:   What has happened since we last spoke?
Pete: I really do enjoy my work. I have received three promotions and am the second in command in my unit.
Dr. G.:   Who do you work under?
Pete: Ralph is still my supervisor.
Dr. G.:   Do you still get along with him?
Pete: Yes. We are very good friends and our families spend a fair amount of time together.
Dr. G.:   You said families. Does that mean you have children?
Pete: Gail and I are the proud parents of two sons, Aaron and Ronald.
Dr. G.:   Does it bother you that you are not in charge of your unit?
Pete: No. You see, I have been assigned to a new research unit and am being trained to head my particular section.

Things had very much worked out for Ben. He was only with Ralph about one half of the week. The rest of his time was spent in a brand-new nuclear research facility located about twenty miles from the plant. This facility was studying various techniques to harness and control nuclear power safely. This was a very special unit and it was quite an honor to be chosen to work in it. Ben's ambition and skills had allowed him to rise up the promotion ladder quickly and this quite pleased him.

Dr. G.:   How does Gail feel about your two jobs?
Pete: Oh, she is all for it. She is always supportive of my career and I love her for it.

Dr. G.:   What about the long hours?

Pete: I don't mind them at all.

Dr. G.:   Doesn't Gail object to your absence from your home?

Pete: Gail has her own career and taking care of the boys keeps her busy. We really don't have any problems.

Dr. G.:   What about your temper episodes? Is that still a problem?

Pete: Not at all. I haven't had an episode in over three years.

Dr. G.:   Are you still seeing Dr. Margolis?

Pete: No.

Dr. G.:   Does your father approve of your termination of therapy with Dr. Margolis?

Pete: He hasn't said anything about it for a long time. Dr. Margolis consulted with Dad before ending the therapy so I guess I'm okay.

Dr. G.:   Has anyone in either of the two facilities you work in found out about your past psychological problems?

Pete: Not a chance. If any knowledge of my treatment were known, I would be removed from my positions.

Dr. G.:   Even though Dr. Margolis feels you are "cured"?

Pete: It doesn't matter what Dr. Margolis thinks. The history of psychological problems would be totally destructive to me professionally.

Dr. G.:   How does Ralph respond to your research position? Is he jealous of you?

Pete: He really is proud of me. After all, he trained me. In answer to your question, I don't feel Ralph is in the least bit jealous of me. Ralph is much more of a family man and he would never work the kind of hours I do.

As we discussed this part of Ben's life I could tell he was really happy. His workaholic tendencies didn't seem to bother Gail, his friends, or his other family members. Ben's father was very proud of him, as were Ben's peers. I, however, was still not convinced that Ben was as psychologically stable as Dr. Margolis had assumed.

Ben had a complete life. He loved his work and enjoyed his family life and his friends when he wasn't working. His ambitions were being fulfilled and unquestionably Ben was in control of his life.

As I progressed Ben forward to a significant challenge or

difficulty in his life some interesting patterns were beginning to emerge.

Dr. G.: What has happened since we last spoke?
Pete: I don't know what I'm going to do about Aaron.
Dr. G.: Aaron, your oldest son?
Pete: Yes.
Dr. G.: What about him?
Pete: He is not doing well at all. He is so bright. There's just no excuse for it.
Dr. G.: What do his teachers say?
Pete: They say he is just not trying. He is preoccupied with other things on his mind.
Dr. G.: How do you handle this situation?
Pete: I tried talking to the boy. He seems to understand me but he just doesn't do anything about it.
Dr. G.: Have you thought of taking him to a child psychologist?
Pete: I don't want even to discuss that option.

As I inquired further into this situation, I seemed to have struck a nerve. Aaron was named after Ben's father. Ben wanted Aaron to excel at everything he did and subconsciously exerted performance pressure on him, which resulted in Aaron's rebelling. By not performing well, Aaron could only go up in his performance. This did not sit well with Ben.

Gail allowed Ben to handle the educational guidance of the boys. The thought of Aaron needing counseling brought back the memories of Ben's treatment with Dr. Margolis. Ben became somewhat frustrated and angry. He came close to losing his temper.

Dr. G.: How did this situation resolve itself?
Pete: Aaron and I had some long talks. I began to treat him differently, letting up on some of the standards I set for him.
Dr. G.: Did it work?
Pete: Yes. He began to improve in school and things went back to normal.
Dr. G.: Did this cause a strain in your relationship with Gail?
Pete: At first it did, but later we worked things out.
Dr. G.: Did this affect your working relationships?

Pete: Well, I guess it did. It is hard working the hours I do.
           Maybe I was a little too sensitive.
Dr. G.:   Could you give me an example?
Pete: Ralph had to correct some of my calculations and
           reports at the plant. I argued with him about it, think-
           ing that he was picking on me.
Dr. G.:   Why would he do that?
Pete: I thought he was jealous of my position at the research
           facility. That was dumb. Ralph is my best friend and
           only wants the best for me.
Dr. G.:   Did you ever have a temper episode with him?
Pete: No, but I felt close to one at certain times.
Dr. G.:   Have you thought about going back to Dr. Margolis?
Pete: Not a chance. I can handle myself now. I do not need
           therapy.

Ben was still quite sensitive about any mention of therapy.
Even the thought of therapy for Aaron made Ben quite upset.
The problem with Aaron did resolve itself nicely without the
involvement of a therapist. It is interesting to note that Pete in
this life is a psychologist but was very averse toward therapy in
his next lifetime.

Ralph didn't seem to be concerned with Ben. The incident was
a minor one and Ralph was used to the egos of some of his crew.
Nobody suspected Ben was having any significant problems.

I progressed Ben forward again to a significant event in dealing with his emotions and his temper.

Dr. G.:   Where are you now, Ben?
Pete: I am at home and arguing with Gail.
Dr. G.:   What is this all about?
Pete: She got into a car accident. It was so stupid. She just
           ran out of the house after we had words and didn't
           think clearly about the other vehicles.
Dr. G.:   Was she hurt?
Pete: No, thank goodness.
Dr. G.:   Did you have a temper episode?
Pete: Yes, and Gail was shocked. She didn't really think it
           was a serious matter. She just wrote it off to the ac-
           cident itself.
Dr. G.:   Have you now thought of seeing Dr. Margolis?
Pete: No, and I don't want to talk about me going back into
           therapy. Is that understood?

Ben was getting very emotional about his psychological state. He even threatened me. I was concerned about his explosive nature and after years of calm, the storm began to rise on the horizon.

I can understand Ben's concern about his career. However, he was acting irresponsibly in not going back to Dr. Margolis. His therapy could still be kept confidential, but Ben wouldn't hear of it.

For the next year or so things quieted down. Ben felt better and he naturally assumed that there would be no further problems. I didn't assume that at all.

I next progressed Ben to another significant event in his life.

Dr. G.:   What is going on with you, Ben?
Pete: (Crying) I don't want to talk about it.
Dr. G: What happened?
Pete: It was such a waste. How could these things happen?
Dr. G.:   What has happened?
Pete: My father was killed in a plane crash. He was return-
          ing from a medical convention.
Dr. G.:   When did you find out about his death?
Pete: Just a week ago. His funeral was very difficult for me
          to attend.
Dr. G.:   And your mother?
Pete: She is taking it a lot better than me. I don't know how
          she does it.

The death of his father was very difficult for Ben. He took some time off work and got to know his family. This was a very emotional time for him. Interestingly enough, Ben did not exhibit temper problems during his grief. He felt emotionally numb but functional.

After several weeks he returned to work. It was business as usual. He worked his long hours, did his job well, and dealt with life. On the surface all seemed to be in order. However, it was clear to me that Ben was repressing his feelings. He was ignoring his inner needs and playing a role. This was not natural and, considering his past psychological history, potentially very dangerous.

To the outside world Ben was fine. His relationship with Gail improved. He was the old Ben, so it seemed. A year later Ben received a very significant promotion.

Dr. G.:   What is your career like now?

Pete: I have been promoted to chief technician at the research facility.

Dr. G.:   How does that affect your other job?

Pete: I now spend all of my time at the research facility. Although I am on call at the power plant, very little of my time is spent there.

Dr. G.:   Are you now working fewer hours?

Pete: Somewhat fewer, but I do spend a lot of time at the research lab.

Dr. G.:   Do you see much of Ralph?

Pete: Yes, we still socialize. He is quite interested in my work and our families do see each other now and then.

Dr. G.:   Ben, tell me about the research facility.

Pete: What do you want to know?

Dr. G.:   Is this work classified?

Pete: No. We just research safe and more effective uses of nuclear power.

Dr. G.:   Is this funded by the government?

Pete: Yes. We have a tremendous budget and we are the most highly regarded research facility in the country.

Dr. G.   Do you worry about being laid off?

Pete: Absolutely not. It is a very secure position. My only concerns are related to doing my work to the best of my ability. After all, I am the chief technician in my unit and a lot depends on my capabilities.

Dr. G.:   What does the facility look like?

Pete: We have a rather large building subdivided into various corridors. Each corridor represents a different division and all divisions are color-coded.

Dr. G.:   Do these divisions have names?

Pete: Yes, of course. There is Norad-Alpha and Norad-Beta, Gani-Alpha and Gani-Beta, and my unit is Teres-Alpha.

Dr. G.:   Is there a Teres-Beta?

Pete: Yes. Didn't I mention that? I apologize for the oversight.

Dr. G.:   Do you occasionally make small oversights at work?

Pete: Now, don't you start that again (getting angry)! I am competent to do my work and I don't need to see Dr. Margolis.

Dr. G.:   I didn't say anything about Dr. Margolis.

Pete: I know, but you were going to, weren't you?

Dr. G.: Ben, have you had any difficulties at all at work?
Pete: Sometimes I miss on a calculation and my men correct me.
Dr. G.: Does that get you angry?
Pete: Not enough that it shows, but, yes, I do get down on myself.
Dr. G.: Are you a perfectionist?
Pete: I don't think so. I just want everything to be done correctly.
Dr. G.: What is the difference?
Pete: I guess none. I will admit to being a perfectionist. Does that make me mentally unfit?
Dr. G.: It could if it makes you angry enough to let your emotions rule your behavior unchecked.
Pete: Well, that doesn't happen, so I guess I'm okay.

Ben went on to tell me more about his position. He was in charge of the Teres-Alpha division, which dealt with researching how to contain nuclear power and more effectively eliminating nuclear waste products. Ben was indeed a good supervisor. He was young, aggressive, knowledgeable, and totally dedicated. If you could ignore his emotional problems, he was absolutely perfect for the job. I couldn't ignore his psychological profile and my concern was growing by the minute.

As I progressed Ben forward he described being in many different types of activities at the facility. He sat in on board meetings, participated in planning major projects, correlated the data from his division, and handled public relations, among others. In other words, Ben had a lot of responsibilities. In my opinion he was "biting off more than he could chew," considering his emotional state.

I progressed him forward to the most significant event in this life.

Dr. G.   What year is this, Ben?
Pete: 2088.
Dr. G.: What is going on in your life at this time?
Pete: I'm really excited about my project.
Dr. G.: What is it exactly?
Pete: I am working on a way to compartmentalize and quantify the flow of nuclear material from one reactor site to another.
Dr. G.   That sounds complicated and dangerous.

Pete: It is. But it is also exciting.
Dr. G.   Are all of your men working on this project?
Pete: No, just me and Chet. I do most of the calculations.
Dr. G.:   Are you putting in a lot of overtime on this?
Pete: Yes.
Dr. G.:   Have there been any problems?
Pete: Just the usual frustrations—nothing major.
Dr. G.:   Does Chet work overtime with you?
Pete: No, he goes home on time. I stay late by myself.
Dr. G.:   So you work better when you are alone?
Pete: You know, I never thought about it, but I do. I really
           do like it better at night when only a skeleton crew is
           around.
Dr. G.:   You mean there aren't people working there at night?
Pete: No, not really. We have the usual security people on
           board in the evening but very few researchers or tech-
           nicians are around at night.

I then progressed Ben forward to an actual event that would
be meaningful to him. He reported being at the facility late one
evening in 2088. He was alone and there were some problems.

Dr.G.:   What is it, Ben?
Pete: Something is very wrong here.
Dr. G.:   Exactly what is it that is wrong?
Pete: The level of nuclear wastes has risen and the diffrac-
           tion chamber I developed isn't working.
Dr. G.:   What do you mean, isn't working?
Pete: Apparently, my calculations were off and there is an
           overflow of the backup of these waste products.
Dr. G.:   Can you handle this emergency?
Pete: I am sure I can. Wait—It isn't working. What am I
           going to do?
Dr. G.:   Move forward, calmly, to your actions.
Pete: The dials are going crazy. The danger signal is about
           to be reached.
Dr. G.:   Can you call for help?
Pete: I can handle this. I can do this myself. After all, I am
           the chief technician.
Dr. G.:   Go on.
Pete: It's no use; the system is backing up.
Dr. G.:   What does that mean?

Pete: A meltdown could occur. Everything will be contaminated. I can't let that happen.
Dr. G.:   What do you do?
Pete: The signal is sounded. The security men will be here shortly. I can't let them see what I have done.
Dr. G.:   What will you do?
Pete: I will isolate myself from them.
Dr. G.:   Is there anybody with you now?

There was silence for a very long two minutes. When Ben finally responded he described a bizarre set of circumstances. There was a security guard making his rounds in the Teres-Alpha unit. Ben knocked him unconscious with a hard metal object. He then went completely out of control.

The frustration of his personal failure got to him. Ben couldn't handle the situation. It was his fault that this meltdown and contamination were occurring. He alone had handled the calculations that resulted in misprogramming the computer. When he calmed down I continued the questioning.

Dr. G.:   What is happening now, Ben?
Pete: I am totally isolated. I have sealed off this unit and it will take hours for them to get in here.
Dr. G.:   What will that solve?
Pete: Nothing, but I must be alone.
Dr. G.:   What have you done to correct this situation?
Pete: I turned all of the power and diffraction switches on high.
Dr. G.:   Won't that add to the overload?
Pete: It sure will. This baby will blow and I'm going with it.
Dr. G.:   Don't you want this to end a different way?
Pete: No. Nobody is going to fire me. Nobody is going to tell me I was wrong.
Dr. G.:   What about the guard and the others?
Pete: I don't care. I don't care.

Ben had a nervous breakdown. He would not listen to reason. Pete, sitting in my recliner, was in no danger. It was Ben who couldn't be reasoned with by logic. As a result of Ben's actions there was a complete meltdown of the research facility. The skeleton crew and Ben were killed. The nuclear contamination from Ben's miscalculations affected the entire Tulsa area. The water supply was contaminated. Concomitantly, the food supplies were then contaminated. Everything was contaminated. From the superconscious mind level I spoke to Ben.

Dr. G.:   Ben, what did you learn from this?
Pete: I learned how to contaminate a major city by my stupidity. I learned nothing but how to hurt innocent people.

Ben didn't quite understand another connection from this future life. He died in August of the year 2088. The eighth month and the year 2088 were very significant associations of the number 8. In addition, he worked in the Teres-Alpha unit. This spells out as Teresa, the name that haunted Pete most of his life.

Pete was brought out of trance feeling drained and unsure of what this all meant. I explained to him that this future life was the real cause of his present contamination compulsion and the origin of his difficulties with the number 8 and the name Teresa. He understood the connection and complimented me on my ability to perceive his true underlying psychological problems when everyone else had been fooled.

However, I wasn't looking for compliments. I pointed out that Ben should have continued to see Dr. Margolis, but even that may not have prevented the blowup. Ben was a powder keg just waiting to explode. Finally, he did.

Pete was confused. How could this future life help him now? It was a terrible thing to look forward to. He sure didn't want to experience this in 100 years. I agreed with him. Although I did effect some cleansing from the superconscious mind level, that wouldn't solve his problem. The answer lay in the application of the principles of quantum physics.

You will recall that in all of the other future life progressions documented in this book, the results were positive. In other words, the resulting life represented a culmination of the patient's achievements. The patient was programmed for this frequency and that became their reality.

But that was just one probability of at least five major probabilities. In Pete's case he perceived a negative frequency or probability though he had at least four others from which to choose. The solution to Pete's problem was really quite simple: All I had to do was to have him perceive the other four choices and then, after he selected the ideal frequency, program this frequency to be his reality. By doing this I would, in a way, help

Pete to switch frequencies so his future would be quite different than if we did nothing.

I realize that this sounds confusing. You may say how can I do this? How can I change the future? What you must consider is that every time you make a choice you are, in effect, changing the future. In Pete's case progressing him forward to the other parallel existences he would have at the end of the twenty-first century would accomplish that very goal.

Pete progressed nicely to four other lifetimes in that same time frame. After each life was reviewed he carefully considered the one he felt was ideal and then I progressed him to that frequency. Remember, Pete was the one who chose the ideal frequency. I will never make that choice. The various environmental factors can be quite similar in these parallel frequencies, as was the case here. However, there will always be major differences and each action by Pete in a certain frequency will have a certain effect on the total outcome of his life.

Thus, there is no predestination. The soul always has free will. What will be somewhat predestined is the basic framework of the frequency. The specifics can be changed by varying the choices along the way but the basic framework can't be altered. You cannot just choose the best aspects of all five frequencies. You can only choose one frequency and accept the good with the bad. That is one reason why I always have the patient make this choice.

The typical pattern of the five frequencies is as follows: one is very bad, one is below average, one is rather neutral, one is above average, and one is excellent (not perfect). It is not difficult for patients to classify their frequencies into the above categories. It is pretty cut-and-dry.

I won't bore you with the details of Pete's other frequencies—just the one he chose. Remember, the basic environmental details were similar. His name, family members, and parents' occupation were identical. It's Ben himself in this ideal frequency who exhibited some noticeable differences.

Dr. G.:   Where are you now, Ben?
Pete: I'm a senior in college.
Dr. G.:   What is your major?
Pete: Nuclear physics.
Dr. G.:   With what goal?
Pete: I want to go to graduate school and become a nuclear physicist.

Dr. G.:   Do you ever get upset and lose control of your tem-
            per?
Pete: No. What a silly thing that is to ask.

In this frequency, Ben didn't settle for just being a technician.
He went for the brass ring and became a nuclear physicist. In
addition, he didn't exhibit any of the signs of emotional instability that he did in the previous frequency. Thus, there were no
visits to Dr. Margolis and no temper episodes.

Gail still entered Ben's life and they got married when Ben
finished graduate school. They were very much in love and Ben's
parents very much approved of this relationship. I next progressed Ben to the year 2084.

Dr. G.:   Tell me about your work?
Pete: Well, I am a nuclear physicist at our new research
            facility outside of Tulsa.
Dr. G.:   How are things going?
Pete: Quite well. I have an excellent staff and couldn't be
            happier.
Dr. G.:   Tell me about your staff.
Pete: My chief technician is someone I have known for a
            few years. He is also my best friend.
Dr. G.:   Who is that?
Pete: Ralph. Ralph Straeger.

So, you see the pattern changed somewhat. Now Ralph had
the position that Ben had occupied in the previous frequency.
Ben was a highly competent and emotionally stable nuclear
physicist who was also Ralph's boss. Ben and Ralph were still
the best of friends. Their families socialized often and Ben was
a very happy man.

Dr. G.:   Tell me about your father.
Pete: Dad is a psychiatrist. We get along real well.
Dr. G.:   Did he ever want you to follow in his footsteps and
            go to medical school?
Pete: He let me decide what I wanted to do with my life.
            He was totally supportive.

I next progressed Ben to the year 2088.

Dr. G.:   Tell me about your family.

Pete: You mean my wife and children?

Dr. G.   Yes.

Pete: Well, my wife, Gail, is a dream come true. We have two sons. I don't know what else you want to know.

Dr. G.:   Do you ever get into big arguments with Gail?

Pete: Not really. We have minor disagreements like all couples do but we never get mad at each other. We are very much in love.

Dr. G.:   How are your children doing in school?

Pete: Just fine. Especially the oldest, Aaron. He is so bright, even I have a difficult time keeping up with him.

Dr. G.:   Does your father spend much time with them?

Pete: What an odd question to ask. My mother and father visit us occasionally. You must realize that my dad is a very busy man. He attends many medical meetings.

This frequency was indeed ideal and different. By August of 2088 things were very different. Ben had no emotional problems. His son Aaron was an excellent student. His father was alive and well. Ben's relationship with Ralph was excellent and all of the previous frequency's problems seem to have been avoided.

I next progressed Ben to the end of 2088.

Dr. G.:   Tell me about your work.

Pete: I have been working on a technique to help divert nuclear waste safely and to more effectively contain nuclear power.

Dr. G.:   How is it going?

Pete: Quite well. Thanks to an excellent staff and my good friend Ralph, we have successfully tested the techniques.

Dr. G.:   So, it is a success?

Pete: A great success.

Dr. G.:   What is the name of your unit?

Pete: Why, it is called Teres-Alpha.

So the pattern was complete. Pete passed the magical year of 2088 without causing the disaster he had in the previous frequency. He, as Ben, still worked in Teres-Alpha but that name didn't act as a jinx. In fact, you might say it was a good-luck charm.

This frequency had many other positive aspects to it but they are not relevant to Pete's problem. I ended the trance and programmed him to this ideal frequency.

Pete made rapid progress after this session. He no longer feared the number 8 or the name Teresa. He understood what it really meant and why the contamination compulsion was so deeply ingrained within his psyche.

Pete's past lives were causative factors. I cannot ignore them. However, I must put a greater weight on his future lifetime as Ben Kingsley as the cause of his former problems. Being the sole cause of the irreversible contamination of an entire city is far more significant than murdering one man or living an immoral life.

Also, Pete made much more progress after experiencing his future life than in perceiving his past lives. There is no doubt in my mind that the future lifetime of Ben was the main cause of Pete's problem.

Pete today is totally recovered. He did this himself with a little assistance from regression and progression therapy. I like this case because it illustrates the principle that the future is now. We can change the future but we must perceive it first.

The new age of Aquarius that we are in gives us the potential for tremendous opportunities. If you ignore them, then your life won't change much. You will stay on your average or below-average frequencies. However, if you follow the laws of karma, you will switch to a much more desirable frequency, which will not only assure you of a better life in this incarnation, but it will result in more positive future lifetimes. The choice, as always, is yours.

CHAPTER TWENTY-THREE

Past Life Therapy
in the Twenty-second Century

KIM'S CASE IS ONE OF MY FAVORITES BECAUSE IT ILLUS-trates so many of the principles of karma and the space-time continuum. It is not that unusual for a patient to express interest in exploring a future life. What is fascinating, more often than not, are the results.

In 1982, a somewhat overweight saleswoman named Kim called my office with such a request. She hadn't read the first edition of *Past Lives/Future Lives* (Newcastle Publishing Co., 1982) but she had heard of it. If there was such a thing as future lives she wanted to experience it.

My explanations of the theory behind future life progression, the space-time continuum, and hypnotherapy were met with enthusiastic interest. Kim didn't have any background in this field whatsoever. She had just heard about me and my work. Kim had never read books on reincarnation or parapsychology, so she began therapy without a lot of preconceptions.

In late July of 1982 Kim began her trip to a future lifetime. She proved to be an excellent hypnotic patient exhibiting REM (rapid eye movement) throughout her trance.

Dr. G.: What do you perceive?
Kim: I see a young female with dark, shoulder-length hair, dark eyes, small frame, and approximately eighteen years old.
Dr. G.: What is your name?

Kim: Barbara. Barbara Parkhurst.
Dr. G.:   What are you wearing?
Kim: I'm wearing a white jumpsuit with a white shoe-boot.
          The clothes are very lightweight. The boot has a spe-
          cial water bubblelike sole for maximum arch support
          and protection.
Dr. G.:   Are these your daily clothes?
Kim: These are my work clothes.
Dr. G.:   What kind of work do you do?
Kim: I work in an underground research facility.
Dr. G.:   What year is it?
Kim: 2219.
Dr. G.:   You stated that you are underground. Is there some
          specific reason for this?
Kim: Yes. We require isolation. We have no contact with
          the outside world.
Dr. G.:   What do you do exactly?
Kim: We are a think tank. Our purpose is to research and
          develop new concepts, which are highly technical, for
          the ultimate betterment of all humankind.
Dr. G.:   Do you work for the government?
Kim: No. We have no political or government affiliation.
          We are an independently funded research organiza-
          tion.
Dr. G.:   Tell me more about your underground location.
Kim: Our complexes are all underground and completely
          indestructible. Should the entire world see holocaust
          we would be completely unharmed. Hopefully, our
          work will preclude human destruction.
Dr. G.:   What about your family?
Kim: We have no families. We are the result of genetic
          engineering. Only genius-level banks are used and
          properly matched. We are all dedicated to science.
Dr. G.:   What do you feel your purpose is?
Kim: Humans in their natural state are destroying their own
          species gradually. We're working to help humankind
          alleviate primal emotion. It is humankind's only hope
          of survival. The thrust of our work involves positive
          emotional responses. We are aware of human behav-
          ioral patterns and select the positive response en-
          hancement for our research.
Dr. G.:   How many of you are there?
Kim: There are many researchers in many areas. We are all

specialists. It is quite rare for someone outside of our
group to appear on the screen.

The screen referred to a monitor for communication from one
area to another. On very rare occasions a scientist from the
surface might communicate with this group.

Dr. G.: What is your specialty, Barbara?
Kim: My work is with light refraction. I specifically work
with ionization of molecular structure.
Dr. G.: For what purpose?
Kim: By altering the molecular structure of certain components of the brain, we hope to permanently remove
destructive human qualities.

I next progressed Barbara to the age of twenty-two. She further described the underground complex as a series of tunnels
(like a maze) ending in laboratories. There were living quarters
for the researchers and viewing screens were set up at strategic
locations in the complex. Transportation within the complex was
provided by small vehicles powered by air cushions. These vehicles did not touch the ground and were nearly noiseless. One
could detect a faint "whooshing" sound when one of these cars
came by. This apparatus had also been developed by one of the
research groups in the complex.

Dr. G.: How do you learn from the others in your group?
Kim: Learning and analysis is by programming discs. There
is no "personal" teaching. All of our work is placed
on discs and we have free access to any disc we
choose.
Dr. G.: What about your personal life?
Kim: There is no male-female relationship as exists above
ground. We do have feelings of deep-rooted respect
and admiration for one another.
Dr. G.: Is there someone you respect and admire more than
the others?
Kim: Yes.
Dr. G.: And who is that?
Kim: Howard Pennington. There is a special, almost in-
describable, feeling on my part for Howard Pennington. It is not physical attraction but one of intense
professional worship. I wish to sit at his feet and

learn—a master-disciple relationship in its pure
form—this is a pure love uncluttered by physical attraction. I wish to spend every free second in his presence.

Dr. G.: What does Howard work on?

Kim: Howard Pennington is so advanced that it is very difficult for us to comprehend his work. He formerly
developed a vibrational response technique to simulate aboveground "family emotional responses." He
was able to place these on discs for our experiments.
He feels my ionization concept may be able to produce similar effects. I am honored that he would be
so familiar with my work.

Dr. G.: What else did he work on?

Kim: Howard has been working on a time biotelemetry
concept.

Dr. G.: What is that?

Kim: He is attempting to condense a thousand years of time
into a few hours. This way a subject can benefit from
the entire spectrum of human emotions in a very brief
period of time.

Dr. G.: Do you want to be his assistant?

Kim: More than anything in the world.

Dr. G.: Why doesn't Howard have an assistant now?

Kim: Because of our response modes.

Dr. G.: What do you mean?

Kim: We are all in awe of Howard Pennington and his work.
This affects our response modes. Most of our response modes fall into a negative range, usually in the
inferiority complex division.

Dr. G.: Are you qualified to work with Howard?

Kim: It's not that simple. My response modes are quite
consistent. My only problem is in the frustration
mode. However, my consistency rates are superior to
all others in the complex. If any of us will be chosen
to work with Howard, it will be me.

During further conversations with Barbara I found out that
she was able to use her own ionization of molecular structure
technique on herself to qualify as Howard's assistant. She began
working with Howard and with her assistance, his work advanced rapidly.

Dr. G.:   How are things going?

Kim: Quite well. We have modified some of our initial approaches to make the outcome more feasible.

Dr. G.:   What do you mean?

Kim: Howard preferred discs to allowing a subject to actually experience different lifetimes for every emotion known. The time it takes to do this is just a few hours.

Dr. G.:   But isn't the subject confused?

Kim: Not really. It is not necessary for the subject to remember or even understand the lives. We are only interested in the emotional cleansing and reprogramming.

Well, it looked as if past life regression therapy were alive and well in the twenty-second century. The principles I practice today are utilized by Howard, with some condensing of time commitments. Barbara and Howard worked very well together. They perfected this technique and had many successful responses from their subjects.

Dr. G.:   What will happen now?

Kim: The results are being sent to the surface and will be used at specific treatment centers.

These treatment centers functioned like psychological clinics. Patients with emotional problems were treated using Howard's past life therapy discs. It proved quite effective.

Dr. G.:   Are you still working with Howard?

Kim: Yes, I'm so excited about his success. Now I'm even more thrilled.

Dr. G.:   Why? Did something else occur?

Kim: Yes. Howard has consented to utilize his technique on me. I can't believe it. Imagine, shortly I will be made to reexperience my past lives and benefit by the resulting emotional cleansing.

Dr. G.:   But won't it be difficult for you to remember them since this is a condensation approach?

Kim: Normally, yes. Because I have been such a help to Howard, he has made special arrangements to slow the procedure down so I can remember these lives.

Thus began the past life explanation of a future life researcher named Barbara Parkhurst. I will attempt to describe the regressions as facilitated by Howard's discs. This most unusual approach proved very informative and therapeutic to Kim.

Barbara regressed back to the early eighteenth century in France. She was a teenage servant girl to a French nobleman named Charles. Her name was Antoinette and the chief servants were Sofie and Josef.

Dr. G.: Tell me about your life, Antoinette. What do you enjoy about it?

Kim: I like being a servant. Charles is kind to all of us. I also like eating the leftover pastries.

Kim had a sweet tooth and the origin of it was not difficult to elicit. Antoinette was very fond of Charles because he treated her and the other servants so well.

Dr. G.: Does Charles ask you to do anything of a special nature?

Kim: If you mean does he take me to bed, the answer is yes. It's part of my duties. I do not mind. Charles is a kind man and I am honored that he allows me to please him.

Apparently, Charles treated Antoinette especially well. She was his favorite and Antoinette fell in love with him. I progressed Antoinette forward to a significant event.

Dr. G.: Antoinette, has anything important occurred since I last spoke to you?

Kim: Yes (crying).

Dr. G.: What is it?

Kim: I'm going to have Charles's baby. I'm so happy.

Dr. G.: What about Charles's wife?

Kim: No one must know that I'm pregnant. Charles's wife is quite frail and all of their previous attempts at children resulted in stillborn babies. She must not know of the child.

Dr. G.: How will you hide this pregnancy?

Kim: Charles is taking me to his summer house. His wife never goes there. Tom, the head of the stable, will look after me. Charles will tell his wife that I was dismissed.

So Antoinette moved into the summer house. Tom took care of her and Charles visited Antoinette about every ten days.

Dr. G.:   Wasn't this a bit unusual?
Kim: Charles took care of everything. It was very lonely but Charles arranged for Tom to marry me so the child wouldn't be a bastard. Only Sofie, Josef, and Tom knew about the baby.
Dr. G.:   What else did Charles do?
Kim: He gave Tom a beautiful horse as well as the servants' quarters for him to live in. I stayed in the big house. Charles told Tom never to touch me and he never did even though I was his wife. Charles could never marry me. He married for land.
Dr. G.:   How did Charles treat you at the summer house?
Kim: He treated me as though I were a lady instead of a servant. He brought me fine clothes, sweets, and exotic foods. He never gave me a wig. He didn't like them on ladies. Charles liked real hair.

I progressed Antoinette forward to the birth of the baby.

Dr. G.:   Tell me what has happened.
Kim: The baby was a boy and we named him David. Charles brought me a ring with a ruby in it. I felt like I was his wife. The women who helped me deliver David were sent away by Tom so that no one would see Charles. He stayed with me for two days. He never did that before and I never wanted him to leave us. He always came to see us when he went hunting, but he always returned the same day.
Dr. G.:   What about other visitors coming to the summer house?
Kim: Charles didn't bring anyone to the summer house anymore. He told these friends that his wife was too sick and all of his socializing was done at the estate.

When David was two years old Charles's wife died in childbirth and their baby died also. Charles decided to remarry to acquire more land.

Dr. G.:   Whom did Charles marry?
Kim: Charles married a foreigner. She was beautiful and

wealthy. She was also quite ruthless and Charles seemed a little afraid of her.

Dr. G.: Didn't that worry Charles?

Kim: No. Since she was a woman, she had no real power as long as Charles was lord.

Dr. G.: What about you?

Kim: Charles didn't really like her. This was strictly a business deal. I was unhappy because I felt jealous, afraid she might have a son and Charles would leave us and forget all about David and me.

Dr. G.: What else did you feel?

Kim: I felt sorry for his other wife. She was so sickly. I felt better than her because I'd given Charles a son. I never feared his first wife. The new woman made me fear losing Charles. She suspected Charles was seeing another woman, but she expected it to be a lady—not me.

Dr. G.: What did Charles do about her suspicions?

Kim: He rejected her because she confronted him and fought with him. She hurt his pride. A French lord should never be questioned by a woman.

Dr. G.: What happened as a result of this?

Kim: He came to us more often and he loved David more and more. He brought us more gifts. We never asked him for anything. Charles kept telling me how much his wife was frustrating him. I started to feel safe again. He told us that he would always take care of us and that his wife would never be able to hurt us.

Dr. G.: Were you always faithful to Charles?

Kim: Yes. I never had any man but Charles and I never asked for any gift except my little goat, Julia. When Charles first brought me to the summer house he said I could have a gift and since I knew I'd be lonely I asked for Julia. I used to play with her at the estate. She was company for me.

Dr. G.: Did he bring Julia to you?

Kim: Yes, he did. I told him Sofie knew which goat was Julia. He had Tom bring her to me over his horse. Besides the goat, I never asked for anything. I did love and appreciate everything Charles brought us. He couldn't stay with us much but he thought he'd done everything to make us happy and he did all he could.

Dr. G.:   Didn't Charles have other lovers?

Kim: He had a lot of women for bedding. He wasn't faithful to anyone, but I think he truly loved us. The rich ones all had a lot of women. Charles wasn't bad, but I still wished he could be faithful to me as I was to him.

As time went on Antoinette became more and more attracted to Charles. She was very much in love with him, even though she was quite aware of his faults and his life-style. I next progressed Antoinette to the most significant event that was to occur in her life.

Dr. G.:   Where are you now?

Kim: Oh, my God! I don't know what to do. Please help me.

Dr. G.:   What happened?

Kim: Charles is dead. He had a heart attack and died in my arms.

After calming her down I tried to follow the next chain of events carefully. Tom helped Antoinette dispose of Charles's body. It could not be found in the house. Tom buried Charles in the woods.

Dr. G.:   What is going on?

Kim: We had to get all of our personal effects out of the house quickly. I packed everything and ran to the servants' house with Tom. I changed into my old clothes and put all of my fancy clothes and gifts from Charles in bags. Tom buried these bags in the woods.

Dr. G.:   Please tell me what is happening.

Kim: Charles's wife was sending four men to look for Charles's kept woman and Tom was afraid they would kill us.

Dr. G.:   But didn't you tell me that all wealthy French lords had many women? Why should she care about you?

Kim: They had many women but a kept woman is something else. I represented more of a threat to her. In addition, she heard rumors about a son by this kept woman and this made me especially dangerous to her.

Dr. G.:   Does she know about Charles's death.

Kim: No, that would be impossible. He just died a few hours ago.

Dr. G.:   What did Tom do next?

Kim: He told me that these men were searching all of
          Charles's houses with orders to kill the girl and the
          child. Tom made us stay in the servants' house. He
          covered my hands with dirt and messed up my hair.
          He dressed little David in old clothes and made him
          look dirty, too. He told me I wasn't to cry for Charles
          or show any emotions when the soldiers came.

I next progressed Antoinette to the arrival of the soldiers.

Dr. G.:   What did the soldiers do?

Kim: The soldiers burst into the big house and searched it.
          Then they came to the servants' house and questioned
          Tom. David and I were working in the garden and we
          could hear Tom telling the soldiers that we were his
          wife and son. He told them a lady came to the big
          house to see Charles a long time ago but hadn't come
          for a long time. He said Charles had never allowed
          him to see her and he didn't know who she was.

Dr. G.:   What happened next?

Kim: The soldiers believed Tom and left. They never came
          back. We were still afraid and never returned to the
          big house. We stayed in Tom's house and wore ugly
          clothes and ate awful food.

Dr. G.:   Did Tom get close to you?

Kim: Oh, no. He stayed in the stable. He was honorable to
          Charles's wishes. Tom acted like our servant.

Later Charles's wife took over the estate. She was quite cruel
and ruthless. The soldiers reported their conversation with Tom
to her. She thought Tom was purposely hiding the true identity
of Charles's kept woman from her. She sent Tom away on a long
journey for special materials for her clothes. Antoinette never
saw Tom again.

Dr. G.:   What did you do?

Kim: I sold the ruby ring Charles gave me to buy food. We
          were cold and had no place to go. David later died.

Dr. G.:   Then what?

Kim: I buried him next to Charles. I then sat in a corner of
          the servants' house and cried. I never ate again.

Antoinette died of starvation pining away for Charles and David. In the superconscious level I was able to find out that Charles was Kim's ex-husband. She divorced him because he "cheated" on her once too often. He was a very materialistic and manipulative man. David came back as Kim's son, Jeremy. They are very close.

The important point in this life was Antoinette's early attraction to sweets. For a servant girl sweets were a welcome change to the dull food normally eaten. As Charles's kept woman they represented a special reward and reminded her of him. The starvation end to that life carried over in Kim's constant and losing battle with dieting.

Barbara Parkhurst was very much affected by this life. Howard Pennington was most pleased with this experience and the following day he "disced" Barbara back into another one of her past lives.

This lifetime took place in Rome in the early part of the sixteenth century. Barbara was a nineteen-year-old guard to the pope and named Paolo. His life seemed without purpose. He did his job well but didn't seem to have any friends; he just seemed to be existing.

Dr. G.: Paolo, tell me about your family.
Kim: I didn't really know my family. I was raised by the Church. My mother was a prostitute in Florence and my father was a nobleman.
Dr. G.: Does that make you a bastard?
Kim: Yes. I'm the bastard son of a nobleman and a prostitute. Some combination, huh!
Dr. G.: Did you ever go back to visit your mother?
Kim: No. The Church forbade me to ever go back to Florence.
Dr. G.: Does that bother you?
Kim: No. I don't miss not having real parents; I just do my job.

I then progressed Paolo forward to a significant time in his life. He reported being sent on some assignment with a number of other soldiers. They were sent by the army to kill the inhabitants of a small village.

Dr. G.: Why are you sent here?
Kim: I do not question my orders.

Dr. G.:   Do you really want to kill these defenseless people?
Kim: No, I don't, but if I disobey my orders I will be killed.

Paolo was the youngest soldier sent to exterminate this village. He had never killed anyone before and didn't want to begin now.

Dr. G.:   Tell me what you do.
Kim: Well, there weren't that many people in the village to begin with. The other soldiers rounded them up and killed them. I was supposed to kill this woman and her child.
Dr. G.:   Did you?
Kim: No.
Dr. G.:   How did you manage that?
Kim: I put my sword into the body of a man lying dead on the street. Then I told the woman and boy to hide and wait for us to go. I also told her to move to another village the following day and never to return to this place again.
Dr. G.:   And your sword?
Kim: The blood on my sword from the dead man's body was used to convince my fellow soldiers that I had carried out my orders.

This plan apparently worked quite well. Paolo returned to Rome and remained a guard in the Vatican.

Dr. G.:   What has happened since I last spoke to you?
Kim: I met a beautiful girl named Julianna. We were married and I am very happy.
Dr. G.:   Do you have any children?
Kim: Yes, we have one son, Antonio.

As the years went by Paolo finally had a purpose. He loved Julianna and Antonio. The problem was his attitude toward his employers. When Antonio expressed interest in becoming a guard like his father, Paolo told him to find another occupation.

Dr. G.:   Why do you discourage Antonio from following in your footsteps?
Kim: These men I guard, they are not holy.
Dr. G.:   Are you referring to the pope?

Kim: No. The Church noblemen I guard now seem to be
          more like politicians. I do not trust them. I do not
          think they are real God-fearing men. I do not respect
          them and I don't care if they live or die.

Dr. G.:   Isn't that a big problem, since you guard them?

Kim: I do my job, but I don't like it. The only thing I care
          about are Julianna and Antonio. Antonio and I some-
          times go to the market. He carries bread and fruit in
          a bag. I love him and feel very proud of him. Nothing
          else in my life has any meaning

Later on Antonio became an apprentice to a craftsman. Paolo
was proud of his son. He was still a guard and quite frustrated
in his job. I next progressed Paolo to a significant time in his
life.

Dr. G.:   What has happened since we last spoke?

Kim: I am very sad.

Dr. G.:   Why?

Kim: My wife and son are gone. They both died of a fever.
          Here I am thirty-five years old and now life is com-
          pletely meaningless.

I asked Paolo about whether he contemplated suicide and he
said no. He did report that he didn't like working with the foreign guards in the Vatican. I then progressed Paolo forward to
the end of his life.

Dr. G.:   Where are you now, Paolo?

Kim: I'm on guard duty.

Dr. G.:   Tell me what happens next.

Kim: I was making my rounds one night and all of a sudden
          someone jumped me by the edge of the building. He
          put his sword through me above the stomach and be-
          tween my ribs. I started to fall when he pulled it out,
          but then I started drifting up and there was no pain. I
          felt free and glad to be free. I knew instantly that I
          was dead and was pleased to be rid of that life.

It is interesting to observe the complete lack of emotion exhibited by Paolo. He was, indeed, most happy to be rid of the
life of a burned-out guard in the sixteenth century in Rome.
From the superconscious mind level Kim (Barbara) reported

that Antonio was her current son, Jeremy. She did not identify Julianna or the village woman and her son whom she had saved. An interesting sidelight to this is that Kim attended a Christian seminary and earned a degree in theology. Although she never used this background professionally, she had a strange attraction to formal study of the Bible. To this day she keeps away from all forms of formal religion.

I did some checking myself on the events in Rome during the early part of the sixteenth century and ascertained some interesting facts. In 1527 Charles V of France ordered the sack of Rome. He took Pope Clement prisoner. Swiss guards along with local guards protected the pope. The *Encyclopedia Americana* stated that the Swiss guards suffered heavy losses in 1527. Paolo mentioned being separated from the foreign guards but on that fateful day being with them.

Another fact of interest in validating the accuracy of this life was the description of the Vatican by Paolo. Paolo did not remember a statue of Saint Paul atop the column of Marcus Aurelius. As it turns out, one of the Popes had the statue of Marcus Aurelius removed and replaced it with Saint Paul's statue in 1589, about sixty-two years after Paolo's death. Thus Paolo correctly would not have seen Saint Paul's statue during his lifetime.

Barbara Parkhurst returned to the twenty-second century a little confused and a little drained. She and Howard discussed these two lives in great detail. She was quite anxious to continue with her past life exploration, so the following day was set aside for her third trip back in time.

Barbara's next past life took her back well over a thousand years. She was a Chinese girl named Soon Lin. Soon Lin was about fourteen years old and worked in rice paddies doing some sort of farming. She was dressed in rough-looking dark clothes that resembled pajamas. She wore no shoes and she spent most of the day standing in water.

Soon Lin described her family as large yet close. They were very poor but proud people. I progressed her to an important day in her life.

Dr. G.:   Where are you now?
Kim: I'm working in the fields. What's that?
Dr. G.:   What's what?
Kim: Those warriors are coming this way.
Dr. G.:   What warriors?

Kim: I noticed them before. It is not uncommon to see warriors ride by the fields. They rarely stop but today is different.

Dr. G.:   Where are they now?

Kim: They stopped by the edge of the fields. They are staring at me and the other girls. I am afraid.

Dr. G.:   What happens next?

Kim: One of the warriors charges into the water and nearly tramples one of my sisters. He's heading toward me. I am afraid—

The warrior grabbed Soon Lin and pulled her onto his horse. He brought her out of the fields and stopped his horse in front of her parents.

Dr. G.:   What did he do next?

Kim: He tossed a small pouch at my father and nodded his head toward me. I guess that meant that he was paying for me with those coins.

Dr. G.:   What did your father do?

Kim: He just nodded in agreement and the warrior rode off with me.

So without a word being said this Chinese warrior bought Soon Lin. He took her with him and joined his fellow warriors and rode away. Some hours later they stopped to set up camp. The warrior took Soon Lin's clothes off and stared at her body. Apparently, this was to see if she was a virgin. She passed the test.

Soon Lin was taken to some kind of village. There she was resold by the warrior to an elderly, obese, and quite ugly Chinese man. Soon Lin fainted when she realized that she had been sold to this grotesque man. The next thing she remembered was waking up in a tent, lying on a bunch of satin pillows.

Dr. G.:   Where are you now, Soon Lin?

Kim: I . . . I don't know. I guess it must be this man's home. His name is Chu.

Dr. G.:   Where is Chu now?

Kim: He is in this tent with two other women. They are older than me and very pretty. Oh—his nails are disgusting.

Dr. G.:   What do you mean?

Kim: He has fingernails that go all the way to the ground.
           It looks disgusting.
Dr. G.:   What happens next.
Kim: Chu comes toward me and hits me across the face.
           Then he rips my clothes off and rapes me right in front
           of the other two women. They laugh as he physically
           abuses me and totally ignore my screams.
Dr. G.:   How long does this continue?
Kim: I don't know. I fainted again and when I awoke I had
           bruises and scratches all over my body.

This went on for over a week. One night Soon Lin couldn't
take it any longer and ran away.

Dr. G.:   Where did you go?
Kim: I ran away to a neighboring village and found a kindly
           old man who lived with his son. He agreed to let me
           stay there and hide away for a while.
Dr. G.:   Did the old man keep his word?
Kim: Yes, for a few days anyway.
Dr. G.:   Then what?
Kim: Some soldiers came later and the boy told me to run
           away fast. His father had accepted some money from
           the soldiers and told them where I was hiding.
Dr. G.:   Did you escape?
Kim: No, I didn't have a chance. The soldiers caught me,
           hit me, and took me back to Chu.
Dr. G.:   What happened to the old man?
Kim: They killed his son for trying to help me. Then they
           took the money they gave him back. He was broken-
           hearted but still alive.

Apparently, Soon Lin was considered Chu's property. She
was bought and now his. He could do whatever he pleased to
her. When she returned to Chu's tent her right leg was broken.
She healed very slowly and walked with a decisive limp. This
was done so she couldn't run away again.

Dr. G.:   What did you do then?
Kim: I stayed and took care of Chu's women. I was some
           sort of a servant but still his toy. He physically abused
           me whenever he felt like it. He made fun of my leg
           and beat me for sport. I hate him.

This went on for about a year. Soon Lin tried to run away again. This time she didn't get very far. She was caught and her right leg was cut off in front of the other women. She slowly bled to death.

From the superconscious level she identified Chu as her ex-husband and the boy who had tried to save her when the old man had sold her out to the warrior, as her son, Jeremy. The lesson she was supposed to learn was humility and submission. She did learn the former but not the latter.

An interesting aside on this life is that Kim later reported to me that she hated long fingernails. She had a favorite aunt who would wear them and she would feel very uncomfortable until her aunt took them off.

Barbara Parkhurst was getting quite a lot out of these past lives. She and Howard discussed them in detail after every session. Howard was beginning to see the benefit of these more slowly done regressions as compared to the instant regressions he had initially programmed into the discs.

The stage was set for another regression. Howard prepared Barbara for her fourth trip back in time.

This time Barbara had also chosen ancient China. She was a male named Yun Chang. He was in training to be an adviser to the emperor. Yun Chang was at some sort of a monastery, surrounded by beautiful statues, Oriental rugs, and other fine things.

Dr. G.: What is it that you study?

Kim: I study everything. The fine arts, history, philosophy, meditation. All knowledge is at my disposal.

Dr. G.: You sound like a man of peace.

Kim: I am.

Dr. G.: But is the emperor also a man of peace?

Kim: I do not know much about him. It does not matter. I will advise him according to my training.

Dr. G.: Do you train with others?

Kim: Yes, there are three others. We will all advise the emperor.

Dr. G.: Is your training identical to that of the other three students?

Kim: No, not quite. We all have our specialties but we also have a common goal.

Dr. G.: And what is that?

Kim: We will advise our leader so that he may best serve the common good.

As the years passed Yun Chang and his three colleagues graduated and advised the emperor. However Wu Dee was not an emperor of peace. He liked war and made it clear to his advisers that he would not take kindly to being advised to keep peace when war was a viable option.

Dr. G.:   If Wu Dee wants to declare war all the time, then why does he need advisers?

Kim: He doesn't look for war all the time. There are many matters of state that require our expertise and we are consulted.

Dr. G.:   But haven't you sold out to the system?

Kim: We have compromised to serve the common good.

So all of Yun Chang's idealism went down the drain. He sold out to the system. His advice was governed by fear—fear for his own life.

I next moved Yun Chang forward to the most crucial time in his life.

Dr. G.:   What is occurring now?

Kim: Wu Dee has called us together to sanction a rather large war.

Dr. G.:   Does Wu Dee need your sanction?

Kim: No, but if we do not agree, he will execute us.

Dr. G.:   How did you decide?

Kim: We took a vote. Two said no and two said yes, including me. I allowed intellect to cloud my judgment and convinced them that we must all say yes to war.

Dr. G.:   Did they all agree?

Kim: Yes, and I was honored for my judgment.

Wu Dee accepted their sanctions and declared war. He was very successful and honored his advisers. Yun Chang was made chief adviser.

Dr. G.:   What else happened?

Kim: I was given a special house to live in with servants. I falsely convinced myself that we were wise to sanction war.

This went on for years. Every time they agreed with Wu Dee they were honored and given additional privileges. From the superconscious level Yun Chang realized he failed to accomplish or display any wisdom. Wisdom is not mere intellect but a combination of intellect, understanding, and compassion.

Yun Chang's intellectual judgment was neither wise nor deserving of honor. He misused his influence over others to allow a unanimous sanctioning of war. Arrogant pride and fear perpetuated this rubber stamping of Wu Dee's ruthless endeavors.

It is most interesting to note that the Yun Chang life preceded the life of Soon Lin. Perhaps the life of Soon Lin was both a karmic retribution as well as a true lesson in the unlearned humility corridor of Kim's karmic cycle.

Meanwhile, back in the twenty-second century, Barbara Parkhurst and Howard Pennington began comparing notes of the former's past lives. They worked well together but nothing romantic developed. This was a different type of society. Barbara had reached her pinnacle of success by working with Howard Pennington.

Howard also benefited by this arrangement. He was able to see his research as it applied to a distinguished colleague, not just a subject sent down from the surface. After a period of further testing, Howard modified his discs to slow down the process of regressing. It wasn't as slow as it is today but it also wasn't as condensed as the "ninety mile-an-hour" method he originally conceived.

Barbara learned a lot from Howard. They worked together for many years in their isolated facility underground. The past life regressions taught her many lessons. She learned about her past, her deficiencies, and her challenges. As Barbara, Kim learned what it would be like to work with a man she held in high esteem, with a higher love.

In spite of Howard's superior mind, Barbara did not shy away from the challenge or allow herself to fall into the negative response mode characterized by an inferiority complex. She rose above this. As a result of the trust and reverence in which she viewed Howard, Howard only reinforced her commitment to dedicate her life to bettering humankind.

But who was Howard in Barbara's past? He did not show up in any of her four past life regressions. Did he suddenly just materialize in the twenty second century? The answer was no. Kim informed me from the superconscious mind level of Howard's real identity. Many years ago Kim dated a man named George. George was a truly kind and beautiful man. They had been engaged to be married.

But fate would not allow this union. George contracted a rare form of leukemia and was hospitalized. Kim visited him every day with tears in her eyes. She prayed every night for his speedy recovery. Perhaps it was a flashback to Antoinette's desire for Charles or Paolo's yearning for Julianna, but George just wasted away and slowly died.

Kim could not hold back the tears as she described this to me. "So close and yet so far" was all she could say. It took her a long time to get over losing George. She never really got over George. Her ex-husband never knew about her previous lover and fiancé. It was for the best that she kept George a secret.

The relationship between Kim and her son, Jeremy, was quite close. Kim could see him as David and the son of the old Chinese man. This was the only saving grace from her marriage.

The result of this future life progression was amazing. Kim lost weight. She dressed better and developed a positive self-image. She made much progress in her career as a saleswoman, giving up her tendencies to procrastinate.

She described her views as follows: "Love is the key to everything. This really makes me feel like I'm on the right track. One aspect of love that I felt for Howard during the progression was complemented by the love I have for God."

Kim improved because now she has a true purpose. It will take 130 years but she will be with George again. George will be Howard Pennington. They will complete their mission together.

The future is now, Kim; enjoy it.

CHAPTER TWENTY-FOUR

What Is It Like to Die?

DEATH IS A DEPRESSING, FEARFUL TOPIC TO MOST PEOple. Yet, we all know that death, like taxes, is unavoidable. In this chapter I will explore accounts of death from my patients who have been regressed or progressed. In nearly every past life regression I have participated in and in many I present in this book there is an inevitable moment of death to explore—and in each patient's account, the findings are always much the same.

Actually, death itself is not a traumatic experience. It is the birth process that is traumatic. Imagine for a moment that you are very ill and lying in a hospital bed. Then imagine your astral body lifting out and all of a sudden you are dead. It takes hours, days, or even weeks to realize that you are, in fact, dead. That is hardly traumatic. All pain and other discomforts are completely removed at the moment of death.

Now imagine yourself being born. The newborn has just acquired a subconscious and has left its cozy womb for a bright, sterile environment that is totally different and most uncomfortable compared to what it has been used to for nine months. The newborn is slapped, footprinted, suctioned, swabbed, processed, and totally dependent on strangers in white uniforms for its very survival. There is no direct data on the actual pain of the birth process, but imagine ice-cold steel forceps around your head, or a premature delivery. Personally, birth seems more intimidating to me than dying.

Eliminating the fear of death is one of the greatest benefits of regression and progression therapy. The realization that death is not an end but a birth into a larger, fuller, and more meaningful life is quite beautiful. Death is merely an exchange of an old body for a new one. Death signifies the beginning of a rest and reevaluation period. It is a form of re-creation and renewal. It is a transition state, not a state of termination. Death may be hard to explain or to understand, but it not to be feared.

Many problems patients ask me to help them with have their origins in past-life death scenes. Once these death scenes are relived, the symptoms disappear accordingly. A traumatic death, such as falling off a cliff, could result in a fear of heights. Reliving this fall often results in the elimination of the phobia.

For the time being I would like you to put aside thoughts of heaven, hell, and even purgatory. Put aside religious convictions and open your mind to what I have to say. Of course, you don't have to accept this information. All I ask is that you consider it with an open mind.

When we die we are really not dead in the common use of the word. We may be nonfunctional on the earth plane but we are quite functional on other planes. We exist then on the astral plane, and eventually we will enter the white light and end up on the soul plane. So, what we think of as death is really shifting to another plane of existence.

Before I go into details about the parapsychological explanations of death, let me give you some medical facts. The cells in our body are dying and being replaced constantly. One of the purposes of the sleep state, at least from a medical point of view, is to re-create the many millions of cells that are killed during each day that we live. We are also replacing lost energy during sleep. Scientists tell us that about every nine months, each and every one of our cells has been replaced at least once.

So, technically, we die every nine months. Our body is completely different from how it was one year ago and will be completely different at this time next year. We obviously don't feel dead and are able to function quite nicely. The process of cell replacement continues along so smoothly that we are not aware of anything different happening. It is our physical perception that is being fooled into thinking that the body is unchanged from year to year.

THE EXPERIENCE OF DEATH

What seems to happen at death is that you experience, at least initially, what you *expect* to experience. In other words, your expectations of what death should be like seem to affect the actual experience or perception of death. A belief in the fires of hell or the clouds of heaven will often manifest themselves, temporarily at least. Fortunately these fantasies disappear quickly and you are joined by Masters and Guides. These angel-like entities will try and help you adjust to the astral plane. They will guide you into a gradual realization that you have died and it is time to move on. You may not even accept that you have died at first, because you really won't feel much different. There is, however, one very significant difference: you are now totally free of any discomfort. Your new environment will be far less limiting than that of the physical plane, which you have just left.

On the astral plane, you may find yourself in the presence of dead relatives or friends. Telepathy is the rule now, so that your true feelings toward that friend or relative will be made known, and vice versa. There is no hypocrisy on the astral plane.

When you go to sleep every night, out-of-body experiences occur and simulate the death experience. This simulated death state is merely training for later. Dreams of flying or falling are conscious remnants of this astral projection.

I alluded earlier to the white light. This white light is an express train to the soul plane—the plane where you will evaluate your past life and choose your next one. Your Masters and Guides and "dead" relatives and friends will advise you to enter this white light. If you do, then all is well and good. But, as I've mentioned before, if you don't, you become what is known as a "troubled spirit" and remain on the astral plane, unsure of who you are and what you are supposed to be doing. You can be observed on the earth plane as a ghost or you can be unobserved and just wander around aimlessly. You will be reminded again and again by your Masters and Guides to enter the white light. But nothing can force you to do so.

Think of it this way. You have just died. Perhaps the moments preceding death were a very traumatic experience. You are immersed with expectations of heaven or hell. Now some unknown entity tries to convince you to enter this blinding white light. You are frightened and resist. Remember that the soul always has free will. It's not difficult to see how someone might be hesitant to jump out of the frying pan and into the proverbial fire, but the white light absolutely must be entered in order to reach the soul plane. The task is now before you. What is real? What is imaginary? What is good? What is evil? Who are the good guys? Who or what are the bad guys? These questions may have to be answered before the soul will decide to enter the white light.

The soul will use its judgment as to who or what to trust. It is the soul alone that will make this decision. The state of mind at death, the karmic cycle, the environment on the astral plane, and other factors will help to make this determination. It may take a few hours or a century for this answer. A more experienced soul that just completed a positive life, karmically, would require less time and would much more likely make the correct decision.

Interestingly, there is rarely any form of correlation between a person's religion and his or her experience of death. In other words, it doesn't seem to matter whether the patient is an agnostic, atheist, Christian, Jew, Hindu, or any other belief; the experiences reported to me are similar.

There are many types of reactions that my patients report to me when they relive a death scene in a past life regression. I will discuss only the most common descriptions my patients have given of the death experience.

CROSSING OVER

First, a floating sensation is almost always described. Whatever physical discomforts the patient may have felt at the moment of death are completely gone. There is no pain or any other feeling at the moment. The patient is simply floating. Feelings of inner peace and quiet, with a complete absence of fear, are quite common. The body below is now viewed as if it were no longer a part of the patient. Indeed, this is exactly the case. Let me repeat, there is absolutely no danger of the patient's really dying, even in very deep trance levels, while reliving the death experience from a past life.

Patients soon realize that they have a body, but a very different type of body, subject to very different physical laws. This astral body possesses the ability to do many things that the physical body cannot. For example, this astral body can move through walls and doors and travel thousands of miles in a matter of seconds. Time is not registered at this level, and the astral body possesses complete knowledge of the former life and can even read the minds of other people who were involved in that life.

THE SILVER CORD

One constant observation that people have reported to me is the presence of a "silver cord." Theoretically, when one experiences an astral projection not related to a death experience, there is a silver cord attached to the back of the head of the astral body and to the solar plexus region of the physical body here on earth. As long as this silver cord is unbroken, the patient's physical body is still alive. Upon death this silver cord is broken.

DEATH SOUNDS

Another observation is auditory. People hear all sorts of noises following death. Buzzing sounds that appear to originate from inside the head are commonly reported; loud ringing sounds, clicks, roars, banging noises, whistling, and musical sounds. One theory that has been proposed states that each plane has a characteristic combination of light and sound, and this will change as one ascends or descends to different planes. The individual's vibrational rate is also changing. At this time many bright colors are often seen. They change frequently and seem to move by at a very rapid rate.

THE TUNNEL

The feeling of moving through a long, dark tunnel is, in my opinion, the most fascinating and important observation of the death experience. Some patients use the term "vacuum." It seems as if the patient is being drawn into this tunnel, and once in this dark structure they are transported to the other side, or astral plane. This may be comparable to a time warp or a black hole.

When I regress or progress patients, I usually suggest they

imagine themselves entering a tunnel that has a bright white light at the end. I suggest that there is a fork at the end of the tunnel. If the patient takes the right fork he or she ends up in a past life. A future life would be the destination if the left fork were taken. This technique is very successful and one of the most commonly used methods of guiding a patient into a past or future life. Whether in a hypnotic state or death, the tunnel clearly seems to represent the passageway to the next level.

THE PRESENCE OF OTHERS

Once the patient is able to stabilize him- or herself after emerging from the tunnel and to adjust to the floating sensation, the presence of others is noted. By "others," I am referring to Masters and Guides who come to offer their help and guidance. Also, the patient may report seeing "dead" relatives and friends who try to help. All communication is by telepathy at this time. A feeling of warmth, security, and inner peace is usually prevalent. The patient is made to feel loved; all fears of death are removed.

THE WHITE LIGHT

The white light is the culmination of the death experience. The patient is shown the white light, which at this time will appear as an almost blinding yet peaceful aura of pure white light. This light is very similar to the image used in various healing techniques on the earth plane. By imagining that they are surrounding the damaged part of the body with this white light, patients have facilitated their own healing. On the astral plane, the patient will benefit most if he or she enters the white light, where he or she will be taken to the soul plane to reevaluate this last life and choose the next one. But, as I have mentioned before, not everyone chooses to enter the white light immediately and some may wander around the lower astral plane for many years or even centuries before they finally do enter.

INDIVIDUAL VARIATIONS

The experiences of death don't always follow the order I've described. Also, there may be time lags between each step. Some people accept the death state quickly and easily. Others require more time and guidance before they will even accept the idea of death, let alone enter the white light.

Remember, it is your expectations of what the death state is supposed to be that will affect the actual experience. If you expect to be surrounded by haloed angels in white robes playing harps, your Masters and Guides will do their very best to create that scene for you because they know that it will make you feel comfortable. It is only when you are comfortable that these higher entities will inform you about where you are and who they are and what you are supposed to be doing.

The main point of this chapter is to demonstrate that death is not an experience to fear. Perhaps it is not something to look forward to, but it is not to be feared.

Accounts of death from past life regressions may not be sufficient evidence for some of you. There have been numerous reports of patients pronounced clinically dead who eventually survived. When asked of their experiences, they have reported startlingly similar observations to those presented here. Yet these people experiencing near-death have usually never heard of past life regression.

If people from different religious backgrounds who are regressed, and people who have clinically died and returned to life, all report similar experiences, the correspondences between these descriptions are more than coincidental. Yet, in the final analysis, you must form your own opinions. Death is an experience you will face many times. It is up to you to interpret this concept to fit your own particular beliefs.

My intention is to remove much of the misconception about the experience, so that when the time comes for you to die, your experience will be as peaceful and serene as possible. In previous chapters, you have seen many reassuringly similar accounts of the death experience. If, by reading this chapter, you have shed even one aspect of your fear, my efforts have been worthwhile.

CHAPTER TWENTY-FIVE

Karma: When Does It All End?

DOES THE CYCLE OF BIRTH AND REBIRTH EVER END? OF course it does. One of the purposes of this book is to show you how to improve your own karmic cycle. By showing you that you will live again, and that your future life will be far more pleasant and fulfilling if you follow the laws of karma wisely, I hope to help you help yourself.

Some of you may still have strong feelings of disbelief, skepticism, and mistrust. Others may gain additional support for their beliefs and hope for the future from reading this book. My hope is that you keep your mind open. It is not hypnotherapists who heal, it is you who have the ultimate responsibility. Past life regression and progression into future lives allow you to expand and explore your awareness and eliminate fear, anxiety, depression, and other negative tendencies, as well as the fear of death.

Hypnotherapy is neither magic nor a panacea. It is a way to help shape the future. By creating your own reality with the knowledge from your subconscious and superconscious minds, you can positively affect your present and future lives.

Karma is simply cause and effect. It is totally just. One might describe it as a practical code of ethics. You are in control of your karma. Every soul plays the part of judge and jury. You can only fool yourself—temporarily. Karma teaches you that you have only yourself to blame or credit for your life. Do not look to somebody else as a scapegoat. "To thine own self be true."

There must be a system to explain our happiness and distress. Some mechanism must be at work to determine who gets what and why. Karma, with its mechanism of reincarnation, is the best answer I have found. Luck doesn't explain the content or the quality of our lives; coincidence doesn't explain them. Karma does. "Do unto others" is a reality and a positive way to live.

With technological advancement there is a trend toward depersonalization in our world. Our lives seem to be numbered, sorted, stamped, and processed without a human mind to mediate the action. But self-identification is still within us all. By tapping our subconscious we can find out who we really are and what makes us tick. It is when we reach our threshold of tolerance of the processed world around us that we rebel with violence, hatred, and fear. By looking within ourselves, we can improve our individual lives and the quality of society as a whole. As a result, we can have an optimistic vision of our collective future.

We sometimes forget that there is a God. God doesn't punish us. We punish ourselves. As one sows, so shall one reap. We will find ourselves in far more pleasant surroundings in our next life if we make the most of our opportunities to serve our fellow men and women now. If we steal in this life, our possessions will be stolen from us. If we kill, we, too, shall die by violence. We will escape our karmic cycle when we end it by learning, loving, and doing.

We have a choice. The soul always has free will. We can choose to do good or evil, right or wrong. We choose our future lives. Who would choose to kill, rape, steal, or cheat if he or she realized the karmic implications? By learning to use these principles of karma to better ourselves, we are bettering the future for us all.

Many people ask me to help them speed up their karmic cycles so that they won't have to come back again. I can't do that. Only you can do that. After reading this book, you have the basic knowledge to speed up your karmic cycle or do anything that you set your subconscious mind to do. Be honest, truthful, and faithful to your own code of ethics. If you follow this simple advice, you are well on your way to the higher planes.

This entire process will end when you fulfill your karma. When you learn all the lessons you have to learn and show kindness and unselfish love to all those with whom you come into contact, the cycle will end. When it ends, you will go beyond the soul plane to the higher planes and, eventually, to God. Karma is merely a process of evolution, of achieving greater levels of perfection. It gives life.

I like to think of karma as opportunities. As one faces each new opportunity, new choices and decisions must be made. It requires much courage to face our shortcomings and an equal amount of wisdom to do something constructive about them. We have these choices. We can dictate our future by acting appropriately in the present. Completing our karmic cycle is not easy, but it is within our grasp. By reviewing each opportunity objectively and by being aware of our karma—with the knowledge gained from past and future lives—imagine how much improved our present lives could be.

Learn these lessons well, and you will have taken the next step toward your destiny.

CHAPTER TWENTY-SIX

Questions and Answers About Past and Future Lives Hypnotherapy

Q. Why can't people consciously recall past lives?
A. All memories about our past and future lives are stored in the subconscious mind. This subconscious mind functions independently of the conscious mind proper. Since your conscious mind proper died along with the body when your last life ended, you start each new life with a virgin conscious mind proper. This conscious mind proper cannot recall any of its past lives simply because it has no memories of them.

It is only your subconscious or superconscious mind that can remember your past or future lives. This mechanism is actually quite protective. Because the mind is exposed to more than one million pieces of new information every day of our lives, think of what it would be like to consciously recall all of this information from our present as well as our past and future lives at any one moment.

There are certain clues to our past lives that we do experience consciously. We all have certain natural talents, likes and dislikes. Certain intuitive tendencies are remnants from past lives. When we dream we often see scenes from past lives. Spontaneous regressions occur to many people in their dreams. Even though we do not consciously remember our past or future lives, there are experiences that give us the knowledge that we have lived before and will live again.

Q. Has anyone not had a past life?

A. There are very few people who request regressions or progressions from me who are not able to achieve one or the other. This does not mean that they have had no past lives. It simply means that I am unable to use hypnosis on them successfully to obtain this information.

When I speak directly to a patient's subconscious or superconscious in trance, I usually receive past or future life data. Never has a patient's superconscious mind denied the existence of past lives. I do not believe, nor have I obtained any evidence, that anyone living today is here for the first time.

Q. Have people been animals in past lives?

A. In all of the regressions and progressions I have performed, I have never had a patient relate a life to me in any other than a human form. The only exceptions to this are regressions of "light people," as described in Chapter 7. Even these "light people" represent human forms, rather than plants or animals.

In certain Hindu and Buddhist schools of Eastern philosophy, transmigration is mentioned. According to these Eastern beliefs, our soul first incarnates as minerals, then plants, then lower animals, and finally the human form is inhabited. This transmigration from minerals to human form is not accepted even by most of the Eastern philosophers today. I personally don't accept it and I have never obtained any evidence to support this theory.

The extraterrestrial concept of reincarnation has gained much acceptance today in many parapsychological circles. This concept is described in Chapter 3 and it nullifies the transmigration theory.

Q. What methods other than hypnosis can help reveal past and future lives?

A. Karmic astrological charts can be constructed for you with the time, place, and date of your birth. This chart will tell you much about your past, present, and future lives. It will give you great insight into your subcycle as well as your total karmic cycle.

Psychics and mediums can often read your Akashic records or at least communicate with your Masters and Guides. In any event, much information concerning your past, present, and future lives can be obtained in this way, too.

Another way we obtain karmic information is from spontaneous regressions and progressions. This experience is infrequent and totally unpredictable, but it is an avenue for karmic data. Dreams represent still another avenue. During the dream state you can witness scenes from past and future lives and consciously remember them upon awakening.

Group meditation is advocated by some. I am not convinced that there is much difference between meditation and hypnosis, except that meditation works better with groups of people and is far less efficient than hypnosis. Both techniques are examples of alpha brain waves.

Automatic writing represents still another method. In this technique you sit quietly with a pencil or pen in your hand resting on some paper. Your hand will move and your subconscious mind will communicate with you by directing your hand movements in the form of words and phrases. I have used this technique with certain patients for various forms of therapy, but I personally have not used it to retrieve information about past or future lives.

Another method is conscious contact with your Masters and Guides. This is quite rare, but there are entirely sane people who claim this ability, and report that they have received information about their past or future lives in this way. Séances represent still another way to obtain this information. I have no personal experience with these phenomena. Apparently, entities from past, present, or future lives can be communicated with directly by way of a séance.

Q. Why are children more likely to remember past lives without the aid of hypnosis?
A. Children don't have as many hang-ups as adults. They are not bothered by what people think. Most importantly, the nervous system is not fully formed in a child until the age of about six. There are small openings in the skull that theoretically allow the soul or subconscious mind to escape and communicate directly with the child. Children, then, are able to consciously remember past lives without having to be formally hypnotized. These openings close by the age of two and a half. There have also been many cases of children having spontaneous past life regressions and other psychic experiences. Children see ghosts and have many more astral projections during daytime hours than adults. Their parents tend to discourage these episodes, which is unfortunate. Children actually make excellent hypnotic patients, and some very interesting regressions and progressions

result from working with them. One of the many exciting things about working with children is that the information obtained often shows knowledge and the vocabulary of an adult. There seems to me to be no other explanation of how these children acquired such knowledge than through past lives.

Q. How can the present population be explained by reincarnation?

A. One theory states that a soul is able to occupy more than one body at a time. If one soul occupied three bodies in the year 3000 B.C., for example, and if each of these subsouls occupied three additional bodies each, it would not be difficult to see how one soul could occupy one and a half million bodies in the matter of thirteen lifetimes.

Q. When does the soul enter the body of a newborn?

A. Although the soul can come and go as it pleases during the entire course of the pregnancy, it is usually within twenty-four hours before or after birth that the soul makes its grand entrance. Remember that the soul leaves our body every night during our sleep state. The soul is never permanently trapped within the body.

Q. Does the Bible mention reincarnation?

A. Yes, it most certainly does. In the third century A.D. there was a teacher by the name of Origen. He promoted the concept of reincarnation. In A.D. 533, however, a Church council met in Constantinople. At this meeting, which was not even attended by the Pope of Rome, Origen's teachings were condemned and most of the references to reincarnation were removed from the Bible. Fortunately, some are still present in the Old and New Testaments, including:

1. John 9:1–3
"And as Jesus passed by, he saw a man which was blind from birth. And his Disciples asked him saying, "Master, who did sin, this man or his parents, that he was born blind?" Jesus answered, "Neither has this man sinned nor his parents. He was born blind that the works of God should be manifest in him.""

2. Obadiah 1:15

"As thou has done, it shall be done unto thee; thy reward shall return thine own head."

3. Revelation 3:12

"Him that overcometh will I make a pillar in the temple of my God and he shall go no more out."

4. Wisdom of Solomon 8:19–20

"Now I was a good child by nature, and a good soul fell to my lot. Nay, rather being good, I came into a body undefiled."

5. Isaiah 26:19

"Thy dead men shall live, together with my dead body shall they arise. Awake and sing, ye that dwell in dust for . . . the earth shall cast out the dead."

6. Daniel 12:2

"And many of them that sleep in the dust of the earth shall awake, some to everlasting life, and some to shame and everlasting contempt."

7. Matthew 17: 1–13

"And after six days Jesus took with him Peter and James and John his brother, and led them up a high mountain apart. And he was transfigured before them, and his face shown like the sun, and his garments became white as light. And behold, there appeared to them Moses and Eli'jah talking with him. And Peter said to Jesus, 'Lord, it is well that we are here; if you wish, I will make three booths here, one for you and one for Moses and one for Eli'jah.' He was still speaking, when lo, a bright cloud overshadowed them, and a voice from the cloud said, "This is my beloved Son, with whom I am well pleased; listen to him." When the disciples heard this, they fell on their faces, and were filled with awe. But Jesus came and touched them, saying 'Rise, and have no fear.' And when they lifted up their eyes, they saw no one but Jesus only. And as they were coming down the mountain, Jesus commanded them, 'Tell no one the vision, until the Son of man is raised from the dead.' And the disciples asked him, 'Then why do the scribes say that first Eli'jah must come?' He replied, 'Eli'jah does come, and he is to restore all things; but I tell you that Eli'jah has already come, and they did not know him, but did to him whatever they pleased. So also the Son of man will suffer at their hands.' Then the disciples understood that he was speaking to them of John the Baptist.''

8. Job 33:15–18

"In a dream, in a vision of the night, when deep sleep falleth upon men, in slumberings upon the bed; then he openeth the ears of men, and sealeth their instruction, that he may withdraw man from his purpose, and hide pride from man. He keepeth back his soul from the pit, and his life from perishing by the sword.''

9. Other reincarnation references:

  a. "Whatsoever a man soweth, that shall he also reap."
     Saint Paul (Gal. 6:7)
  b. Saint Augustine in *Confessions* 1:6
  c. Saint Jerome in his *Letter to Avitus*

There are cases today of people in the Roman Catholic Church accepting reincarnation without being declared heretical. (An example of this is the late Cardinal Mercier [Prelate of Belgian Catholics] and the late Dean Inge of Saint Paul's Cathedral in London.

Q. Does a belief in reincarnation conflict with a belief in God?
A. I hope that throughout this book you have noted my many references to God. My work as a hypnotherapist specializing in past life regression and progression into future lives has only strengthened my personal belief in God. It is hard for me to imagine someone working in this field not having a very strong belief in God. If more and more people studied parapsychology, especially the karmic cycle, I'm confident that we would see a renaissance in monotheism (a belief in one God).

Q. Does one always improve in one's next life?
A. Not necessarily. If you fail to learn the lessons that you are supposed to master, then you will have to face these same lessons in either this or a future life. Also, in the process of dealing with other entities, you could incur negative karma. This would add to your karmic cycle rather than help it. Since the soul always has free will, you are not guaranteed improvement with each life. That we have thousands of lives and still much karma

to work out highly suggests that we do not constantly improve in our karmic cycles.

Q. Why are progressions more difficult than regressions?
A. I am not sure why progressions are more difficult. Perhaps it is because we are all programmed to believe that the future hasn't occurred yet. Another reason might be that the actual mechanism involved disorients our subconscious mind's thought process. I hope further research will give us some insight into this question.

Q. Do we ever change sex in our karmic cycle?
A. We must change sex at least once in order to complete our karmic cycle. Even though we do change sex at least once, most of our lives are lived as one sex. This change of sex roles in our karmic cycles offers one possible explanation for homosexuality. Another possible karmic explanation for homosexuality is that people have been ridiculed, ostracized, and punished for sexual behavior in previous lives.

Q. How do you know these past lives are not figments of the imagination? Might not some of your patients just be making these lives up?
A. My patients are able to overcome negative habits and eliminate phobias as a result of past lives regressions. If they were simply imagining these scenes, these problems would not disappear. The remission of symptoms seems proof enough to me. Second, the lives my patients report to me are hardly complimentary to themselves. Most of these lives are tedious and dull, rather than glamorous, hardly the kind of lives one would fantasize about to enhance one's self-image.

In addition, I have never regressed a patient who lived the life of a celebrated historical figure. This only adds to the validity of hypnotic regression. One would naturally question the possibility of regressing Napoleon, Cleopatra, and George Washington all within the same year. The odds against regressing a famous person from history are astronomically high. Since I have performed thousands of regressions and none of these accounts have been of historical figures, I feel that this precludes the idea of patients using their imagination. But you must make your own determination about what you accept when it comes to karma.

Q. How do I find a qualified hypnotherapist?

A. I would like to close this book with some advice to those of you who will seek out hypnosis to explore past or future lives. Although I know of no case in which hypnosis has ever harmed anyone, I highly recommend that you seek out a qualified hypnotherapist. The term *hypnotherapist* should only be used by someone with a doctorate in the health sciences. It may be a D.D.S. (such as myself), it may be a Ph.D. (such as a psychologist), or an M.D. (a physician), or other health professional.

The term *hypnotist* refers to those without professional training other than their training in hypnosis, which rarely exceeds four days. The reason I recommend a doctor is because doctors live by very strong ethical codes. A lay hypnotist may or may not have these standards. Second, our background includes much training in psychology and other behavioral sciences.

The second quality I would look for in a hypnotherapist is a very extensive background in the field of parapsychology. He or she should be knowledgeable about all aspects of karma and able to answer your questions and offer the appropriate guidance.

The third quality to look for is experience. The therapist should have done regressions or progressions many, many times before. They should also be experienced in shielding (white light protection) techniques, which should precede any regression or progression.

Fourth, trust your instinct about the therapist. If the therapist is qualified but you don't like or trust him or her, leave immediately. Not only will you not succeed with that particular therapist, but you might just be susceptible to his or her negative karma.

Since 1958, the American Medical Association has formally accepted hypnosis as a reputable clinical aid. The British Medical Association accepted hypnosis in 1955. No longer are hypnotherapists thought of as charlatans or stage entertainers. When I first began practicing hypnotherapy, patients would seek my services as a last resort, usually after traditional medicine and psychotherapy had failed. Today I'm more often approached initially, before other traditional forms of therapy are considered. Of course, I refer my patients to physicians to rule out possible physiological causes of their complaints. When the physical causes of illness are eliminated, I begin my therapy. Any therapist you meet should take this clinical approach.